CONFLICT AMONG REBELS

Conflict Among Rebels

WHY INSURGENT GROUPS FIGHT EACH OTHER

Costantino Pischedda

Columbia University Press

New York

Columbia University Press
Publishers Since 1893
New York   Chichester, West Sussex
cup.columbia.edu
Copyright © 2020 Columbia University Press
All rights reserved

Library of Congress Cataloging-in-Publication Data
Names: Pischedda, Costantino, author.
Title: Conflict among rebels : why insurgent groups fight each other /
Costantino Pischedda.
Description: New York City : Columbia University Press, [2020] | Includes
bibliographical references and index.
Identifiers: LCCN 2020015562 (print) | LCCN 2020015563 (ebook) |
ISBN 9780231198660 (hardback) | ISBN 9780231198677 (trade paperback) |
ISBN 9780231552745 (ebook)
Subjects: LCSH: Insurgency. | Allegiance.
Classification: LCC JC328.5 .P57 2020 (print) | LCC JC328.5 (ebook) |
DDC 355.02/18—dc23
LC record available at https://lccn.loc.gov/2020015562
LC ebook record available at https://lccn.loc.gov/2020015563

Cover image: Santa Maria della Salute, Venice, Italy.
Cameraphoto Arte Venezia/Bridgeman Images.

Chapters 1, 2, and 4 in this book draw from Costantino Pischedda, "Wars Within
Wars: Why Windows of Opportunity and Vulnerability Cause Inter-rebel Fighting
in Internal Conflicts," *International Security*, 43, no. 1 (Summer 2018): 138–76. © 2018
by the President and Fellows of Harvard College and the Massachusetts Institute of
Technology. Published by The MIT Press. Used with permission.

I dedicate this book to my sister and my parents
—Alessandra, Mattia, and Peppino.

Contents

Acknowledgments

I owe a great debt of gratitude to many individuals and institutions for help and encouragement along the path to this book. Jack Snyder, Page Fortna, and Bob Jervis expertly advised me in the first phase of the project at Columbia University. Laia Balcells, Dick Betts, Brian Blankenship, Daniel Corstange, Andrea Gilli, Mauro Gilli, Laura Gomez-Mera, Morgan Kaplan, Amaney Jamal, Austin Long, Zachariah Mampilly, Massimo Morelli, Luigi Moretti, Joe Parent, Stefano Recchia, Will Reno, Joan Ricart, John Paul Russo, Randy Schweller, Lee Seymour, Paul Staniland, Daniel Verdier, Manuel Vogt, Michael Woldemariam, and Matias Mednik provided helpful feedback at various stages. Dara Kay Cohen, Theodore McLauchlin, Nuno Monteiro, Benjamin Valentino (participants in my book workshop, which was hosted by Helen Milner and Amaney Jamal at Princeton University,) and Peter Krause offered detailed and insightful comments on a previous draft.

Kamal Soleimani heroically translated from Kurdish the three-volume memoir of Nawshirwan Mustafa, Farid Asasard's *Political Atlas of the Kurdistan Region*, and the PUK Declaration of Formation in long meetings at Columbia University's Butler Library. Joan Ricart kindly created the maps in chapters 3 and 4.

I am enormously grateful to my interviewees, too many to list here, who generously offered their time and memories. Wolde-Yesus Ammar, Leonardo Arriola, Pamela DeLargy, Patrick Gilkes, Gebru Tareke,

Günter Schröder, Lahra Smith, and Michael Woldemariam helped me establish contacts with many of my interviewees in Ethiopia. Zana Ali, Noah Arjomand, Lawen Azad, Ermione Gee, Mariwan Hama-Saeed, Michael Knights, Mohammed A. Salih, and Caitlin Talmadge helped me get in touch with many of my interviewees in Iraq. Abdurrahman Bapir, Mohammed Ghafour, and Abdulla Hawez worked as translators for several of my interviews in Iraq. Simone De Santi and Hajar Khoshnaw provided logistical help and hospitality in Erbil.

I did much of the writing for this book at the University of Miami, where I found a friendly and stimulating academic environment. I am thankful to Louise Davidson-Schmich and Joe Uscinski for their mentorship. I gratefully acknowledge the financial support provided by the University of Miami's Department of Political Science and College of Arts and Sciences as well as by Princeton University's Niehaus Center for Globalization and Governance.

I thank Caelyn Cobb at Columbia University Press for rounding up an excellent set of reviewers and ensuring a smooth process from review to production, with the skillful help of Monique Briones, Marisa Lastres, and Anita O'Brien.

CONFLICT AMONG REBELS

1

Wars Within Wars

We must not fight two-sided; it is better to fight one-sided.
—MAO ZEDONG[1]

I
n early January 2014 the news media were buzzing with reports of
battles between Sunni rebel groups taking part in Syria's civil war.
Observers immediately pointed out that the government of President
Bashar al-Assad would be the ultimate beneficiary, noting that "rebel
infighting is a boon to regime forces and clearly detrimental to the overall strength of the Syrian opposition."[2] Subsequent developments con-
firmed this assessment, as the government made major gains in the
following months of inter-rebel clashes. For example, in the span of a few
weeks of fighting among rebels, the al-Tawhid Brigade, the largest rebel
force in Aleppo, lost 500 men compared to 1,300 in the previous two
years of antigovernment struggle, enabling the Assad regime to tighten
its noose around the rebel stronghold.[3]

Analyses of the causes of the infighting, however, were not as insightful as the predictions of its consequences. The initial narrative of moderate rebels fighting against the extremist organization known as the
Islamic State of Iraq and Syria (ISIS) became untenable as evidence
emerged that the anti-ISIS coalition included several Salafi groups and

even al-Qaeda's Syrian affiliate, the al-Nusra Front.[4] Why would rebel groups sharing ethnosectarian identities and religious ideology engage in "fratricide"? More generally, why do rebel groups divert resources from their common struggle against a powerful foe to fight one another? Why does inter-rebel war occur?

Large-scale clashes between rebel groups are not peculiar to the Syrian civil war, which over the years has become infamous for the complex alignments of dozens of rebel formations, progovernment militias, and meddling third-party states. In fact, instances of inter-rebel war abound in contemporary history. During the Algerian war of national liberation against the French, the National Liberation Front (FLN) targeted its local competitor, the Algerian National Movement (MNA). More recently, the Tamil Tigers wiped out rival Tamil groups fighting against the Sri Lankan government, and Kashmir insurgent groups fought one another as they also battled India's security forces. The fight between al-Qaeda in Iraq (AQI) and other rebels in Anbar province in the mid-2000s is perhaps the episode of inter-rebel violence that has attracted the most attention in the media and policy circles, given the involvement of U.S. forces in the war and the fact that the infighting may have contributed to the subsequent reduction of insurgent activity in the country by causing massive defections from the rebel ranks.[5]

Yet inter-rebel war is not a constant feature of civil wars. By my own count, inter-rebel war has taken place in about one out of four civil wars involving multiple rebel groups in the post–cold war era.[6] Moreover, while some civil wars do not experience large-scale inter-rebel clashes at all (e.g., the civil wars in Argentina and El Salvador), in the cases characterized by rebel infighting mentioned above, phases of peaceful coexistence and even cooperation among insurgent groups preceded violent conflict.[7]

Existing studies do not provide entirely satisfactory explanations for the observed variation in inter-rebel war, despite the important stakes for international intervention in civil wars and counterinsurgency. This book aims to address this lacuna in our understanding of civil war processes by presenting a novel theory of the onset of inter-rebel war, weaving together insights from international relations theory and the study of ethnic politics, and testing it with a combination of case studies and statistical analysis.

The Puzzle and Limits of Existing Explanations

The occurrence of inter-rebel war is puzzling from several theoretical perspectives. Strategic logic (encapsulated by the adage "the enemy of my enemy is my friend") should dissuade rebels from diverting scarce resources from the struggle against their common enemy. In particular, balance-of-power thinking should push rebel groups to ally against the government, which is usually the strongest warring party: inter-rebel squabbles should be set aside until the government's threat recedes.[8]

These instrumental considerations should be reinforced by the enhanced social cohesion in the rebel camp caused by the shared experience of violence at the hands of government forces.[9] When civil wars occur along ethnic lines, this effect should be especially strong, as ethnic violence "hardens" identities and deepens interethnic hostility and fear.[10]

Inter-rebel violence is also baffling because it often entails image costs for the insurgents before domestic and international audiences. Rebels' domestic and foreign supporters may be disheartened by the incomprehensible internecine violence. The government, on its part, may be better able to resist international pressure to address the rebellion's grievances by pointing out that the insurgents are themselves divided and claiming that the struggle between rebels and the government is not the main axis of violence.

Although recent political science scholarship has shed much light on a broad range of civil war dynamics, existing answers to the puzzle of inter-rebel war tend to either lack a fully fleshed out theory of inter-rebel war or run into significant empirical difficulties.[11] In the only published cross-national study on inter-rebel war, Hanne Fjelde and Desirée Nilsson find that insurgent groups are more likely to be involved in inter-rebel fighting when they are either strong or weak relative to other groups; they have exclusive control of some territory; they fight in areas with drug cultivation; and government authority is weak.[12] While constituting an important contribution, these statistical findings are correlations in search of a theory, as they are not integrated in an overarching explanation of inter-rebel violence.

Fotini Christia has advanced a parsimonious theory of civil war alliances, a phenomenon closely related to, though distinct from, inter-rebel war.[13] (Alliances and inter-rebel war are not each other's mirror images: two rebel groups may not cooperate and thus not form an alliance, while also abstaining from fighting each other. However, arguments that make predictions about rebel alliances typically imply predictions about inter-rebel fighting, as allies, by most definitions, do not wage war on each other.) Christia argues that alliances follow a minimum winning coalition (MWC) logic in which shared identity plays no role: warring parties strive to be part of the smallest possible alliance sufficient to win the war, both to maximize their shares of the spoils of victory and to reduce their vulnerability to strong allies. When the MWC threshold is passed, one or more belligerents will abandon the dominant coalition in search of an optimally sized one. The implication for inter-rebel war is that rebel groups should tend to fight one another only when at least one of them is stronger than the government. Many well-known instances of groups fighting one another while facing an unambiguously more powerful government, however, cast doubt on the ability of MWC theory to solve the puzzle of inter-rebel war.[14] For example, in Algeria the FLN wiped out the MNA, despite the overwhelming power of the French army.[15] Similarly, the National Front for the Liberation of Angola (FNLA) and the Popular Movement for the Liberation of Angola (MPLA) fought each other rather than cooperate against the vastly superior Portuguese forces.[16] This pattern is not limited to anti-colonial wars. For instance, in the 1990s Kashmir insurgent groups fought one another notwithstanding the clear military edge of the Indian government.[17]

Finally, Peter Krause theorizes about how the distribution of power within national liberation movements affects their prospects of success.[18] Krause supports his argument with case studies of four movements, showing that they were most effective when hegemonic (i.e., with a single significant organization). One of the mechanisms in Krause's theory—nonhegemonic rebel movements are more likely to experience internecine violence—suggests a prediction about inter-rebel fighting consistent with the argument presented in this book: inter-rebel war is unlikely once a rebel group has firmly established itself as the hegemon.[19] In competitive movements (i.e., with more than one significant organization), Krause argues, relatively weak rebel groups should be particularly inclined to initiate infighting as a way to improve their power position, even if internecine violence is detrimental to the national liberation cause. There is remarkable variation in infighting, however, that Krause's argument cannot explain: on the one hand, relatively strong groups like the FLN and the Tamil Tigers seem to initiate their fair share of episodes of inter-rebel war; on the other, weak groups engage in infighting in some moments but get along with their rivals in others.

This book aims at advancing our understanding of the internal dynamics of rebel movements by presenting (and then testing) a theory of the logic driving inter-rebel war, which specifies more fully than existing arguments the conditions under which competition between rival organizations is likely to escalate to large-scale violence, even in the empirically common context of a government enjoying clear military superiority over the insurgents.

The Stakes for Policy Makers

Unraveling the puzzle of inter-rebel war not only is important for theoretical reasons; it also has significant implications for external intervention in civil wars and their outcomes. When contemplating intervention in ongoing civil wars, policy makers will typically want to have a sense of the probability of inter-rebel fighting and of what policies could be adopted to induce cooperation or violent conflict among rebels, based on an intuition that infighting could make a decisive difference for developments on the ground. Going back to the case of ISIS with which this book opened, a key element of President Barack Obama's strategy against the group in Syria was to induce other rebel organizations to fight it.[20] By contrast, forging an alliance between Muslims and Croats was the lynchpin of the U.S. intervention strategy in Bosnia's civil war, ultimately aiming to put pressure on the Serbs to negotiate a settlement.[21]

Inter-rebel fighting has indeed the potential of powerfully influencing the outcome of civil wars. In the course of infighting, insurgent groups redirect part of their resources from their struggle against the counterinsurgent toward other rebels. The government may then be able to take advantage of the internecine fight to regroup or to intensify operations and expand its territorial control, as the Syrian regime did in the wake of large-scale clashes between Sunni insurgents in 2014. Moreover, inter-rebel violence may lead to insurgent side-switching, as the group being defeated turns to the government for help.[22] "Insurgent defection" not only entails a shift of manpower from the insurgent to the counterinsurgent side but also often provides the government with precious intelligence on the groups that continue to oppose it and thus can have a substantial impact on counterinsurgency outcomes. This point is well illustrated by the insurgencies in Iraq and Sri Lanka. In Iraq, the decision by Anbar province's rebels to side with U.S. and Iraqi security forces against their erstwhile ally AQI marked a key turning point in the counterinsurgency campaign, paving the road to a substantial reduction in insurgent activity in the province and in the rest of the country.[23] In Sri Lanka, the Tamil Tigers' eastern commander's "flip" in 2004 facilitated the subsequent government offensive, culminating in the Tigers' complete defeat in 2009, after almost thirty years of intermittent fighting and negotiations.[24]

Inter-rebel war is not, however, an unalloyed good for the counterinsurgent. If a rebel group manages to quickly defeat its rivals, rather than being bogged down in a long war of attrition, it may come to represent a more formidable foe for the government by obtaining unhindered access to its constituency. For example, after wiping out their various coethnic competitors, the Tamil Tigers reached the apex of their political and military strength: by 1990 the group had unchallenged control of Sri Lanka's Northeast (one-third of the country's land area) and could hold its own in conventional battles against government forces, in addition to conducting a campaign of devastating suicide attacks deep inside enemy territory in Colombo.[25]

Understanding the causes of inter-rebel war thus holds the promise of providing policy-relevant insights about the conditions under which rebel-on-rebel violence is more likely and strategies that local counterinsurgent and external interveners could adopt to intensify or mitigate the risk of infighting as well as to shape its impact on the trajectory of the civil war.

The Argument and Contributions to the Literature

I argue that inter-rebel war is a calculated response by rebel groups to opportunities for expansion and threats emanating from their environment. Specifically, inter-rebel war tends to break out when rebel organizations face "windows of opportunity" and "windows of vulnerability."[26]

Windows of opportunity are situations in which a rebel group is markedly more powerful than its coethnic rival(s) and the government does not pose an immediate and serious threat but is also not so weak as to be experiencing major territorial losses, let alone to be approaching defeat. Under these circumstances, the stronger rebel organization will be tempted to launch a "hegemonic bid" to lock in its advantageous position—that is, to use force to eliminate a coethnic rival (or rivals) at low cost and ultimately establish itself as the ethnic rebel hegemon. The relevant costs are not limited to the risk of exposing the rebel group weakened by infighting to an attack by the government; they also include the opportunity costs of forgoing major gains on the battlefield against government forces "on the ropes." Thus, even when facing a much more powerful government, the attacker stands to benefit from inter-rebel fighting if it can prevail rapidly and the government faces constraints to escalating its war effort on short notice.

Windows of vulnerability occur when a rebel group that is relatively weak and/or confronts a significant government threat faces the prospect of a dramatic decline in power relative to a coethnic rival. If no other option appears viable (e.g., forming alternative alliances, attracting new sources of external support, or developing more effective popular mobilization techniques), the group will be tempted to resort to force against the rival or start a course of action entailing a high risk of inter-rebel war in a desperate attempt to extricate itself from the difficult situation. I call this typology of inter-rebel war "gambling for resurrection."[27]

In both cases, rebel organizations' calculus about infighting is influenced by whether they are facing coethnic insurgent groups. Somewhat counterintuitively, coethnic rebel groups represent both especially frightening threats and enticing opportunities for expansion for one another. The fact that coethnic organizations aspire to control the same population makes their conflict of interest stark and immediate: rebel group A has reason to believe that coethnic rival group B values highly extending its control over the ethnic community, including the absorption of A's social resource base (in particular, the social networks from which A obtains intelligence, recruits, and material support, but also some of its rank and file). Moreover, rebel group A knows that group B would have a good chance at harnessing A's social resources after defeating the rival and then at making further progress in controlling the ethnic community as a whole, which in turn would strengthen B's position in its fight against the government. Rebel group B's perspective is the mirror image of group A's. Therefore a gamble for resurrection offers some hope of halting a rebel group's dangerous decline relative to an ambitious competitor, while a hegemonic bid promises an improved threat environment and unencumbered access to more resources by eliminating the competition. By contrast, owing to their less immediate conflicts of interest and inability to expand at one another's expense, generally non-coethnic organizations lack comparably strong motives for inter-rebel war.

This is not to say that we should expect non-coethnic rebel groups to never fight one another. There may indeed be pathways to inter-rebel war among non-coethnics beyond those envisioned by window theory. For example, rebel organization C may decide to use force to take over a piece of territory controlled by non-coethnic organization D because large numbers of C's coethnics live there or because that territory has strategic value independent of its demography (e.g., it contains important natural resources such as oil, or its control ensures the defensibility of the organization's strongholds). The key point is that, other things being the same, non-coethnic rebel groups should have significantly weaker incentives for violent conflict; thus window theory suggests that inter-rebel war should be less likely among non-coethnic rebel groups than among coethnic ones.

The relative ease of taking over the social resource base of defeated coethnic rivals is a function of the well-documented phenomenon of ethnic parochialism: *individuals'* tendency to be particularly cooperative with and favor members of one's own ethnic group. Thus when a rebel organization eliminates a coethnic rival, the victor is likely to be able to recruit and extract resources at a relatively low cost from the coethnic population previously under the defeated group's control and coopt segments of the latter's membership, as the two organizations have similar ethnic credentials. There may be instances in which other types of shared identity (e.g., political ideology) have comparable effects as ethnicity, but I expect this generally not to be the case. This is because, as suggested by various evolutionary perspectives discussed in the next chapter, evolution has endowed our brains with a particular focus on shared ethnic identity.[28] In the pithy words of evolutionary biologist Joseph Henrich, "our minds are prepared to carve the social world into ethnic groups, but not classes or ideologies."[29]

Though the key moving parts of window theory of inter-rebel war—power and ethnic identities—are common to many existing studies, they are conceptualized and combined in distinctive ways, with far-reaching theoretical implications. Unlike most analyses of civil war dynamics that adopt some variant of balance-of-power logic, this book conceptualizes belligerents' power as both dynamic and contextual. Starting from the plain observation that rebel groups' power may wax and wane, window theory of inter-rebel war brings into the study of civil war processes insights from the rich literature on the commitment problem, power shifts, and preventive war in international relations.[30] This book also identifies a hitherto unexplored path for the growth of rebel power. Insurgents start operating from a position of weakness vis-à-vis the incumbent (i.e., the government), but they expect to grow as they carry out political and military activities. As counterinsurgency theorist and practitioner David Galula writes, "The protracted nature of a revolutionary war does not result from a design by either side; it is imposed on the insurgent by his initial weakness."[31] Infighting is one of the processes through which rebel groups can grow in strength, as the winner can acquire resources previously controlled by defeated coethnic rivals and further extend its hold on the ethnic community.

Contrary to balance-of-power logic, this book argues that inter-rebel aggression in a context in which the government is militarily much stronger than the insurgents is not necessarily a high-risk course of action; rather, it might enable a rebel group's growth without exposing it to unacceptable risks. This is because the incumbent's power is contextual: its superior aggregate resources do not automatically translate into ability or willingness to wield decisive force on short notice anywhere in the country's territory. Political, logistical, and military constraints may limit government power projection, so that the incumbent may not represent a serious and immediate threat to rebel groups fighting one another. An important, related quality of window theory of inter-rebel war is that it provides an explanation for both the fundamental decision to engage in inter-rebel war and the timing of its initiation: a mix of expansionary ambitions and fear induced by shared ethnic identity constitutes the underlying motive for inter-rebel aggression, while the relative power among rebel groups and the level of threat posed by the government influence decisions about timing. By contrast, other arguments using the metaphor of windows often only provide an explanation for when, but not why, war occurs.[32]

This book questions two influential views on the effects of ethnic identity on civil war dynamics. One view envisions shared ethnicity as a powerful source of solidarity and cooperation. In particular, the ethnic security dilemma literature expects individuals to flock to their ethnic side under conditions of state collapse or large-scale violence, so that ethnic groups can be treated as cohesive actors in their interactions with one another and the state.[33] The other, more recent, view contends that ethnicity does not have an important effect on civil war behavior but rather tends to be a façade for more mundane, often purely materialistic or individual survival-maximizing considerations.[34] My contention that coethnicity affects the risk of inter-rebel violence by increasing the benefits of infighting challenges the view of ethnicity as largely epiphenomenal in civil war dynamics. At the same time, it turns on its head the earlier view positing a causal impact of ethnic identities: the cooperation-inducing effect of shared ethnicity at the individual level produces competitive dynamics at the organizational level that, under some circumstances, can lead to war between coethnic rebel organizations.

This book also complements existing works on the structure of opposition movements, in particular Krause's study suggesting that national liberation struggles dominated by a single organization (the hegemon) are more likely to be successful.[35] Window theory provides an answer to the question: Under what circumstances and how do ethnic insurgent hegemons emerge? Infighting, rather than always being a wasteful diversion of resources from the struggle against the government, may lead to the consolidation of the rebel movement under the control of a single organization, which in turn can facilitate ultimate rebel victory.

Defining Key Terms

Before proceeding further, it is important to explicitly define key concepts. *Inter-rebel war* is purposeful, leadership-endorsed, large-scale combat between distinct rebel organizations fighting against the same government. This conceptualization distinguishes inter-rebel war from low-level clashes/skirmishes, which are far more common in civil wars. In some cases, skirmishes can be considered accidental, as they occur at the initiative of foot soldiers and junior commanders rather than organizations' leaders. In other cases, low-level clashes may be part of an organization's "coercive diplomacy," a conscious attempt to use threats and limited force to intimidate a rival and make some gains at its expense without engaging in an all-out military confrontation. Inter-rebel clashes qualify as large-scale combat if repeated battles between units of different organizations or a major battle with hundreds of fighters occur in a given year (the involvement of most members would suffice for smaller organizations), or if one group attempts to overrun the headquarters of another group.

Rebel groups are independent non-state organizations engaged in large-scale armed conflict against the incumbent, that is, civil war.[36] I consider rebel organizations as independent if they make their own decisions about alignments with other organizations and about the strategic use of force (i.e., initiation and termination of their antigovernment activities as well as their military strategy) and they have exclusive authority over their armed forces (that is, their top leaders are not formally subordinate to other decision makers). Independence distinguishes rebel groups from subunits, i.e., factions, of which rebel organizations are composed.

Drawing on Max Weber's seminal insight, I define *ethnic groups* broadly, as large collectives whose members share a sense of belonging on the basis of a subjective belief in a common culture and descent.

Markers of common culture and descent include somatic similarities, shared religion, and a common language.[37] Thus in some instances the cleavage separating ethnic groups is linguistic (e.g., Catalans and Basques in Spain), while in others it is religious (e.g., Iraq's Sunni Arabs and Shia Arabs). In other cases, politicized religion is better thought of as a form of political ideology, rather than ethnicity, as in disputes about the interpretation and political role of a shared religion within a given community. For example, in overwhelmingly Sunni Muslim Algeria, the place of Islam in politics was the key bone of contention in the nonethnic civil war that ravaged the country in the 1990s.

I consider rebel organizations *coethnic* if their announced political aspirations directly relate to the same ethnic group's fate and if the majority of their rank and file *or* of the leadership belongs to the same ethnic group (i.e., both ethnic goals and membership criteria need to be met).[38] In the presence of "subethnic" divides, I consider rebel groups as coethnic if (besides the basic requirement of the majority of their rank and file or leadership belonging to the same ethnic group) their political goals relate to the fate of the ethnic group as a whole and they recruit (or are willing to do so) across subethnic cleavages. For example, Iraq's Kurdistan Democratic Party (KDP) and Patriotic Union of Kurdistan (PUK) were coethnic rebel organizations even if the former had its stronghold in Iraq's Kurmanji-speaking territories, whereas the latter recruited mostly from Sorani-speaking areas, as both met these criteria.

An *ethnic rebel hegemon* is an insurgent organization in an undisputed position of dominance, i.e., without rivals in its ethnic community. Hegemony does not equate to absolute monopoly of organized armed resistance to the state. Much like being a "regional hegemon" in international relations does not imply exercising sovereign control over a world region but simply being the only great power in that region and being able to "dictate the boundaries of acceptable behavior" to much weaker states,[39] rebel hegemons often tolerate coethnic organizations as long as they are extremely weak and unlikely to grow rapidly, thus not posing a meaningful threat. In other cases, hegemons may demand the dissolution of these puny organizations. The key point is that, regardless of what the hegemon decides to do, we should not expect to see infighting between it and organizations below a threshold of extreme weakness: their lack of meaningful military capabilities implies that the probability of mounting successful resistance to the hegemon is virtually zero, making acquiesce a preferable option to the organizations themselves.

Scope and Methods

This book is about inter-rebel relations in the context of multiparty civil wars, i.e., settings in which at least two rebel groups are engaged in large-scale armed struggle against the government. Relations among counterinsurgent militias (i.e., armed actors engaged in sustained cooperation with the incumbent's counterinsurgency effort by directly fighting the rebels in coordination with government forces) lie beyond the scope of this book, as the incentive structure of this type of nonstate actor typically differs from that of rebel groups—counterinsurgent militias' declared enemies are insurgents, not the government.[40] Moreover, counterinsurgent militias often have limited decision-making autonomy from the incumbent.[41] Similarly, window theory does not apply to relations between rebel groups and nonstate armed organizations that are not fighting the government (e.g., those between ISIS and the Kurdish militias in Syria), owing to the heterogeneity of their respective incentive structures: as the two sets of actors are not engaged militarily against a common enemy (the government), the most powerful consideration cautioning against infighting is removed from the equation. Thus conflicts of interest and other types of impulses that window theory would expect not to be significant enough to cause inter-rebel war may suffice to bring about large-scale clashes between rebel groups and other armed nonstate actors.

This book adopts a mixed-method approach to examine the empirical validity of window theory and competing explanations of inter-rebel war, combining case studies and statistical analysis. Testing my argument requires fine-grained and contextual measures of the inter-rebel balance of power and government threat, which are exceedingly hard to collect for a large number of cases over time. Therefore, in-depth case studies of post–World War II Kurdish insurgencies against Iraq and rebellions in the northern Ethiopian provinces of Eritrea (1961–1991) and Tigray (1975–1991) play a prominent role. The case studies combine secondary literature with primary sources collected during fieldwork, including interviews with former insurgent leaders, their memoirs, and archival materials.

I used Iraq's Kurdish insurgencies in the years 1961–1988 for theory development, that is, to develop my argument about the causes of inter-rebel war through a combination of deductive reasoning and inductive insights from fieldwork in Iraq and the secondary literature. The case is particularly useful for this purpose because it represents a glaring anomaly for intuitive understandings of inter-rebel relations as driven by balance-of-power logic or ethnic solidarity.[42] The Kurdish rebel groups notoriously fought one another while facing the militarily superior forces of the Sunni Arab–dominated and mass killing–prone regime in Baghdad. Moreover, the case displays useful variation in inter-rebel war. The fact that the Kurdish rebels clashed among themselves on several occasions but peacefully coexisted in other moments offers multiple opportunities to observe the mechanisms envisioned by window theory, while controlling for a number of confounders, and guarantees a minimum of representativeness vis-à-vis the larger population by including instances of both inter-rebel war and peace.[43]

Besides displaying substantial variation in inter-rebel war, too, northern Ethiopia is an ideal setting for a preliminary test of window theory as multiparty ethnic rebellions occurred at the same time in two adjacent provinces.[44] That Tigrayan and Eritrean rebels operated in physical proximity to both coethnic and non-coethnic rebel groups allows me to assess whether interactions between rebel groups vary depending on whether they cross ethnic lines, as window theory predicts.

To explore whether window theory travels beyond Iraq and Ethiopia, I present ancillary case studies, based on the secondary literature, of the civil wars in Lebanon and Sri Lanka as well as of ISIS's relations with other rebel groups in Syria. Moreover, I test the theoretical implication that, other things being equal, coethnic rebel groups should be especially likely to fight one another with statistical analysis of all rebel organizations facing the same government in the post–cold war era.

Each of the three ancillary case studies—all multiparty civil wars with multiple instances of inter-rebel fighting—offers distinct benefits. Lebanon's civil war (1975–1990) provides an additional opportunity to test the coethnicity part of the argument, as the case features both coethnic and non-coethnic armed groups operating in close proximity and thus with opportunities to fight one another. The multiparty phase of Sri Lanka's Tamil insurgency (1983–1990) offers a chance to explore inter-rebel dynamics beyond the Middle Eastern and African scope of the other cases of this book. Analyzing ISIS's relations with other rebels pitted against the Syrian government (2013–2014) permits me to assess whether window theory is relevant to Jihadist groups, a relatively common feature of civil wars since the U.S. invasion of Iraq in 2003.

Plan of the Book

The rest of the book is organized as follows. Chapter 2 fleshes out window theory of inter-rebel war, elaborating on the constitutive elements of windows of opportunity and windows of vulnerability. It pays particular attention to the mechanisms through which coethnicity affects rebel groups' calculations and the underlying microfoundations related to ethnic parochialism. Furthermore, the chapter makes the case about the utility of using case studies to test window theory.

Chapter 3 presents the case study of the Kurdish insurgencies against Iraq, which I used for developing my argument. Relying on interviews with insurgent leaders, their memoirs, and the secondary literature, it shows how the opening of windows of opportunity and windows of vulnerability caused multiple episodes of inter-rebel war among coethnic (Kurdish) rebel organizations intensely competing with one another for control of their ethnic constituency.

Chapter 4 presents the main theory-testing case studies—the insurgencies in the adjacent Ethiopian provinces of Eritrea and Tigray. Combining interviews with rebel leaders, other primary sources, and the secondary literature, it traces rebel groups' decision-making processes and shows that the dynamics of intense competition that led to intra-ethnic rebel war were absent in interactions among non-coethnic rebel groups operating in close physical proximity.

The next two chapters assess the broader validity of window theory beyond Iraq and Ethiopia. Chapter 5 presents ancillary case studies of the multiparty civil wars in Lebanon and Sri Lanka as well as of ISIS's relations with other groups fighting against the Syrian government up to the point when ISIS found itself at war with virtually the entire Syrian opposition. Collectively, these case studies reveal that window theory can indeed explain patterns of inter-rebel relations in a variety of geopolitical contexts. Through an analysis of all multiparty civil wars since 1989, chapter 6 shows that coethnic rebels are especially prone to clashing against one another, thus providing support for an important observable implication of my argument. The concluding chapter summarizes the empirical record of window theory and discusses its implications for international relations theory and the study of civil war dynamics as well as for counterinsurgency, international intervention in civil wars, and the conduct of rebellion.

2

Windows of Opportunity, Windows of Vulnerability, and Inter-rebel War

But when dominions are acquired in a region that is not similar in language, customs, and institutions, it is here that difficulties arise; and it is here that one needs much good luck and much diligence to hold on to them.

—NICCOLÒ MACHIAVELLI[1]

None whatever. We agree perfectly. We both want control of Italy!

—FRANCIS I OF FRANCE (IN RESPONSE TO INQUIRIES ABOUT THE DISAGREEMENTS BEHIND FREQUENT WARS WITH SPAIN'S CHARLES V)[2]

Rebel groups exist in an anarchic environment: there is no overarching authority enforcing agreements and providing protection, as they have challenged the state's monopoly of organized violence. Much like sovereign states in the world envisioned by realism in international relations theory, insurgent organizations must rely on themselves and cooperation with other self-regarding actors to survive and achieve their goals.[3] This characterization is arguably more fitting for civil wars than for the contemporary international system: in civil wars, the balance-of-power game is played especially hard, and participants frequently "fall by the wayside," i.e., they are destroyed.[4] By contrast, "state death" (that is, the formal loss of foreign policy–making power to another state) is a rare occurrence.[5] Balance-of-power logic would lead one to expect rebel groups to be natural allies, given that they typically face a stronger common enemy. So why do inter-rebel wars break out?

This chapter lays out my answer: window theory of inter-rebel war. Rebel groups initiate inter-rebel war when facing windows of opportunity to get rid of weaker coethnic rivals on the cheap or windows of vulnerability produced by a sharp decline in power relative to a coethnic rival. I should note that though my dependent variable (that is, the phenomenon I intend to explain) is the onset of inter-rebel war, the closing of windows of opportunity and vulnerability should increase the probability of termination of inter-rebel war too. There may be, however, an element of inertia associated with psychological biases: having committed to initiating inter-rebel fighting, rebel leaders may be slow to update their initial beliefs that they could easily defeat a rival or had a chance of forestalling the decline of their group in the face of contrary evidence. Moreover, intense emotions of fear and vengefulness produced by their clashes may push rebel groups to continue fighting past the point at which it makes strategic sense.

The next section details the combination of material factors (the inter-rebel balance of power and the level of government threat) and ideational factors (rebel groups' ethnic identities) that shape the rebel calculus and give rise to windows of opportunity and windows of vulnerability. A discussion of my approach to testing window theory with case studies follows.

Window Theory of Inter-rebel War

Window theory stems from two simple conjectures. First, rebel groups may have various instrumental motives for resorting to violence against one another. Second, the costs of doing so vary, rather than always being prohibitively high. Therefore, in some circumstances, the benefits of acting on those motives and starting inter-rebel war may be worth the costs. My argument identifies factors shaping rebel groups' calculations (both strictly military considerations and the existence of shared ethnic identities between rebel groups) and specifies the conditions under which inter-rebel war is likely to ensue, namely, when windows of opportunity and windows of vulnerability open.

Motives for inter-rebel war are primarily a function of conflicts of interest among rebel groups, resulting from differences in ideology and values, disagreements over strategy, different priorities, and overlapping ambitions. Groups with the same "strategic goals" (e.g., regime change) can have conflicting "organizational goals" (e.g., increasing their respective membership and funding).[6] In fact, while typically having similar strategic goals, coethnic rebel groups tend to have especially immediate and intense conflicts of interest about organizational goals: they aspire to control the same population and know that they could absorb with relative ease the social resource base of defeated coethnic rivals (and then further extend their hold on the ethnic community), which in turn would improve their chances in the fight against the government. Given that coethnic rivals may represent existential threats as well as pose serious obstacles to growth for one another, both defensive and expansionary motives predispose rebel groups to resort to force to destroy or at least weaken coethnic rivals. Conversely, non-coethnic rebel groups lack intrinsic, powerful motives for fighting one another: they do not necessarily have overlapping ambitions over the same community, and they have little reason to believe they could easily absorb the social resources of a defeated group.

In terms of costs, the possibility that inter-rebel war might weaken the rebels and expose them to a devastating attack by overwhelmingly powerful government forces generally looms large. By contrast, when the government is faring poorly on the battlefield, infighting could entail the major opportunity cost of forgoing significant gains and even outright victory against the incumbent. The costs of inter-rebel war can be relatively low, however, for a group enjoying marked superiority over its rival(s) and facing a strong government that is nonetheless unwilling or unable to intervene rapidly and take advantage of infighting. In fact, the government's aggregate military superiority does not translate automatically into ability or willingness to launch well-timed, decisive offensives against rebels engaged in infighting, owing to political, logistical, and military constraints to power projection.

Both types of windows are situations in which the expected benefits of inter-rebel war outweigh the costs for the initiator.[7] Windows of opportunity entail high expected benefits and low costs for the group launching a hegemonic bid (top-left quadrant in figure 2.1): by quickly and cheaply destroying a weaker coethnic rival (or rivals) without exposing itself to an unacceptably higher risk of government victory and without forgoing opportunities to make major gains against the incumbent, the would-be hegemon at the peak of its power expects to cement its dominant position and cash in on the major benefits of removing the threat posed by coethnic rivals and acquiring more resources.[8]

A rebel group that is relatively weak and/or confronts a significant government threat may also resort to inter-rebel aggression to forestall the deterioration of its power relative to a coethnic rival when no other solution appears possible—a gamble for resurrection in the face of a

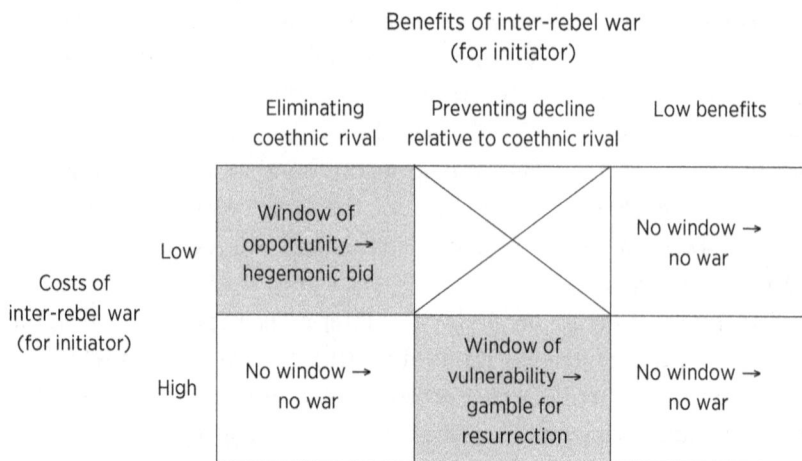

FIGURE 2.1 Window theory of inter-rebel war. The shaded quadrants correspond to scenarios in which window theory predicts inter-rebel war. Inter-rebel war yields low benefits for an initiator that already has established itself as the ethnic rebel hegemon or that would be targeting a non-coethnic group. The center-top quadrant is empty because when the costs of inter-rebel war are low for the initiator, the group faces a window of opportunity to launch a hegemonic bid regardless of whether it is experiencing decline relative to a coethnic rival: getting rid of the rival both addresses the immediate threat posed by its relative growth and provides the long-term benefits of reduced competition and access to a larger social resource pool.

window of vulnerability. The "gambler" may hope to inflict a debilitating blow on its adversary or to conquer militarily strategic territory, whose control would radically alter the inter-rebel balance of power. Though choosing a risky course of action in the face of a window of vulnerability is consistent with an expected-utility perspective (a steep decline in relative power represents a serious threat to the viability of a rebel group), risk-acceptant behavior motivated by loss aversion could also contribute to the decision to gamble for resurrection. As prospect theory suggests, individuals may be willing to take risks to recoup or prevent losses that they would consider excessive when trying to attain gains.[9]

Gambles for resurrection are not limited to the initiation of violence but also include remedial courses of action with a high probability of provoking a violent response by a coethnic rival, such as creating a fait accompli by deploying forces in strategic disputed territory.[10] The ensuing boost to the power of the gambler would create a window of vulnerability for its rival, prompting it in turn to violently oppose the fait accompli rather than acquiesce.

Windows of vulnerability are characterized by both high expected costs and benefits (the center-bottom quadrant in figure 2.1). The prospect, however remote, for a rebel group to reduce the urgent threat of a rising coethnic rival by picking a fight with it may warrant paying the steep costs and running the serious risks involved in inter-rebel war in the absence of a favorable balance of power and/or a limited government threat. Desperate times call for desperate measures. Window theory predicts no inter-rebel war between non-coethnic rebel groups or when a rebel group has already established itself as the ethnic rebel hegemon given the low expected benefits (right quadrants in figure 2.1).

Both hegemonic bids and gambles for resurrection follow a "better-now-than-later" logic, albeit with an important difference.[11] Whereas gambles for resurrection represent a rebel group's desperate response to a relative decline in power, hegemonic bids are efforts to consolidate a group's dominant position before a window of opportunity closes, even if there is no indication of an imminent deterioration of the balance of power or intensification of government threat.[12]

Shifts in the inter-rebel balance of power may have various causes. Some rebel groups may simply be better than others at recruiting and mobilizing the population, owing to the resonance of their political message or their particular effectiveness in rewarding their affiliates and intimidating their rivals' supporters. Furthermore, rebel organizations may see their growth propelled by access to profitable resources (e.g., smuggling networks, drug cultivation, oil, precious metals and gems). Third-party states can also affect the inter-rebel balance of power; foreign largesse may fatten some groups, while others may starve as their external lifeline is cut off. Moreover, an imminent direct external intervention in support of rivals may signal the prospect of a group's sharp decline in relative power.

Rebel groups launch hegemonic bids without delay when a window of opportunity opens. By contrast, gambles for resurrection are responses of last resort. Insurgent leaders typically would go to considerable lengths in search of a less risky way out of their predicament, for example, engaging in diplomatic initiatives to break hostile encirclements and gain new allies, experimenting with different mobilization strategies in the face of dwindling popular support, striving to improve their cohesion and battlefield effectiveness, or even engaging in low-level coercive actions to extract from adversaries concessions that may help forestall relative decline.[13]

While my argument is about the causes of inter-rebel war, it also has implications for the outcomes of clashes between rebel groups. As window theory does not assume a systematic bias in rebel leaders' assessment of the balance of power and threat environment, hegemonic bids should tend to be successful, given that they are launched by a preponderant rebel group in a context of limited government threat.[14] Conversely, gambles for resurrection should fail more frequently, as they represent desperate attempts by increasingly vulnerable groups to improve their difficult position.

I now turn to a more detailed discussion of the factors shaping the cost-benefit calculus of rebel groups—coethnicity, government threat, and the inter-rebel balance of power.

Coethnicity and the Benefits of Inter-rebel War

Coethnicity provides defensive and expansionary motives for inter-rebel war, as it holds the promise of both an improved threat environment and a larger social resource pool for the initiator. As a result of overlapping ambitions to control the same ethnic community, coethnic rebel groups tend to see one another as direct competitors and thus as obstacles to their goals and even as existential threats. Coethnic organizations might interfere with their respective mobilization efforts and derail the struggle against the government by spoiling negotiations, reducing the clarity of rebel demands and the credibility of threats to the incumbent, and they may even flip to the government's side.[15] A rebel group would therefore consider using force to reduce the threat posed by a coethnic rival. Refraining from doing so at an opportune moment may mean not only forgoing a chance to address the problems just discussed but also exposing the group to the future risks of an attack by the rival or of having to make unpalatable concessions to it from a position of weakness.

The high level of perceived threat that characterizes relations among coethnic rebel groups is compounded by the "cumulativity" of their social resources—that is, these resources can be extracted at low cost, and their possession allows a group to protect itself and grow stronger.[16] When a rebel organization wipes out a coethnic rival, it can often coopt large segments of the latter's membership. More important, the organization that prevails in inter-rebel war is likely to be able to recruit and extract resources at a relatively low cost from the coethnic population previously under its rival's control: undisputed access to a rebel group's ethnic constituency is the key asset, as waging guerrilla warfare (the most common way in which insurgents fight) typically does not require large armies. A pliable support base can provide intelligence, safe havens, money, and logistical support, in addition to recruits. Moreover, some elements of defeated groups may be considered irreconcilable, making less experienced but more reliable new recruits preferable. Therefore achieving hegemony through a quick and cheap fight against coethnic rivals holds the prospect of strengthening the victor for its ongoing fight against the government.

By contrast, an organization perceived by the social base of support of a defeated organization as an out-group or a "foreign occupier" is likely to experience difficulties with recruitment and extraction activities and will have to devote substantial manpower to policing the population, potentially leading to a net drain of its resources.[17] The point is not that foreign occupiers simply cannot recruit and elicit support from the population in the occupied territories,[18] but rather that the corresponding costs are likely to be high.[19] For this reason, the existence of long-term conflicts of interest between non-coethnic rebels groups (for example, about the distribution of power among a country's ethnic groups) does not tend to prompt inter-rebel war: their settlement is better left to the postwar phase, as infighting would disproportionally benefit the government.[20] I should note that window theory does not assume civilians to be indifferent about cooperating with, joining, or being under the control of different coethnic rebel groups: inhabitants of a certain area may well have a preference for a given rebel group over its coethnic rivals. The argument, rather, posits that once her preferred coethnic organization no longer exists, the average individual should be relatively willing to cooperate with and join another existing coethnic organization, but not non-coethnic organizations.

As an illustration, compare ISIS's experience in dealing with Sunni Arabs, on the one hand, and Kurds, on the other. ISIS's Sunni Arab constituency in Iraq initially welcomed the Jihadists as liberators from the oppression of the Shia-led Iraqi government. A Sunni resident of Mosul summarized the attitude of many inhabitants of Iraq's second largest city toward ISIS fighters thus: "We thought they were Sunnis who had come to help their fellow Sunnis." By contrast, Kurds living in the outskirts of Mosul fled their homes before ISIS's arrival.[21] Moreover, ISIS's internal documents indicate that it perceived Syrian Kurds as a fifth column for the U.S.-led coalition and the Kurdish-dominated Democratic Union Party (better known by its Kurdish acronym, PYD), prompting the Islamic State's decision to expel the Kurdish population from key areas under its control.[22]

What are the microfoundations of the cumulativity of resources controlled by coethnic rebel groups? An individual's propensity to join and support coethnic rebel organizations can be traced to ethnic parochialism, the tendency for people to be particularly cooperative with and favor members of their ethnic group.[23] As a result, in ethnically heterogeneous clientelist democracies and electoral autocracies, elections are often ethnic censuses, with ethnicity providing a remarkably precise predictor of voting behavior.[24] In addition, patronage and public goods are distributed along ethnic lines.[25] Moreover, rulers of developing countries often resort to "ethnic stacking" (i.e., filling key government and military positions with coethnics) to ensure the loyalty of the security apparatus.[26]

While these empirical patterns are widely acknowledged, there is much debate over their causes. The dominant view in political science holds that individuals cooperate with coethnics because of the prospect of material gain. In particular, agreements between coethnics are more easily enforced because of their especially dense social networks facilitating information flows.[27] Moreover, given their relative visibility and stickiness, ethnic markers can be used by individuals as quick and crude information shortcuts to gauge the likely behavior of their counterparts; if people come to believe that coethnics tend to cooperate with one another, ethnic favoritism becomes a self-fulfilling prophecy.[28] A second view, rooted in social identity and political socialization theories, postulates that individuals have genuine, emotionally laden attachments to their ethnic group.[29] These attachments prompt people to support organizations representing their ethnic group's interests even at high personal costs, in particular during large-scale ethnic violence.[30]

Window theory of inter-rebel war is agnostic about the relative importance of the two families of mechanisms just described: both are likely to operate simultaneously, making individuals more willing to join and cooperate with coethnic rebel organizations, and thus contribute to promote inter-rebel war. After rebel group A's defeat of coethnic rival B, the latter's supporters would tend to be drawn to group A in the expectation that it would be a bulwark against a government controlled by ethnic-others threatening the security, well-being, and dignity of the ethnic community. Moreover, rebel group A's members would benefit from existing expectations of cooperation among coethnics and would be able to tap into ethnic information networks, making threats of punishment and promises of rewards credible, which in turn would facilitate control of the population previously under rebel group B's sway.

An important question about coethnicity needs to be addressed: Why doesn't the cooperation-inducing effect of shared identity among individuals extend to relations among rebel leaders, thus failing to discourage inter-rebel war? The answer lies not in different degrees of ethnic identification or in-group bias of rebel leaders compared to followers—the former may well be as ethnoparochial in their attitudes as the latter (or even more so). Rather it has to do with leaders' distinctive outlooks and incentive structures. Insurgent leaders are uniquely placed to grasp the constraints and incentives provided by their strategic environment.

The brutal facts of rebel groups' life stare insurgent leaders in the eyes and induce them to adopt a strategic and consequentialist outlook: the imperatives of organizational survival and success in the struggle against the government warrant a dispassionate and forward-looking approach to inter-rebel relations and justify actions toward coethnics that would not be acceptable in interpersonal relations.[31] Moreover, the personal interests of leaders are inextricably intertwined with those of their organization: even if they are genuinely committed to the well-being of the broader ethnic community, leaders stand to benefit more than coethnic rank and file or civilians from their organization's survival and success; thus rebel leaders should be inclined to use force against coethnic rival organizations in the advancement of their organization's interests.

Government Threat, Balance of Power, and the Costs of Inter-rebel War

Inter-rebel war also has its costs. Besides the direct expenditure of blood and treasure, these consist of increased vulnerability to the incumbent and forgone opportunities to make military gains against it. In particular, the government could take advantage of the situation and attack the squabbling rebels, or it could let them bleed one another white and then take on the debilitated victor.[32] Moreover, inter-rebel fighting could push the group that is losing to turn to the government for help, strengthening the counterinsurgency effort. Inter-rebel war would entail major opportunity costs if it diverted resources from the antigovernment struggle when a sustained effort could bring about important territorial gains or even victory for a rebel group (or multiple groups), thus offering a chance for the incumbent to regroup.[33]

The costs of inter-rebel war should be low, however, when three conditions are jointly present: (1) there is a marked imbalance of power among rebel organizations, (2) the government does not represent a serious and immediate military threat, but (3) it is not so weak as to suggest major opportunity costs. In the face of these low costs, the more powerful group may be tempted to wipe out its coethnic rival(s) to become the rebel hegemon. Under these circumstances, the image costs in the eyes of the relevant ethnic community of committing "fratricide" are likely low too: the decisive fight will be over quickly, and the hegemon will be in a favorable position to emphasize the importance of unity against the government.[34]

The government is typically the strongest warring party, but this superiority does not mean a constant willingness and ability to unrestrainedly bring to bear its military power. Political, military, and logistical constraints may limit government power projection, so that it may not represent a serious and immediate threat to the rebels. In some instances, the low level of government threat faced by an insurgent movement is largely beyond the incumbent's control, as when security forces are busy dealing with a foreign enemy, paralyzed by internecine struggle, or simply in the midst of challenging logistical preparations and training for a future major offensive. In others, the government may consciously adopt a low-threat stance, as putting maximum pressure on the rebels is not a top priority. As Paul Staniland notes, "States are often content not to devote their full resources to internal war." For example, the prospect of high domestic political costs discouraged the Indian government from launching large-scale offensives against the United Liberation Front of Asom and the Naxalite insurgents for years.[35]

Rebel groups can gauge whether the government poses a serious and immediate threat based on recent or ongoing battlefield trends and troop deployments, as well as on intelligence about the incumbent's plans. The typical scenario of serious and immediate threat would be when the government is engaged in (or about to launch) a major offensive. Even if government forces are not making major territorial headway, an intense fight in which the insurgents are stretched thin to resist the government's onslaught would not represent a permissive environment for inter-rebel fighting: diverting resources to inter-rebel war (even if short and decisive) may pave the way for the government's battlefield success. By contrast, in a context characterized by sporadic, limited clashes or stable battle lines, insurgent leaders may see the diversion of resources to inter-rebel fighting as entailing an acceptable short-term increase of vulnerability.

The typical scenario of high opportunity costs is one in which a rebel group is poised to capture important territory from government forces or victory appears within reach if it sustains maximum pressure against the government. In these situations, the prospect of forgoing major military gains should deter the group from inter-rebel aggression.

The inter-rebel balance of power affects the prospective costs of inter-rebel war, too. Attacking clearly weaker rebel groups promises a cheap victory. By contrast, groups of comparable strength are likely to put up a serious fight. The ensuing long war of attrition would weaken the rebels, thus creating the conditions for a successful government offensive. Therefore a favorable inter-rebel balance of power is a requirement for launching a hegemonic bid.[36] By contrast, rebel groups gamble for resurrection when facing an unfavorable distribution of power and/or a serious and imminent government threat, that is, when inter-rebel war is likely to be very costly.

Questions About Window Theory of Inter-rebel War

A few questions about window theory remain to be addressed. First, what prevents coethnic rebel groups from finding a negotiated solution to their conflicts of interests?[37] The answer, in a nutshell, is: coethnic rebel groups' intense fears that any agreement reached today to avoid inter-rebel war may amount to just a scrap of paper tomorrow, i.e., the so-called commitment problem in anarchy. In the presence of a window of opportunity, the only acceptable alternative to launching a hegemonic bid for the stronger group would be the de facto capitulation of its weaker coethnic rival, lest the latter come to pose a serious threat under changed circumstances. On its part, the weaker group would reject these terms, as fighting holds the prospect (albeit dim, given the imbalance of power) of a better outcome than negotiating itself out of existence.

When facing a window of vulnerability, the group in relative decline should be willing to remain at peace if offered credible guarantees that its core interests would not be trampled over by its coethnic rival down the road. The underlying shift in the balance of power, however, would undermine the credibility of promises to that effect, given that the rising group would have an incentive to renege on them later on.[38] The declining group may be concerned not only (or even primarily) about the risk of an eventual attack by its coethnic rival but also about the prospect of having to make unpalatable concessions in the future owing to a deteriorating bargaining position.[39] While these concerns could be assuaged if the declining group acquired some asset (such as a territory with strategic value) capable of propping up its strength, the rival would be likely to oppose violently such a development: with roles reversed, in this scenario the hitherto declining power could not commit not to take advantage of its newfound source of power in the future.[40] Thus a group's attempt to escape its window of vulnerability with a fait accompli acquisition of strategic territory would risk creating a window of vulnerability for its rival and therefore a new, war-provoking commitment problem.

The commitment problem is inherently less intense in relations among non-coethnic rebel groups, due to their less stark and immediate conflicts of interest and the difficulty for rebels of mobilizing a non-coethnic population. Rebel group C would have less of a reason to be concerned about a power shift in favor of non-coethnic rebel group D, as D would not have a strong incentive to try to squeeze C out of the rebel camp or to attack it. By contrast, a nonnegligible commitment problem between coethnic rebel groups would exist even in the absence of the other elements of windows of opportunity and vulnerability: there is always the *possibility* of future changes in the inter-rebel balance of power and the level of government threat. However, inter-rebel war among coethnic groups in the absence of the other elements of windows of opportunity and vulnerability is generally deterred by its prohibitively high costs relative to the benefits.

Second, in contexts with more than two coethnic rebel groups, should we expect hegemonic bids only when the preponderant organization can marshal greater military power than all others combined? No, a large, unambiguous margin of superiority vis-à-vis the "second-ranked" rebel group would typically be sufficient, as serious collective action and coordination problems are likely to hamper joint defensive efforts against the would-be hegemon.[41] Each of the weaker rebel groups has an incentive to sit on the sidelines or limit its contribution in the hope that someone else "catches the buck." Moreover, for any given level of contribution to the coalition, coordination problems at the strategic, operational, and tactical levels are likely to arise, thus reducing its military effectiveness.[42] By contrast, when the first- and the second-ranked groups are roughly equally powerful, we should normally expect them to abstain from launching hegemonic bids against other weaker groups, lest their "peer" got involved in the fight and thus found themselves bogged down in a long, costly inter-rebel war.

Third, do windows of opportunity for one group correspond to windows of vulnerability for other groups? The answer: typically not, but it may happen. When that is the case, we should be more likely to see a hegemonic bid than a gamble for resurrection, given that, as noted above, gambles for resurrection are responses of last resort. The reason the two types of windows normally will not coexist is that a window of vulnerability is not merely a situation in which a rebel group faces the risk of attack by a stronger coethnic rival; rather, it entails a clear prospect of a drastic deterioration of the group's power relative to a rival, which induces the declining group into now-or-never thinking. Under these circumstances (and in the absence of a major first-strike advantage), the rebel group experiencing a relative rise would not face a window of opportunity to attack; it would have instead an incentive to refrain from using force while its power grows.

A possible scenario in which a window of opportunity for a rebel group would correspond to a window of vulnerability for others is one in which a group has sufficient power to take on its weaker coethnic rivals sequentially and would then grow stronger by absorbing the social resource base of one rival at the time: the preponderant rebel group would then face a window of opportunity while the other groups would face a window of vulnerability, due to their prospect of further decline after each bilateral fight. A hegemonic bid, however, would be more likely than a gamble for resurrection in this scenario, as the weaker groups would be reluctant to act until less risky paths out of their quandary have been ruled out. Moreover, the declining rebel groups would experience collective action problems in mounting a joint attack, while the would-be hegemon would have an incentive to act swiftly.

Fourth and finally, why should we expect coethnicity to have a different effect on inter-rebel relations than other forms of shared identity, such as those based on social class and ideology? My answer stems from both empirical and theoretical considerations. Empirically, studies documenting systematic in-group bias in a variety of political outcomes—voting, patronage distribution, and stacking of the security apparatus—emphasize ethnic rather than other types of cleavages.[43] Theoretically, three distinct, but complementary, evolutionary processes suggest that ethnic identity should have an especially powerful effect on individual behavior in ethnic civil wars: kin favoritism (or inclusive fitness), culture-gene coevolution, and group-level selection through war.

A predisposition for preferentially caring for one's kin is adaptive as it helps spread one's genes and thus the predisposition itself.[44] Several theorists envision ethnic parochialism as an extension of kin favoritism through widening circles of attachment, from the nuclear and the extended family to the tribe and then the broader ethnic community.[45] As humans have spent almost all their time on earth as hunter-gatherers in extended family groups (clans), in turn part of larger endogamous groups characterized by egalitarian relations among members and a shared culture (tribes), "what proved adaptive then constitutes our biological inheritance."[46] Though blood ties among members of the tribe were not nearly as close as those among family members, dense networks of intratribe marriages ensured that there would be much closer kinship among in-groups than with out-groups, and thus a corresponding in-group favoritism. The kin-favoritism basis for ethnic parochialism was significantly strengthened by a cultural twist. As in ancestral times culture was local and tightly correlated with kinship, tribe-specific culture worked as an efficient and reliable cue for recognizing relatively close kin.[47] Today's ethnic groups can be thought of as quasi-tribes—larger groups of individuals sharing a sense of kinship and common culture—capable of harnessing our evolved tribal psychology.

Culture also played a different role in shaping our ethnically parochial minds. From early on in our evolutionary history, humans have been a uniquely cultural species, whose ability to learn from others shaped individuals' life chances and in turn directed genetic evolution—a dynamic known as culture-gene coevolution.[48] As culture begun to accumulate over generations, a key "selection pressure on genes revolved around improving our psychological abilities to acquire, store, process, and organize the array of fitness enhancing skills and practices that became increasingly available in the minds of the others in one's group."[49] Natural selection thus endowed us with a tendency to preferentially interact with those who share our tribal/ethnic markers regardless of genetic relatedness, as these individuals would be more likely to possess locally relevant, fitness-enhancing know-how.

Violent intertribe conflict—war—may have contributed to spread norms requiring prosocial behaviors within the group through a process of group-level *cultural* selection. Archaeological and anthropological evidence suggests that war was very frequent and deadly among ancestral humans;[50] tribes with social norms fostering internal cooperation would have fought more cohesively on the battlefield and thus driven out, eliminated, or assimilated tribes with different norms.[51] Moreover, through a process of group-level *gene* selection, war may have facilitated the spread of the trait of "parochial altruism"—a combination of hostility toward outsiders and willingness to help members of one's tribe/ethnic group at a cost to oneself.[52] Ancestral tribes with a prevalence of parochial altruists would tend to be involved in war and to prevail in it, owing to superior numbers of committed fighters. Parochial altruism would then proliferate, as battlefield success offered group members both a higher chance of survival and more opportunities for reproduction. Without war, willingness to sacrifice for group members may not have proven adaptive, as it would have had the effect of selecting out individuals who possessed the trait faster than helping them through higher group survival and reproduction rates.

In sum, in the course of our long history as members of tribes—egalitarian groups knit together by blood and marriage ties as well as a common culture and frequently engaged in violent intergroup conflict—evolution has equipped us with a propensity to offer preferential treatment on the basis of shared ethnicity rather than other types of identity. There may well be instances in which other types of identities take on a quasi-ascriptive character and operate similarly to ethnicity.[53] Based on the theory and evidence discussed, however, I posit that this should be the exception rather than the rule. In the following chapters I assess empirically the effect of shared political ideology as an alternative explanation for inter-rebel war.

Importantly, the fact that our ethnoparochial psychology has deep evolutionary roots does not imply that existing ethnic groups are timeless monoliths. To the contrary, they are shaped by processes of social construction, so both their boundaries and cultural content can change over time. Moreover, individuals' ethnic repertoires often include multiple identities (one can be simultaneously, say, Sardinian, Italian, European, and white), whose relative salience may vary based on the situation.

Nonetheless, it makes sense to speak of rebel organizations affiliated with specific ethnic groups, particularly when insurgents make claims on behalf of and recruit from those ethnic groups: large-scale violence across ethnic lines heightens the salience of the corresponding identities and hardens ethnic boundaries, thus justifying an assumption of ethnic groups as exogenously given for my theoretical purposes.[54]

Testing Window Theory with Case Studies

Convincingly testing window theory requires paying heed to fine-grained measures of belligerents' capabilities and battlefield developments as well as to rebel groups' constituencies. Thus this book puts particular emphasis on case studies of various civil wars, presented in the following three chapters. (Chapter 6 uses statistical analysis to test, on a broader range of civil wars, a specific implication of window theory—that coethnic rebel groups should be particularly prone to infighting.)

Windows of opportunity and windows of vulnerability shape rebel groups' behavior indirectly, through the perceptions and beliefs of their leaders. Thus the ideal evidence for testing my argument is information on rebel leaders' calculus.[55] Window theory would be strongly supported by evidence that (1) rebel leaders launched an attack as a result of their perception of an opportunity to cheaply eliminate weaker coethnic rivals or of an urgent need to forestall a decline in power relative to a coethnic competitor despite the potential steep costs; and (2) they refrained from attacking because comparable opportunities and vulnerabilities were absent. I gathered relevant data by conducting interviews with individuals who had taken part in (or were directly informed about) rebel groups' decision making.[56] I address concerns about subjects' (conscious or unconscious) biases and defective memories by triangulating information across interviewees that belonged to different organizations (and thus presumably had divergent incentive structures) and with accounts provided in rebel publications and the secondary literature.[57]

Information from the secondary literature is useful not only for cross-checking purposes, but also for coding the existence of windows in the various instances in which data on rebel leaders' assessments of the inter-rebel balance of power and government threat is not available.[58] In the absence of information on rebel leaders' perceptions of the defining features of windows, I adopt the following coding criteria to identify them, independently of whether inter-rebel war occurred. I measure the inter-rebel balance of power along four dimensions: (1) rebel groups' number of fighters; (2) access to weapons; (3) organizational cohesion (measured as relative absence of splits and feuds among leaders and pervasive indiscipline among the rank and file); and (4) tactical-operational skills (proxied by battlefield experience and reports of battlefield prowess).[59] As extant theory does not provide clear indications about the relative importance of these aspects of rebel military power, I consider a rebel group stronger if it clearly outranks a rival in a net number of dimensions of power for which I have information.[60] I code a sharp shift in rebel relative power—a key element of windows of vulnerability—if there is evidence of an unmistakable trend in flows of recruits or weapons or an impeding international intervention in favor of specific rebel groups.

In cases in which rebellion takes the form of guerrilla warfare, I code a low level of government threat if insurgents typically initiate contacts with security forces (by launching hit-and-run attacks), which implies that the rebels can choose when and where to fight and thus control the pace of their losses. In conventional warfare, a permissive threat environment typically would be characterized by static battle lines, which, based on previous interactions, the insurgents know they can comfortably defend in the absence of indications of significant government escalation in the near future. I code high opportunity costs of inter-rebel war if a rebel group has just made substantial territorial gains or conquered several towns (suggesting a clear favorable battlefield trend, which the insurgents should be wary to jeopardize) or is engaged in an offensive to take a major town or an area on an international border (suggesting the prospect of making potentially decisive gains against the incumbent).

My qualitative approach to coding the existence of windows of opportunity and windows of vulnerability has a drawback: reasonable analysts may disagree in their interpretation of the evidence, thus reaching disparate conclusions about the presence of windows in some instances. This could be avoided if strict numerical coding criteria were adopted specifying, for example, that a government escalation amounting to a shift from a permissive threat environment for the insurgents to a nonpermissive one requires a certain percentage increment of government forces conducting counterinsurgency operations. However, the benefit of "reliability" (that is, ensuring that different analysts would reach the same conclusions about the existence of windows) risks coming at the cost of sacrificing the contextual and nuanced measurement of complex concepts, which may undermine "validity" (the close correspondence between the concept of interest, i.e., the existence of windows, and the chosen indicator). Though the secondary literature and the evidence of rebel calculus emerging from my interviews significantly limit the room for individual analysts' interpretation, I acknowledge the trade-off between validity and reliability of measures of the existence of windows.[61] I seek to minimize concerns about reliability through transparency of my coding decisions.[62] I welcome debates about my historical interpretations that may ensue.

Finally, I consider a rebel group as below a threshold of extreme weakness, thus representing a negligible threat for the ethnic hegemon, if it has less than one-third as many fighters as the most powerful coethnic rebel group (i.e., the hegemon) *and* no immediate prospects of rapid growth, which would typically be the case if the group operates in territory under the control of the hegemon or in sparsely populated areas and has no independent access to external support. The same holds for relations between coethnic rebel groups other than the hegemon. For example, the second strongest rebel group would tend to perceive a coethnic group of less than one-third its size as not poising a meaningful threat, in the absence of indications that the small group is about to rapidly grow. I adapt this coding criterion from Krause's approach to identifying hegemonic national liberation movements, requiring at least a 3:1 power advantage for the strongest group over each of the others. Krause notes that international relations scholars typically require that a state be 50–80 percent as strong as the most powerful state in the international system to be considered a great power, but he suggests that a much starker measure of dominance is appropriate in the context of national liberation movements and civil wars, as the balance of power among nonstate organizations is much more volatile than among states.[63] It makes sense to use a unidimensional, numerical measure of extreme weakness because often very little is known about marginal rebel organizations.

Moreover, even in cases in which information about other aspects of the inter-rebel balance of power is available, there are no obvious ways to establish that a group enjoys three times the level of firepower, tactical-operational skills, or cohesion as another group. When even estimates of group size are unavailable, I code rebel groups as below the threshold of extreme weakness when sources explicitly report them as inconsequential, irrelevant, or tiny, or key works on the corresponding civil war fail to even mention the groups.

Selection Issues

This book is about multiparty civil wars, which are a subset of all civil wars. Various processes determine the number of active rebel groups and thus whether a given armed conflict is selected into the universe of multiparty civil wars. What are the implications of this selection for my argument and analysis?

Different rebel groups may be expressions of distinct social cleavages, ethnic or otherwise, and corresponding preferences about distribution of power and wealth as well as public policy.[64] For example, in the late 1980s the Uganda People's Army (UPA) and the Lord's Resistance Army (LRA) mobilized the politically discriminated Iteso and Acholi ethnic groups, respectively, while the Communist Party of Nepal-Maoist took up arms in 1996 after breaking away from the United People's Front, which had hitherto pursued class struggle with nonviolent means.[65]

Perhaps more surprising to some readers, civil wars often feature multiple rebel organizations representing the same ethnic community. This is because, as Staniland has shown, would-be rebel leaders typically build their organizations atop preexisting social networks that are embedded in a broader ethnic group, such as political parties, religious organizations, kinship ties, and veteran associations.[66] For example, the Jammu and Kashmir Liberation Front (JKLF) and the Hezb-ul-Mujahideen (HuM)—both claiming to fight on behalf of the Muslim population of India-controlled Kashmir—were built on a network of members of the Islamic Students' League and the religious organization/political party Jamaat-e-Islami, respectively, which had existed long before the onset of armed conflict. Moreover, existing rebel groups may fragment giving rise to coethnic splinters.[67] In the early 1990s multiple rebel groups splintered off the JKLF amid leadership disputes and a membership hemorrhage.

The presence of more than one rebel organization affiliated with the same ethnic community could be the result of particularly strong underlying intra-ethnic tensions, leading to organizational splintering or to the independent emergence of multiple rebel groups; these tensions, in turn, could be the driver of inter-rebel war among coethnic rebels, rather than shared ethnicity per se, potentially introducing a selection bias in my analysis.[68] In practice, two sets of considerations suggest this is unlikely to be a serious problem. First, the existence of multiple organizations affiliated with the same ethnic group is the rule rather than the exception: the average number of organizations in self-determination movements in a given civil war year in the period 1960–2005 was 4.8, while only in less than one out of five self-determination movement-years in a civil war context was there just one active organization.[69] The high frequency of fragmented ethnic movements suggests that studying civil wars with multiple rebel groups from the same ethnic community does not automatically imply selecting cases with an exceptional propensity to inter-rebel war among coethnics. Second, inasmuch as it is plausible that intra-ethnic tensions are particularly high when coethnic rebel groups emerge from an organizational schism rather than as separate organizations from the outset (a divorce may lead to more bitterness than an engagement that never takes place), I can assess the split-induced intra-ethnic tensions as an alternative explanation in both case studies and statistical analysis by taking into account rebel groups' origins.

Competing Explanations

In the following chapters I assess how well window theory can explain the observed pattern of inter-rebel war compared to competing explanations. Christia's minimum winning coalition theory represents a clear alternative to my argument, suggesting that rebel groups, spurred by the survival imperative under anarchy, would ally with one another when facing a stronger government.[70] From this perspective, inter-rebel war should occur only when at least one rebel group has a clear margin of military superiority vis-à-vis the government. Krause's argument about the internal dynamics of national liberation movements with competing organizations suggests an alternative power-driven explanation for infighting: relatively weak rebel groups (which he dubs "challengers") should tend to be the initiators of inter-rebel war in the hope that the ensuing shake-up of the intramovement balance of power would allow them to climb to a position of dominance.[71]

Arguments positing the unconditional power of shared ethnic identity to draw people together in the context of large-scale violence suggest a potential explanation for the *absence* of inter-rebel war: regardless of what specific factors drive rebel organizations to fight one another, coethnicity should reduce the risk of inter-rebel war, as intra-ethnic solidarity and hostility toward out-groups should promote cooperation and suppress conflict among coethnics.[72]

Other alternative explanations focus on individual rebel leaders' characteristics and rebel groups' features (in particular, their degree of internal cohesion and ideology). Leaders' worldview, temperament, personality, and mental health may affect the propensity of their organizations to engage in inter-rebel war.[73] For example, highly insecure or aggressive leaders may embark on more inter-rebel wars than, say, empathic ones. Decentralized or undisciplined organizations may be especially prone to inter-rebel war as skirmishes initiated by foot soldiers or low-level commanders might escalate to the point of engulfing entire organizations. Conversely, groups lacking tight centralized control may be less likely to experience inter-rebel war as their leaders' decision to attack another organization may not be carried out by operatives on the ground.

Certain ideological leanings may predispose rebel organizations to violence in their relations with any rebel group or only with groups embracing different ideologies, regardless of ethnic identities. For instance, Islamist rebel groups may be generally prone to inter-rebel aggression or only when dealing with secularly oriented organizations. It may also be that ideology conditions the effect of shared ethnic identity, prompting coethnic organizations to turn against one another only when they hold different ideological visions for their ethnic community.[74] Alternatively, a shared ideology could have a comparable effect as shared ethnicity, pushing rebel groups with overlapping ideologically defined constituencies to compete with and fight one another.[75] A further variant of the ideological argument centers on the distinction between rebel hardliners ("hawks") and moderates ("doves") as the source of disagreement that may escalate in inter-rebel war.[76]

As discussed in the previous section, the path through which multiple coethnic organizations come into existence may also offer an alternative explanation for the inter-rebel war. In particular, it may be that organizations that emerge from the fragmentation of a preexisting organization are particularly prone to infighting, as a result of tensions produced by the splintering process or those that brought it about in the first place.

A different set of alternative explanations focuses on other actors: third-party states and the incumbent. Both actors could try to induce inter-rebel violence or cooperation by deploying carrots and sticks at their disposal (e.g., promises of aid or recognition, threats of increased military pressure or reduced support).[77] The incumbent could also bring about inter-rebel war by creating the perception that some rebel groups are in cahoots with it, thus increasing distrust inside the rebel movement.[78] Alternatively, as Kristin Bakke, Kathleen Cunningham, and Lee Seymour argue in the context of self-determination movements, a rebel group may attack a rival in the hope of government concessions, as a reward or as an acknowledgment of the group's strength signaled by success in inter-rebel war.[79]

It is important to note that while some alternative explanations are incompatible with window theory, others are not necessarily so. In particular, evidence that rebel groups follow minimum winning coalition logic (fighting one another only if one of them was stronger than the government and disregarding ethnic identities) would falsify my argument. Similarly, if intra-ethnic solidarity appears to suppress, rather than propel, inter-rebel competition, window theory would be falsified. By contrast, evidence that rebel groups, say, with certain ideological leanings, decentralized organizational structures, or aggressive leaders are distinctively prone to inter-rebel war would not necessarily falsify window theory. My argument would be falsified only if these extraneous factors tend to be so powerful as to prevent inter-rebel war in the presence of windows or to bring it about in their absence.

The same holds for alternative arguments pointing to the influence of the incumbent or third-party states on relations among rebel groups: these actors' influence on inter-rebel relations is unproblematic for my argument, as long as it does not tend to overcome the effects of windows of opportunity and windows of vulnerability. In fact, window theory envisions specific ways in which third-party states and the incumbent can affect the risk of inter-rebel war—by influencing the balance of power among rebel groups and their threat environment and thus the presence of windows of opportunity and windows of vulnerability. The fact that groups may mistrust one another because of the possibility (or actual fact) that they are in contact with the government (and may at some point even cooperate with it to other groups' detriment) is also fully consistent with window theory, as the risk of defection is one of the factors, postulated by my argument, that make rebel groups see one another as threatening. Window theory would be falsified only if fear of defection caused inter-rebel war regardless of the presence of windows.

Summary of the Argument

Inter-rebel wars erupt when an insurgent organization faces a window of opportunity or a window of vulnerability, while inter-rebel peace tends to prevail in the absence of windows. Windows of opportunity require three conditions: (1) an imbalance of power among coethnic rebel groups, (2) a limited government threat, and (3) low opportunity costs for the relatively strong group (i.e., it is not poised to make major strategic gains against the government on the battlefield). In this situation, the relatively strong rebel group will be tempted to launch a hegemonic bid to get rid of a coethnic competitor.

Windows of vulnerability arise when a rebel group that is relatively weak and/or faces a high government threat experiences a sharp power decline relative to a coethnic rival, which cannot be forestalled by peaceful means. The group will then be tempted to gamble for resurrection—i.e., initiate a course of action likely to set it on a collision course with the rival or directly use force against it—in a desperate attempt to improve its difficult situation. Far from being a mere façade for material calculations, rebel groups' shared ethnic identity provides both defensive and expansionary motives for inter-rebel war, as it affects rebel groups' threat perception and ability to acquire resources at their rivals' expense.

Let us now turn to this book's first case study to observe window theory in action.

3

Inter-rebel War in the
Shadow of Genocide

THE KURDISH INSURGENCIES IN IRAQ

Excluding Anfal, more Kurds in Iraq have died at the hands of fellow Kurds than of Arabs.

—SENIOR KURDISTAN DEMOCRATIC PARTY MEMBER[1]

I would never allow Barzani to forcefully impose his hegemony on Kurdistan.
    I rather let it all go to hell.

—JALAL TALABANI[2]

A t various points in the second half of the twentieth century, Iraq's Kurdish rebel organizations fought one another to exploit opportunities to launch hegemonic bids or to extricate themselves from positions of deepening vulnerability. All these inter-rebel fights occurred despite the presence of an overwhelmingly powerful common enemy—the Iraqi government—with a penchant for ethnic mass killing. Rather than promoting solidarity and cooperation against Baghdad, coethnicity stoked violent competition among Kurdish rebel organizations for control of their common constituency.

I used the history of relations between Iraq's Kurdish rebel groups in the years up to 1988 to develop my window theory of inter-rebel war. In this chapter, I present this case in significant detail for two reasons, before turning to the main theory-testing case studies of Ethiopian insurgencies in the next chapter. First, exploring whether the opening of windows of opportunity and vulnerability cast light on the trajectories of war and cooperation among Kurdish rebel groups represents an opportunity for an initial probing of my argument. Contrary to a prevailing understanding of the case study method, "peeking" (i.e., seeing the evidence before complete formulation of the theoretical argument) makes neither confirmation inevitable nor falsification impossible if what one is trying to explain are complex phenomena characterized by multiple data points.[3] Contending otherwise would imply denying any value to qualitative research on cases that are well known (think of World War I or the end of the cold war) and more generally to historians' efforts to provide "historical interpretations" of specific events *after* carefully studying the available evidence.[4] As Marc Trachtenberg comments, "It is not as though observations are like dots on a piece of paper that can be connected to each other however one pleases. Only certain connections can legitimately be drawn: the sort of picture that can legitimately be painted on the basis of those data is limited by the fact that 'the world is what it is'—or, in the case of history, by the fact that the past was what it was."[5]

Moreover, the fact that my theory-development exercise excluded the 1990s, owing to the unwillingness on the part of my Kurdish interviewees to discuss the dramatic issue of intra-Kurdish fighting in that period, offers the opportunity for an out-of-sample test of window theory in Iraqi Kurdistan itself: relying on the secondary literature, I conducted an ancillary case study of relations between Kurdish rebel groups in the 1990s, with which I was not familiar when I developed my theoretical argument.

The second reason for delving into the details of the case is to contribute to advancing the understanding of the complex pattern of infighting among Iraq's Kurdish rebel groups in the second of half of the twentieth century. This aspect of Iraqi and Kurdish history remains relatively understudied,[6] yet it is highly policy relevant, due to its close connections to continuing divisions in Iraq's Kurdish region and more broadly to ongoing developments in the Middle East.[7]

The next section presents an overview of the Kurdish rebellions against Iraq. The following two sections assess the empirical fit of window theory and alternative arguments. The final section summarizes the main findings.

Overview of Iraq's Post–World War II Kurdish Rebellions

The fall of the Hashemite monarchy in 1958 raised hopes of loosening the tensions that had characterized relations between the central government and the Kurdish minority since Iraq's independence in 1932. Yet these hopes were soon shattered by the eruption in 1961 of the first Kurdish rebellion against Iraq in the post–World War II era.[8]

The new president, General Abdul Karim Qassem, forged an alliance with Kurdish leader Mullah Mustafa Barzani, and the new provisional constitution acknowledged the Kurds' national rights for the first time in Iraqi history. This honeymoon period, however, was short-lived. Qassem became concerned with Barzani's expanding influence among the Kurds, and the latter grew frustrated with the lack of progress toward Kurdish autonomy. Following skirmishes between Barzani's forces and the army, in September 1961 the government launched a major offensive in Kurdistan.[9]

In addition to being a powerful tribal leader and a charismatic ethnonational figure, Barzani was the honorary president of the Kurdistan Democratic Party (KDP). However, the party was under the actual control of urban intellectuals, in particular Ibrahim Ahmed (KDP secretary general) and Jalal Talabani (KDP politburo member).[10] After initial hesitation, the Ahmed and Talabani group decided to join Barzani's fight against Baghdad in early 1962 with their own separate forces.[11] As the two armed groups (Barzani's and Ahmed-Talabani's) made independent strategic decisions and controlled their own troops (known as "peshmerga," that is, "those who face death"), they should be considered distinct rebel organizations, even though both operated under the banner of the same political party; thus in this early phase of the Kurdish struggle the KDP is better thought of as an alliance between two rebel organizations rather than a single armed group.[12] The Ahmed-Talabani group was popular in the urban centers of the Sorani-speaking areas (central and southern Iraqi Kurdistan), while the Barzani group drew most of its support from Kurmanji-speaking tribes in the Badinan region (northern Iraqi Kurdistan).[13]

The first two years of the war displayed a seesaw pattern of government offensives that would get bogged down in the mountains and Kurdish counterattacks in moments of government military weakness or turmoil in the Iraqi capital. Then, in February 1964, Barzani reached a ceasefire agreement with the new Iraqi government emerging from a coup. The Ahmed-Talabani group denounced Barzani as a sellout and argued that the Kurds should press their military advantage. In the following months, the long-simmering struggle for control of the Kurdish movement came to a head: in July Barzani forces attacked the headquarters of the Ahmed-Talabani group, whose members fled to Iran after defeat.[14] This was the first episode of Kurdish inter-rebel war.

Subsequently, negotiations between Barzani and Baghdad over Kurdish self-administration stalled, and the government launched a new offensive in April 1965. Barzani then allowed the members of the Ahmed-Talabani group back into Kurdistan, absorbing the rank and file in his organization while keeping its leaders under close surveillance (Ahmed remained in exile). In a stunning turn of events, however, Talabani and a group of followers left the Barzani camp in January 1966 and started fighting against the Barzani group in close cooperation with government forces.[15]

The following three years witnessed similarly indecisive fighting between the Barzani group and the government, with an alternation of massive, yet unsuccessful, government offensives and phases in which Baghdad "outsourced" most counterinsurgency operations to the reestablished Ahmed-Talabani group, with government forces providing support when needed. (Since 1961 the government had also relied on Kurdish militias mostly formed from tribes hostile to Barzani, mockingly referred to by the rebels as "jash" or "little donkeys.")[16] In 1969, after yet another coup, the Baath Party government, newly in power, realized that Iraq's armed forces were not strong enough to deal at the same time with an increasingly combative Iran across the border and the ongoing Iranian-supported Kurdish insurgency in the north of the

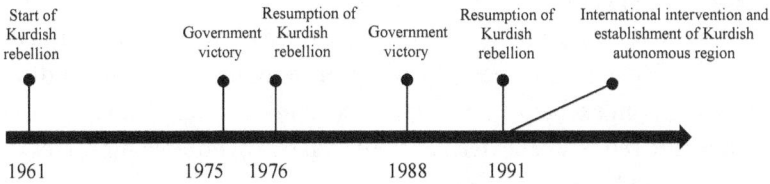

(a) Rebels vs. government

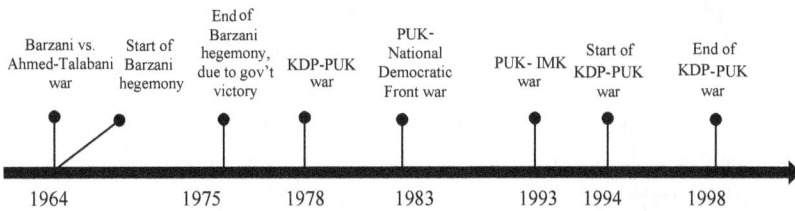

(b) Rebels vs. rebels

FIGURE 3.1 Timeline of Kurdish rebellions in Iraq, 1961–1998. Part A presents key events in the interaction between Kurdish rebels and the government. Part B reports periods of inter-rebel war and rebel hegemony.

country. The Iraqi government thus decided to appease Barzani by granting significant autonomy to the Kurds, enshrined in the March 11 1970 Agreement.[17] Among other important concessions, Baghdad ceased its support for the Ahmed-Talabani group, and its members were absorbed as individuals into a KDP under Barzani's unchallenged control.[18]

Disputes between Barzani and the Iraqi government over implementation of the agreement and other unresolved issues emerged soon afterward.[19] Emboldened by promises of U.S. and Iranian support, Barzani stiffened his bargaining position. War re-erupted in the spring of 1974, and a government offensive made substantial inroads. By the winter the Kurdish forces were reduced to a strip of territory near the Iranian border, which they could defend only with Iranian artillery support.

Baghdad became convinced that the only solution to its Kurdish "problem" was to placate its neighbor, while Tehran calculated that the time had come to reap the diplomatic benefits of the pressure it had imposed on Iraq through its Kurdish allies.[20] In March 1975 the two governments caught the world and Barzani by surprise with the announcement of the Algiers Agreement, by which Iran undertook to stop aiding the insurgency in exchange for Iraqi concessions in a long-standing border dispute. Bereft of vital external support, Barzani ordered his forces to stop fighting and the rebellion collapsed.[21]

New Kurdish organizations emerged in the power vacuum created by the defeat and the ensuing dissolution of Barzani's KDP. In the summer of 1975 Talabani announced from Damascus the formation of the Patriotic Union of Kurdistan (PUK), which started military operations against Iraq the following year. In 1976 Barzani's sons, Idris and Massoud, in cooperation with other former KDP elements, re-created the KDP, which resumed operations in Kurdistan shortly after the PUK. In the second half of 1979 the Socialist Party of Kurdistan (henceforth Socialist Party) and the Kurdistan Branch of the Communist Party of Iraq (henceforward Communist Party) established a military presence in Sorani areas, where the PUK also operated.[22]

In the years preceding the Iran-Iraq War, there were skirmishes between the KDP and the PUK, as Talabani's group tried to extend its activities from the Soran region to the Badinan region—the KDP's stronghold in northern Iraqi Kurdistan. These low-level clashes culminated in a major battle in the spring of 1978, in which the PUK was badly mauled—the second episode of Kurdish inter-rebel war.[23]

As the Iran-Iraq War started in the fall of 1980, the various rebel groups took advantage of the redeployment of the Iraqi army from Kurdistan to the southern front to rapidly expand their forces and areas of operations. For a few years after their fight in 1978, the antagonism between the KDP and the PUK was largely confined to hostile propaganda and competing initiatives to court third-party states, as neither organization frontally challenged the rival's control of its stronghold.[24]

In the spring of 1983 a complex series of alliance maneuvers in the Kurdish camp and battlefield developments in the Iran-Iraq War prompted the resumption of large-scale intra-Kurdish fighting—the third episode of inter-rebel war. The PUK found itself surrounded by hostile forces: it was fighting the Iraqi government while also facing the National Democratic Front, an increasingly assertive alliance of all other armed organizations active in Kurdistan, led by the KDP, and feared an

FIGURE 3.2 Map of Iraqi Kurdistan

imminent invasion of Iraqi Kurdistan by Iran, which was hostile to the PUK and supported the KDP. The PUK reacted by attacking the Socialists' and Communists' headquarters and expelling their forces (and those of the KDP that they were hosting) from Soran region.[25]

Though successful in virtually defeating the Socialists and the Communists, this fight, coming on the heels of six years of antigovernment struggle, left the rebel group in an unsustainable position. In late 1983 Talabani thus decided to accept Baghdad's offer to negotiate the terms of

Kurdish autonomy, leading to a government-PUK ceasefire. Negotiations, however, broke down a year later, and the PUK resumed its fight against Baghdad.[26]

As it had done before, the PUK strove to avoid fighting on multiple fronts and thus made conciliatory gestures toward the KDP and Iran. By now Tehran was more willing to cooperate with the PUK, as Iran's hopes of a rapid military victory against Iraq had been shaken by the emergence of a grinding stalemate in the spring of 1984.[27] After several extremely costly and ultimately unsuccessful attempts at breakthrough on the southern front, in late 1987 Iran refocused its effort against Iraq on the Kurdish front: it launched major offensives there and intensified its support for the Kurdish insurgents, leading to some territorial advances by the anti-Baghdad forces in early 1988.

The tide would turn in Iraq's favor in the spring, however, when Iraqi forces were able to retake much of the territory lost in the previous months in Kurdistan. More crucially, the thinning of Iranian defenses in the South (due to Iranian redeployments to Kurdistan) created the conditions for a series of successful Iraqi offensives—the first ones since 1981. As Baghdad's forces were now in a position to threaten Iranian territory and military victory by Tehran appeared impossible, a militarily and economically exhausted Iran accepted Iraq's standing ceasefire proposal. Following the withdrawal of Iranian forces from Iraqi Kurdistan, in the late summer Iraq crushed the Kurdish resistance with a series of attacks against the remaining rebel strongholds, indiscriminately targeting militants and civilians on a massive scale in the course of the infamous "Anfal" campaign.[28]

In 1991 the U.S.-led intervention to reverse Iraq's occupation of Kuwait created a new opportunity for Kurdish rebellion. This time, armed resistance took the form of a spontaneous mass uprising in March. The two strongest Kurdish rebel groups—the KDP and the PUK—quickly joined the fight and managed to wrest control of most of Kurdish-inhabited territory from Baghdad, only to be pushed back by a government offensive before the end of the month. As Iraqi forces retook the region, hundreds of thousands of Kurdish civilians fled to the mountains on Iraq's borders with Turkey and Iran. The ensuing humanitarian emergency prompted another international intervention, leading to the creation of a Kurdish autonomous region in northern Iraq outside of Baghdad's control.[29]

Intra-Kurdish peace prevailed until 1994, with the exception of a brief fight in December 1993 between the PUK and the Islamic Movement of Kurdistan (IMK), a small Kurdish organization—the fourth episode of inter-rebel war. However, as a land dispute between supporters of the KDP and the PUK in May 1994 escalated, fighting between the two groups set the whole region ablaze. The fifth instance of inter-rebel war would last until the KDP and the PUK signed the Washington Agreement in September 1998.[30] The KDP and the PUK would then rule their respective halves of Iraq's Kurdish region until the creation of a unified Kurdish Regional Government (KRG) following the U.S.-led overthrow of Saddam Hussein in 2003.

Assessing the Empirical Fit of Window Theory

The previous section identified five onsets of inter-rebel war and six periods of inter-rebel peace (see table 3.1). To what degree can window theory explain this pattern of relations among Kurdish rebels? As the analysis shows, my argument has remarkable explanatory power: all but one instance of inter-rebel war and absence thereof are consistent with the expectations of window theory.

From Inter-rebel Cooperation to War, 1962–1964

Window-of-opportunity logic explains the first episode of inter-rebel war in 1964 and the absence of large-scale Kurdish infighting in the preceding years. In July 1964 the Barzani group attacked and expelled into Iran its weaker coethnic rival—the Ahmed-Talabani group—taking advantage of a lull in the fight against the government. The two groups were coethnic, as both aspired to autonomy for Iraq's Kurds and had exclusively Kurdish memberships. The Barzani group had been stronger throughout the rebellion, but the significant threat posed by the government did not warrant a hegemonic bid until the spring of 1964. Before the February 1964 ceasefire, at different moments the rebels had confronted major government offensives, observed an ominous military

TABLE 3.1 Inter-rebel Relations in Iraqi Kurdistan, 1962–1998

Observed Outcome (war/no war)	Type of Window	Correct Prediction?
No war, Barzani–Ahmed-Talabani, 1962–1963	No window (coethnic, imbalanced power, but high government threat, no power shift)	✓
War, Barzani–Ahmed-Talabani, 1964	Window of opportunity (coethnic, imbalanced power, low government threat, low opportunity cost)	✓
No war, PUK–KDP, 1976–1977	Window of vulnerability (coethnic, balanced power, but power shift; PUK's initial attempts to address decline without force)	✓
War, PUK–KDP, 1978	Window of vulnerability (coethnic, balanced power, and high government threat, but power shift)	✓
No war, PUK–KDP, 1979–1982	No window (coethnic, balanced power, high government threat, no power shift)	✓
War, PUK–National Democratic Front, 1983	Window of vulnerability (coethnic and balanced power, but power shift and no alternative alliance options for PUK)	✓
No war, PUK–National Democratic Front (1984–1988)	No window (coethnic, balanced power, no power shift)	✓
No war PUK–KDP, 1991	No window (coethnic, balanced power, no power shift)	✓
No war, PUK–KDP, 1992–1993	Window of vulnerability (coethnic, balanced power, but power shift; PUK's initial attempts to address decline without force)	✓
War, PUK–IMK, 1993	(Insufficient evidence)	?
War, PUK–KDP, 1994–1998	Window of vulnerability (coethnic, balanced power, but power shift)	✓

Note: Each row indicates an episode of inter-rebel war or inter-rebel peace involving rebel groups operating in Iraqi Kurdistan. The years 1961 and 1965–1975 are not included as the only rebel group was Barzani's (in 1965–1975 the Ahmed-Talabani group operated as a counterinsurgent militia).

buildup in Kurdistan, or faced a new government of untested determination and strength—all situations in which Barzani could not be confident that Baghdad would be unable to inflict a decisive blow on the insurgents if they had started fighting each other. By contrast, there is no indication of a clear shift in the balance of power in 1962–1964 that might have prompted a gamble for resurrection.

The Barzani group maintained a clear military edge over its rival throughout this period. At the onset of the rebellion, Barzani's fighters numbered five thousand, while the Ahmed-Talabani group had little in the way of a military organization. From early on, Barzani saw the Ahmed-Talabani group as a potentially threatening rival but favored Ahmed and Talabani's decision to join the fight against Baghdad, as he thought he could not afford to forgo the military contribution of the smaller group against Baghdad's offensive. By the summer of 1962 the Kurdish ranks had expanded to fifteen thousand armed men; both groups had experienced rapid growth, but Barzani group controlled the bulk of the fighters throughout the period.[31] The stark imbalance of power in favor of Barzani clearly emerges from interviews with former Kurdish rebels. For example, Khursheed Shera—a fighter on Barzani's side from 1961 and later KDP commander—reported that in 1964 Barzani controlled ten thousand troops, while the Ahmed-Talabani group had about forty-five hundred armed men.[32] (The secondary literature and my interviewees tend to focus on troop numbers when discussing the balance of power between the two groups, without indications that the Ahmed-Talabani group had an edge in other dimensions of military power, that is, tactical-operational skills, cohesion, and weaponry).[33]

For most of this period, the rebels faced a serious and immediate government threat. After being squeezed in the mountains by government advances in 1961, the insurgents gradually extended their operations to large swaths of Kurdistan in the spring and summer of 1962. Throughout 1962, however, government troop strength in the region increased: Iraqi forces in Kurdistan doubled in size by the end of the year, from four to eight brigades, as Baghdad prepared for a new major offensive. Even if this buildup did not translate into battlefield trends favorable to the government, it is likely to have figured prominently in Barzani's calculations and to have induced him to caution vis-à-vis the Ahmed-Talabani group.[34]

In February 1963 a coup brought to power the Baath Party, whose ability and resolve to conduct effective military operations were untested. There were, in fact, signs for the Kurds that the new government might represent a more relentless foe than its predecessor. Baath's ideology had long opposed significant concessions to the Kurds, considering any potential cooperation with them only as a tactical arrangement to get rid of President Qassem.[35] The Baath, furthermore, shared the widespread dissatisfaction in the officer corps with Qassem's conduct of the war against the Kurds, seeing its lack of success as a consequence of the constraints on the army's freedom of movement as well as on ammunition and other supplies imposed by the prime minister.[36] After the coup the Iraqi military argued that Qassem "did not want to defeat" the Kurds but rather intended to "keep the army away from Baghdad"; provided that the military were now granted enough weapons and troops, "the Kurdish rebellion would be eliminated in the space of a week."[37] Moreover, in 1963 Iraqi troops kept flowing north, so that by May 1963 three quarters of the army were deployed against the guerrillas.[38] Thus Barzani probably did not see the months of negotiations between the Kurdish movement and the Baath government following the coup (February–June) as propitious for a hegemonic bid.[39]

As war resumed in June 1963, the government launched an offensive larger than the previous ones, making significant territorial headway in the course of the summer. In October, however, a substantial number of troops were redeployed from Kurdistan to Baghdad to deal with political turmoil there, which enabled rebel territorial gains. Between the November 1963 coup and the February 1964 ceasefire with the Kurdish rebels, the new government was barely able to prevent further rebel advances, as Iraqi forces had been significantly weakened by infighting during the coup and purges in its aftermath, as well as by the withdrawal of a supporting Syrian brigade.[40] The government would not be able to launch a serious offensive with an army in such weak condition. The existence of a moment of opportunity for Barzani to liquidate his rivals was further signaled by Baghdad's statements and actions following the ceasefire: Iraqi president Abdul Salam Aref threatened force against elements opposed to the cessation of hostilities between him and Barzani—a thinly veiled reference to the Ahmed-Talabani group—and shortly afterward the government provided some weapons and money to Barzani.[41]

Important military figures on Barzani's side confirm that the Kurdish leader understood that the new government in Baghdad was weak and needed a break from the fight to reorganize in the aftermath of the coup, as illustrated by the following interview excerpt with Sa'id Kaka, one of Barzani's commanders:

> *Author*: Why did Barzani want peace with the government in 1964?
> *Sa'id Kaka*: People were really tired of war. You have to do what the people demand and they demanded a break.[42] It was just a tactical pause.
> *Author*: Did Barzani fear that Baghdad would take advantage of the fight with the Ahmed-Talabani group?
> *Sa'id Kaka*: Baghdad did not want to fight because it was hurting too and so there was no fear of that sort for Mullah Mustafa.[43]

Dr. Mahmoud Osman, Barzani's close collaborator, represents perhaps the best source to gain insight on the calculus of the Kurdish leader, given that Barzani did not write a memoir and refused to have his oral recollection of past events taped.[44] Osman's account clearly suggests that after the 1964 ceasefire Barzani perceived the existence of a moment of opportunity to get rid of the threatening rival:

> Barzani had intended to attack the politburo [the Ahmed-Talabani group] since 1963 but could not do that then because the Kurds were engaged in heavy fighting against the Baath. Barzani and the politburo had been engaged in a power struggle. Barzani wanted to be in control of the party; the politburo wanted to do the same and use Barzani as a symbol to attract popular support for its cause. . . . Both sides were concerned about the other's plan to take control of the movement. There was a lot of mistrust on both sides.[45] . . . Barzani signed the February [ceasefire] agreement with the clear objective of getting rid of the politburo. He took advantage of a pause in the fight with the government.[46]

After the expulsion of the Ahmed-Talabani group from Iraq, Barzani consolidated his control of the Kurdish movement and large swaths of Kurdish-inhabited territories that government forces were unable to penetrate ("liberated areas"), without encountering any resistance in areas previously under his rivals' control.[47] As Chris Kutschera puts it, with unchallenged authority in the Kurdish countryside, throughout the following decade "Barzani was the uncrowned king of Kurdistan."[48]

In sum, the available evidence strongly supports the interpretation of the 1964 inter-rebel war as a hegemonic bid by Barzani. The key elements of a window of opportunity were present in the spring of 1964 but not before. First, all sources agree that the military balance was clearly in favor of Barzani's group throughout the rebellion. Second, in early 1964 the government threat abated, as the Iraqi armed forces were weakened by the coup and the withdrawal of the supporting Syrian unit. As one of Barzani's commanders pointed out, the Kurdish leader understood that the government needed a break from the fight and thus would not be able to launch an opportunistic attack during the inter-rebel war. Moreover, a close collaborator of Barzani explicitly stated that the Kurdish leader saw the pause in the fight against the government as an opportunity to eliminate a threatening rival for the leadership of the Kurdish movement. Finally, consistent with the expectation that coethnic rebel organizations' social resources are relatively cumulative, Barzani was able to extend his authority to areas formerly under his rivals' control without facing any resistance from the local population.

Drifting Toward the 1978 Inter-rebel War

Window-of-vulnerability logic sheds significant light on the second episode of inter-rebel war in Iraqi Kurdistan as well as the lead-up to it. At first the PUK attempted to address without violence its decline relative to the KDP, due to the PUK's lack of access to outside support; these initial efforts having met no success, the PUK embarked on a gamble for resurrection.

Relations between the two groups were tense from the beginning of their operations in 1976.[49] PUK leader Talabani needed to mobilize a population that was deeply disillusioned in the aftermath of the Kurdish defeat at the hands of the government in 1975.[50] His approach to this challenge was to draw a sharp distinction between the new organization and the "feudalist, tribalist, and rightist" leadership of the previous rebellion, which he held responsible for the debacle.[51] The KDP responded with propaganda attacks of its own.[52]

Both organizations were initially extremely weak, with a few hundred poorly armed men facing the formidable Iraqi military machinery.[53] The KDP concentrated its early activities in Badinan, while the PUK was most active in Sorani areas, the Ahmed-Talabani group's erstwhile stronghold. Despite their profound reciprocal distrust, we should not expect either organization to launch a hegemonic bid, given the rough balance of power (or better, weakness) between them. Moreover, in particular after the government launched a counterinsurgency campaign in the spring of 1977, the rebel groups were under significant military pressure from the Iraqi armed forces, making large-scale inter-rebel violence additionally unappealing.[54]

The 1978 inter-rebel war, however, can be explained as the result of a PUK's gamble for resurrection—a desperate attempt to deal with the window of vulnerability it was facing. The PUK launched a major expedition to establish a supply route through the Badinan region to Syria and thus obtain badly needed weapons and ammunition. The KDP predictably perceived the PUK's move as an encroachment on its stronghold and feared the shift in the balance of power that would ensue. The KDP thus resorted to force to block the PUK's initiative.

The PUK had faced a window of vulnerability since the beginning of its guerrilla activities. Essential supplies (ranging from sleeping equipment to ammunition and weapons) had to come from Syria, the group's main external supporter.[55] However, Iraq's border with Syria was under tight government control. The only way to Syria for the PUK, therefore, was via Badinan and then southern Turkey, where the KDP and allied tribes held sway (at this stage, the Iraqi government was unable to effectively seal the border with Turkey).[56] The KDP did not face comparably tight constraints to its future growth, as Ankara tolerated the group's bases in southern Turkey, where the KDP enjoyed logistical support from local Kurds.[57]

The PUK initially adopted a "salami-slicing" approach to establishing a presence in Badinan: in 1976 and then 1977 it deployed two small units, to be gradually reinforced, in areas straddling the border with Turkey.[58] The PUK forces, however, were wiped out by either government forces and militias or local tribes and KDP affiliates.[59] The available information on these small-scale clashes and the identity of their initiators is patchy, but it would make sense, as PUK sources suspect, that the KDP resorted to limited force as a form of coercive diplomacy to deny access to Badinan and Syria to its rival.[60]

The PUK repeatedly tried to find some form of understanding with the KDP that would allow it to operate in Badinan, explaining that its only enemy was the government and it did not want to have problems with the KDP.[61] At a meeting in London between the two groups' leaderships, the KDP committed to investigate the events surrounding the disappearance of the PUK small unit in Badinan in1976, allegedly ambushed by the KDP.[62] Eventually in March 1977, with Syrian prodding, the PUK and the KDP agreed to assist each other's operations in their respective strongholds and establish monitoring mechanisms to ensure the equal distribution of weapons brought in from Syria among the groups.[63] Shortly afterward, however, the KDP reneged on the agreement, accusing the PUK of bringing weapons to Kurdistan clandestinely. The KDP then refused to facilitate PUK's movements from and to Syria through Badinan, and the second PUK small unit transporting weapons from Syria into Kurdistan was ambushed, allegedly by KDP affiliates.[64]

While access to Syrian supplies was essential for the PUK to fight against the government, it would inevitably affect the balance of power between the PUK and the KDP, generating an intense commitment problem. The KDP leadership perceived the PUK as aggressive and would thus see with apprehension an expansion of PUK's firepower, as the newly acquired weapons could be used against the KDP.[65] Even if one discounted as self-serving the KDP's accusation that the PUK harbored aggressive intentions, the mere existence of a deep conflict of interest between the two—both wanted to have more influence in the Kurdish struggle against Baghdad—would still imply an intense commitment problem: the PUK could not credibly commit not to throw its weight around after establishing a supply route to Syria; thus the KDP may have preferred using force to forestall the unfavorable shift in the balance of power to living with its consequences (i.e., acquiescing to a subordinate position in the rebel camp or fighting from a position of weakness). Moreover, even if the KDP leadership were certain (which most likely was not) that the PUK did not have aggressive or hegemonic intentions at that time, it could not rule out that its rival's appetite would grow with its power or that new, more hostile leaders would emerge in the future.[66]

Much debate took place within the PUK leadership following the breakdown of the 1977 agreement with the KDP, with options being discussed ranging from violent retaliation to complete abandonment of Badinan. Despite many meetings and resolutions, no clear decision was reached about the PUK's next move and how to address the group's acute logistical needs.[67] According to PUK's unofficial deputy leader at that time, the late Nawshirwan Mustafa Amin, Baghdad's decision to resume its depopulation campaign of the Kurdish border areas eventually forced the PUK's hand. The group's leadership vowed to oppose the government initiative (scheduled to start in July 1978) by arming the people in the affected areas, which in turn required finding a way to get guns from Syria.[68] Having assessed the KDP's strength in border areas between Iraq and Turkey, its influence among the local tribes, and the deployments of Iraqi, Iranian, and Turkish forces along the route, the PUK decided to send an expeditionary force of about a thousand men (half of them unarmed) to pick up a major cache of arms coming from Syria and establish a base in Bradost, an area of Badinan where the Iraqi, Turkish, and Iranian borders meet.[69] In the hope of avoiding a military confrontation, Talabani sent letters to the KDP leadership explaining that the expedition was not against the KDP and its sole purpose was transporting weapons from Syria to fight the government more effectively.[70] However, after having been harassed en route by Iraqi and Iranian forces, the PUK contingent was ambushed by a large KDP force and affiliated tribes on Turkish soil. Hundreds of PUK members were killed or captured (including several leaders) or surrendered to the government, while the remaining forces retreated in disorder to Sorani areas.[71] It would take years for the PUK to recover fully from the blow, and the group would not attempt again to establish a supply route to Syria.[72]

All PUK-related subjects I interviewed agree that the KDP was not the expedition's target and that the participation of a large number of armed men was just a precaution in case the group came under attack (by the KDP, Iraq, or its neighbors): the PUK had a contingency plan to respond to an attack by the KDP, but it preferred not to fight.[73] However, the most empathic PUK-related interviewees readily acknowledge that the KDP would inevitably perceive the PUK's move as threatening because the growth of PUK's power following the establishment of the supply route could lead to further encroachments in Badinan.[74]

In sum, the available evidence supports the interpretation that the 1978 clash occurred as an unwanted result of the PUK gambling for resurrection to get access to Syrian support. The key elements of window-of-vulnerability logic are present. The PUK faced the prospect of not keeping up with the KDP and withering away without access to supplies, ammunition, and weapons; these could only be obtained from Syria, which could be reached only by crossing KDP-dominated areas. As initial, less provocative attempts at establishing a supply route to Syria failed in 1976 and 1977, the PUK leadership reluctantly embarked in 1978 on a major expedition to transport a large cache of weapons back to Kurdistan, knowing that there was a risk of a military clash with the KDP. With no guarantee that the PUK would not take advantage of its increased power, the KDP attacked the PUK's contingent and inflicted a major blow to its rival.

From Peaceful Coexistence to Inter-rebel War, 1979–1983

The fight between the PUK and the other major rebel groups operating in Iraqi Kurdistan in 1983 can be understood through the lenses of window-of-vulnerability logic, too. An isolated PUK resorted to force in a desperate attempt to forestall the sharp decline in relative power foreshadowed by the impending intervention in Kurdistan by Iran, which was hostile to the PUK and supported its archenemy, the KDP. The absence of windows of opportunity and vulnerability, conversely, helps explain the absence of inter-rebel war in the years 1979–1982.

The negative consequences of the 1978 clash for the PUK were not limited to the loss of a large share of its fighters.[75] The military debacle exacerbated pre-existing tensions among PUK's constitutive factions. The leaders of one of them, the Social Democratic Movement, which had just lost two key figures and a great deal of members, criticized Talabani's leadership and eventually decided to break away in the spring of 1979, forming a new organization—the Socialist Party.[76] The constellation of rebel groups active in Kurdistan became even more complex in late 1979, when the Communist Party established a presence in Sorani areas after having been expelled by the Baath from the ruling National Patriotic Front and started military operations the following year.[77] I consider the Communist Party a Kurdish rebel group as it had openly espoused the Kurdish cause since the 1950s (in addition to its broader program of radical political and economic change for Iraq as a whole) and its fighters were almost exclusively Kurds, with Kurds well represented in the leadership, too.[78]

We should not expect any of the four Kurdish rebel groups to have launched a hegemonic bid in the years 1979–1983, as none of them had a large, unambiguous military advantage over the others, even if from 1980 the government threat receded significantly, with Iraq focusing its attention on the war against Iran.[79] Unfortunately there are no precise year-by-year data on the rebel groups' sizes for this periods; even less information is available about the other dimensions of the inter-rebel balance of power. It is nonetheless clear that by 1981 the PUK enjoyed at best a marginal advantage over the second strongest group, the KDP. One source reports that in 1981 the PUK and the KDP controlled, respectively, three thousand and two thousand fighters,[80] while another source estimates the PUK's fighting force at two thousand to twenty-five hundred in 1982.[81] Moreover, most of my interviewees, regardless of political affiliation, answered questions about the relative strength of the two groups by saying that they were both strong in their respective strongholds (Soran and Badinan regions), suggesting a rough balance of power.[82] The fact that now two new organizations existed, which could help the KDP in case of a PUK attack, should have disabused the PUK of any notion that an attack on the stronghold of the KDP would have a better outcome than the calamitous clash of 1978. (The Socialist Party and the Communist Party reportedly each had two thousand fighters in 1981.[83])

On the other hand, the concerns that had driven the PUK to gamble for resurrection in 1978 had since largely dissipated. The turmoil caused by the Iranian Revolution weakened Tehran's tight grip on the border with Iraq, thus providing the PUK with the outlet to the outside world it had long sought. In addition, with the drastic reduction in Iraqi troop presence in Kurdistan caused by the outbreak of the Iran-Iraq War, the insurgents gained significant freedom of movement. Though these developments were a boon for all the Kurdish rebel groups, the PUK appears to have benefited the most, as it quickly recovered from its massive losses in membership due to inter-rebel war in 1978 and fragmentation in 1979 to become at least as large as the KDP.

Developments in the rebel camp, the worsening of relations between the PUK and Iran, and the latter's looming intervention in Iraqi Kurdistan, however, would conspire to create a new window of vulnerability for Talabani's group and once again bring about inter-rebel war. As the Socialist Party and the Communist Party were actively competing with a PUK in full recovery for members and influence in Soran region (where all three had bases), in late 1980 the two new Kurdish rebel groups formed the National Democratic Front, an alliance with the KDP that purposefully excluded the PUK.[84] Though the Socialists' and Communists' decision may have been primarily driven by a desire to keep the PUK in check, the latter could not help but perceive a worsening of its threat environment, as it now faced an alliance led by the KDP, with superior aggregate military power.[85]

Relations between the PUK and the National Democratic Front deteriorated in the following two years as they got involved in a spiral of accidents and skirmishes.[86] Of particular concern for the PUK was the fact that the Socialists and the Communists appeared to be acting as a Trojan horse for KDP's penetration of Soran, by inviting KDP peshmerga to their areas of operations; these troop movements may have been conducted to more effectively fight the government forces (as the Front's members claimed), but inevitably the PUK felt threatened.[87] At the same time, the Socialists and Communists resisted PUK proposals to establish closer ties among the three of them, voicing fears that this would be the first step for the PUK to absorb them, which the PUK considered disingenuous.[88] In February 1983 Syria and Libya managed to broker an agreement between all Iraqi opposition forces (including the PUK and the Front's members) to coordinate their struggle, but it broke down a few days later.[89]

In parallel to the escalation of tensions in the rebel camp, PUK-Iran relations took a turn for the worse. The PUK's relationship with Tehran had never been as smooth as the KDP's, but it deteriorated significantly in 1981, when Ayatollah Khomeini ousted Abdulhassan Banisadr, revolutionary Iran's moderate first president.[90] According to Nawshirwan Mustafa, until then the PUK had managed the difficult balancing act of getting some support from Iran while continuing its cooperation with

Iranian Kurdish rebel groups, in particular the Iranian Kurdistan Democratic Party (KDPI). After Khomeini's consolidation of power, however, Teheran became inflexible in demanding the PUK's help against the KDPI. The PUK did not budge as it was skeptical that Tehran would ever adopt a friendly attitude toward a group that it saw as flawed in ideological, ethnic, and religious respects—"Communist, Kurdish, and Sunni."[91] Iran responded by severing relations.[92]

The threat posed by Iran to the PUK significantly increased in the course of 1982. Having contained Baghdad's offensive (1980–1982), Tehran launched its own summer offensive against Iraq on the southern front while striving to wrestle control of Iran's Kurdish North from the KDPI, which was supported by Baghdad.[93] The PUK sent a contingent in a desperate attempt to prop up its ethnic brethren's defenses against the Iranian onslaught, but this only served to buy some time for the KDPI's withdrawal into Iraq.[94] In March 1983, Tehran launched another operation, clearing residual KDPI forces from Iranian soil.[95] An Iran emboldened by its recent successes against the Iraqi forces and further antagonized by the PUK's involvement in its fight against the KDPI was now just across the border—an ideal position to intensify its support for the KDP and invade Iraqi Kurdistan.

In this context, after a new series of skirmishes with the Communist and Socialist forces following the breakdown of the February 1983 agreement, at the beginning of May the PUK launched a major attack against the two groups' headquarters. It inflicted substantial losses to the National Democratic Front's units and forced them to flee to Badinan and mountainous areas on the border with Iran.[96] The PUK's attack thus eliminated the local forces that could have provided support to a future incursion into Sorani areas by Iranian and KDP forces.

Talabani's right hand, Nawshirwan Mustafa, claims that the PUK's attack was preemptive: "In February 1983, the KDP forces, with the help of Iran, came close to Nawzang [where the PUK's headquarters were located], took the high ground and threatened to occupy the region. . . . All the indications [in late April] were telling us that the National Democratic Front's forces were about to launch an attack. . . . We had no choice but to fight for our life."[97]

We should, of course, be wary of Nawshirwan Mustafa's claims, given his incentive to present the PUK's actions in a positive light. However, the basic features of the PUK's strategic situation in the spring of 1983 are hardly disputable: the PUK had bad relations with all the other armed groups active in Iraqi Kurdistan; its only ally (the KDPI) had been defeated by Tehran; and a hostile Iran had taken back control of the border, from where it could more easily support the KDP and invade Iraqi Kurdistan.[98] Thus even if we dismiss as self-serving Mustafa's claim that an attack on his group was imminent, it is hard to escape the conclusion that by the spring of 1983 the PUK was facing the prospect of a dramatic deterioration of power relative to the rival alliance, and in particular to the Iranian-supported KDP—the kind of predicament that should prompt a gamble for resurrection.

Nawshirwan Mustafa claims that the people in areas of operations of the Socialist and Communist Parties welcomed PUK forces after the expulsion of the other groups.[99] This is consistent with window theory's expectation about the cumulativity of social resources held by coethnic rivals. No other source mentions this development, however, so it should not be given undue weight.

To summarize, despite the absence of incontrovertible evidence of PUK's decision making, the available information is consistent with an explanation of the 1983 inter-rebel war as a gamble for resurrection of the PUK driven by window-of-vulnerability logic. Key implications of the argument can be observed: as diplomatic attempts to break its encirclement and improve relations with other rebel groups and Iran failed, the PUK embarked on a risky path to address its vulnerability to the impending increase in Iranian support for the KDP, attacking and expelling the KDP's Communist and the Socialist allies from Sorani areas.

The Absence of Inter-rebel War in 1984–1988

The lack of windows of opportunity and vulnerability goes a long way in explaining the absence of inter-rebel war in the years 1984–1988. With the attack on the KDP's allies in Soran, the PUK dampened the impact of increased Iranian support for the KDP. Yet the PUK's position remained difficult. As it feared, in the summer and fall of 1983 Iran launched two major offensives in Iraqi Kurdistan with the support of the KDP.[100] Faced with the prospect of being crushed between the Iraqi and Iranian millstones, the PUK leadership reluctantly reached a ceasefire with Baghdad and started negotiations on Kurdish autonomy in December 1983.[101] Negotiations between the PUK and the Iraqi government made significant progress until late 1984, when Saddam Hussein, under Turkish diplomatic pressure, eventually refused to sign the agreement.[102] The two sides benefited from the ceasefire while it lasted: the PUK got an opportunity to recuperate and reorganize its forces, while receiving weapons from Baghdad; the government was able to move a large number of troops from Kurdistan to the main front against Iran in the South.[103] In early 1985 the PUK resumed operations against the government and started a gradual reconciliation with the members of the National Democratic Front and with Iran. Increased coordination rather than violent confrontation was the main pattern of interaction between the PUK and the Front in the years 1985–1988.[104]

Quite clearly, there was no window of opportunity in these years. Thanks in part to its ceasefire with Baghdad, the PUK managed to keep up with the growth of the Iran-supported KDP. All sources consistently suggest that the PUK and the KDP (with, respectively, roughly five thousand and six thousand fighters at their disposal by 1985) were comparably powerful, and both groups were well entrenched in their respective strongholds.[105] There was no reason to expect an all-out fight between the PUK and the KDP to lead to a quick and cheap victory for either group.

Less obviously, the window of vulnerability that the PUK faced in 1983 had closed by 1985. The accounts of PUK leaders consistently point to two major reasons for the group's improved condition. First, the PUK had significantly weakened the Socialist and Communist Parties in 1983; by 1985 the PUK controlled five thousand troops, while Communists and Socialists had each about a thousand armed men.[106] As part of an overall effort to improve its relations with the Front and Iran, the PUK now allowed the Socialists and the Communists to resume operations in Sorani areas, but the arrangement under which this occurred reflected the major imbalance of power that now existed between the PUK and the two groups: the Socialists and the Communists would be financially dependent on transfers from the PUK rather than raising their own taxes, which was one of the issues that had caused friction between them and the PUK in the past.[107] The Socialists and Communists thus were too

weak to pose a meaningful threat to the PUK and had less of an opportunity than in the past to operate as a Trojan horse for KDP penetration
of Sorani areas.

The second reason for the PUK's improved position was a significant
warming in relations with Iran, which drastically reduced the threat
directly posed by Tehran to the PUK and may have contributed to the
group's reconciliation with the KDP.[108] As PUK foreign emissary Faridoun Abd-Al Qader observed, Iran became much friendlier after the
PUK resumed its fight against Baghdad: Tehran was now willing to talk
to the PUK and gradually started providing military support to the
group.[109] PUK-affiliated subjects point to the deterioration of Iran's military position in 1984-1985 compared to 1983 as an explanation for Tehran's change of heart: while in 1983 the Iranian forces had successfully
been on the offensive for almost two years, in the spring of 1984 they
exhausted themselves in an inconclusive, major assault, followed by
smaller (and similarly unsuccessful) offensives.[110] Another important
factor behind Iran's more cooperative stance was the de facto disappearance of a major bone of contention between the PUK and Tehran—the
PUK's refusal to turn against the KDPI. By the time the PUK resumed its
fight against Baghdad, the KDPI was based in Iraq and was a spent force,
thus no longer representing a serious threat to Iran.[111]

In sum, there is evidence that the absence of windows of opportunity
and windows of vulnerability can explain the absence of inter-rebel war
in the years 1984–1988. The window of vulnerability that had prompted
inter-rebel war in 1983 had closed by 1985, as the Communists and Socialists no longer posed a serious military threat and Iran was now willing to
cooperate with and support the PUK.

Inter-rebel Relations After the Anfal Campaign

If there is a moment in Kurdish history in which one would be justified
in expecting intra-ethnic solidarity to prevail over competition between
Kurdish rebel groups, this would be the aftermath of the Anfal campaign crushing the Kurdish rebellion in 1988. Anfal is notable even by
the gruesome standards of Iraq's treatment of the Kurds. Between February and September 1988 government forces killed 50,000–100,000

Kurds and destroyed thousands of villages, forcibly displacing over one million people.[112] And yet peaceful inter-rebel coexistence was short-lived: from 1994 to 1998 the KDP and the PUK engaged in a new, bloodier round of infighting. This time their clashes occurred before the mystified eyes of the international community, which had become more familiar with the plight of Iraq's Kurds following Saddam Hussein's repression of their uprising in 1991 and the establishment of the safe haven in Kurdish-inhabited northern Iraq.

Window theory offers important insight on intra-Kurdish relations in the aftermath of the Anfal campaign, although, as I discuss below, it may not explain the PUK-IMK fight in 1993. Initially, in the absence of windows of opportunity and vulnerability, the KDP and the PUK abstained from inter-rebel war. Then in 1994, facing a sharp decline in relative power that inter-party negotiations had failed to address, the PUK resorted to force in a desperate attempt to confront a window of vulnerability. As noted, this part of the case study relies exclusively on the secondary literature and thus provides less fine-grained evidence compared to previous phases of the Kurdish struggle. Yet this limitation is compensated for by the fact that I developed window theory before diving into the corresponding empirical material; therefore support for the argument should substantially boost our confidence in it.

In a narrow sense the post-1991 period lies outside the scope of window theory because the KDP and the PUK did not engage in large-scale fighting against the Iraqi government at the same time, i.e., there was no multiparty civil war. However, the high risk of a new government invasion of Kurdistan suggests that my argument should be relevant in this period, too. The Iraqi army remained deployed just south of the region, "keeping inhabitants of the 'border' areas in a perpetual state of insecurity."[113] Kurdish leaders were painfully aware that Saddam Hussein was simply waiting for the international protection force deployed in Turkey (nicknamed Operation Poised Hammer) to be withdrawn.[114] Moreover, actual protection from Saddam's forces was highly uncertain even while the international mission was in place, as illustrated by fact that when the Iraqi army shelled Kurdish villages in April 1992, Turkey did not allow coalition airplanes to take off and intervene.[115] Therefore the KDP and PUK faced the concrete possibility, like in an active multiparty civil war, that the government would launch an offensive to take advantage of infighting. As it turned out, Saddam Hussein did just that in the summer of 1996, when, upon invitation from the KDP leader Massoud Barzani, the Iraqi army intervened to help the KDP wrest Erbil from the PUK and briefly take control of the whole Kurdish region.[116]

Peaceful Coexistence in 1989–1991

Window theory correctly predicts the absence of inter-rebel war in the immediate aftermath of Anfal. The Kurdish rebels emerged significantly weakened from the brutal counterinsurgency campaign. Government forces were in complete control of Kurdistan, whose countryside was virtually depopulated. The two main rebel groups, the KDP and the PUK, were left with just a few hundred fighters and could only execute sporadic hit-and-run attacks, without being able to hold any territory.[117]

The fact that the two groups were of roughly equal strength and the government had a tight grip on the region indicates an absence of a window of opportunity, as inter-rebel war would have been prohibitively costly. No window of vulnerability existed either, in the absence of any clear prospect of one of the two groups rapidly outgrowing the other.

In 1990–1991 Saddam Hussein's foreign policy blunders offered the Kurdish rebels an unexpected chance to regroup. With the invasion of Kuwait and the ensuing international crisis, Iraq withdrew most of its forces from Kurdistan, thus enabling a rapid expansion of the peshmerga. The Kurdish uprising in the wake of the Iraqi defeat in the Gulf War saw even faster growth of the rebels, going from 15,000 fighters to around 100,000 in the span of a few days as a result of the mass defection of the Kurdish progovernment militias.[118] Window theory correctly predicts continued inter-rebel cooperation under these circumstances. As there is no indication that the PUK and the KDP were experiencing markedly different growth rates, neither one probably faced a window of vulnerability; and the two groups' roughly equal strength implied that inter-rebel war would be have been long and costly. Moreover, infighting in a moment in which the Kurdish rebels were in the process of rapidly wresting control of the region from the government would have entailed major opportunity costs.

The ensuing Iraqi counteroffensive brought about a complete, albeit short-lived, reversal of the rebels' territorial expansion. Owing to international intervention on the behalf of the Kurdish population in April 1991, the KPD and the PUK reestablished control over most of Iraqi Kurdistan by the fall of 1991. Window theory correctly suggests that the high opportunity cost of forgoing the Kurdish gains enabled by external intervention, following the phase of serious and immediate government threat during the onslaught of the Iraqi army, should have discouraged inter-rebel war.

The Path to the KDP-PUK War, 1994–1998

The emergence of a de facto autonomous Kurdish region under international tutelage in 1991, combined with the vagaries of history and geography, created a window of vulnerability for the PUK and thus brought about a new bout of intra-Kurdish fighting. The outcome of historic elections in Iraqi Kurdistan in 1992 was a draw between the KDP and the PUK, resulting in a power-sharing arrangement between the two.[119] In a context of deep uncertainty about the reliability of the promise of international protection from the government forces massed on the southern border of the region, in Iraqi Kurdistan "money" was "the true source of power . . . [allowing] to purchase weapons and loyalties."[120] The KDP and the PUK, rather than the new regional government, remained largely in control of the financial resources of their respective territories.[121] The two groups were clearly in a category of their own in terms of power: none of the other Kurdish organizations secured enough votes to pass the 7 percent threshold for parliamentary representation and their manpower was more than an order of magnitude smaller than the KDP's and the PUK's, besides being less well-armed.[122]

While Iraqi Kurdistan suffered under the double embargo imposed by the international community on Iraq and by Baghdad on the region, contraband trade, in particular of Iraqi oil, flourished between areas under KDP control and Turkey. As the long-standing KDP stronghold, Badinan, abuts Turkey, the KDP was able to raise significant revenues by imposing tolls on cross-border flows.[123] By contrast, the PUK leader Talabani "wasn't getting a penny because no part of the oil smuggling route passed through his corner of Kurdistan,"[124] and thus he saw with growing concern the "KDP's financial ascendancy."[125]

Tensions between the KDP and the PUK mounted as they failed to find a negotiated solution to the problem of asymmetric revenues in the course of 1992 and 1993.[126] In the summer of 1993 a realignment of Kurdish parties might have shattered the PUK's hopes of addressing its predicament by prevailing in the elections scheduled for 1995: the merger of three smaller Kurdish parties with the KDP, Gareth Stansfield observes, "sent shock waves through the PUK camp and altered the balance" in favor of the KDP, providing the latter with a potentially decisive future advantage at the polls, which resulted in a stiffened negotiating position in the meantime.[127] In May 1994 a land dispute between supporters of the two groups provided the spark for inter-rebel war, which would go on, amid multiple international mediation attempts, until 1998.[128]

David Romano, a prominent scholar of Kurdish politics, provides an account of the episode that captures the logic of window of vulnerability, implying that the PUK launched a resurrection gamble: "Because the KDP enjoyed a higher income from its control of the border trade with Turkey, the PUK felt itself being gradually squeezed out of power and starved of finances. Hence the PUK was probably the party that initiated the 1994 civil war, in an attempt to redress the worsening balance of power in Iraqi Kurdistan."[129]

Other secondary accounts are less explicit as to whether the PUK or the KDP initiated the inter-rebel war (often using murky expressions like "fighting erupted" or "clashes broke out") but typically note that the root cause of the fight was the asymmetric access to custom revenues of the two groups, as window theory leads us to expect.[130] Moreover, the PUK's pattern of behavior on the battlefield and at the negotiating table is strongly consistent with window-of- vulnerability logic. In May 1994 the PUK captured the parliament and then, in December, it took over the rest of Erbil, using its hold on the Kurdish capital as a bargaining chip to obtain concessions on revenue sharing from the KDP throughout the conflict.[131] According to Robert Baer, a CIA agent stationed in Iraqi Kurdistan at time and with access to KDP and PUK leaders, during the inter-rebel war Talabani thought that "the dirty oil money was giving Barzani an insurmountable cash advantage" and that in spring 1995 he had to launch "a do-or-die effort against Barzani and his KDP before the PUK's stocks of weapons and ammunition ran out completely."[132] In addition, according to Ambassador Robert Pelletreau, the U.S. diplomat tasked with reconciling the PUK and the KDP in September 1996, the reason Talabani violated a U.S.-brokered ceasefire agreement earlier in the year was to coerce the KDP to share custom revenues, thus address-ing the PUK's predicament.[133] After the PUK, with Iranian help, man-aged to retake Sulaimania and part of the Erbil province (but not the capital itself), which it had lost to the joint forces of the KDP and the Iraqi government in the summer of 1996, Talabani embarked on one last attempt (Operation Vengeance Storm) in the fall of 1997 to coerce the KDP into making immediate concessions on revenue sharing; this time Turkey intervened with airpower to stop the PUK's advance and then help the KDP recover its lost territory.[134]

Talabani's use of force amounted to a gamble for resurrection rather than a hegemonic bid, given that he had no reason to expect a cheap and quick victory. While Baghdad may not have posed an immediate and serious threat (as there was no specific indication of an impending gov-ernment invasion of Iraqi Kurdistan in 1994), the "fairly even balance of power between the two groups" suggested that the fight would be a dif-ficult one for the PUK.[135] If anything, Talabani's group controlled a lower number of peshmerga than the KDP, although the PUK compensated for its numerical inferiority with heavier weapons at its disposal.[136]

This episode of inter-rebel war did not result in a military victory by either side, so we cannot observe fully the cumulativity of coethnic rebels' social resources. We can, however, get a glimpse of the ease of mobilizing resources previously under the control of a coethnic rival in Sulaimania, the long-standing center of the PUK's power that the KPD took over for a few weeks in 1996. While thousands of PUK affiliates fled or were expelled by the KDP, upon the arrival of KDP leader Massoud Barzani Sulaimania's "population, assembled en masse in the streets, looked at its new master without any particular anxiety."[137] This evi-dence, while admittedly fragmentary, suggests that the KDP probably would not have experienced significant trouble operating in its rival's strongholds had it completely defeated the PUK.

The Washington Agreement of September 1998 that brought the intra-Kurdish war to an end did not completely close the PUK's window of vulnerability.[138] Although the agreement clearly stated that until the cre-ation of a new Kurdish government following multiparty elections the KDP should transfer financial resources to the PUK to address their rev-enue asymmetry, disputes about the interpretation of the terms of the agreement stalled its implementation after one initial payment by the

KDP.[139] Four years of indecisive fighting, however, probably had clarified that the PUK was not strong enough to defeat its rival or coerce it into additional revenue-sharing concessions.[140] The PUK's gamble for resurrection had clearly failed, and the group did not restart the intra-Kurdish fight.[141] On its part, the KDP had no reason to expect to be able to achieve a quick and decisive victory any time soon, and it had strong incentives to refrain from infighting as its financial advantage over the PUK grew. In the absence of new windows of opportunity and windows of vulnerability, relations between the KDP and the PUK would remain peaceful, if tense, in the years leading to the overthrow of Saddam Hussein.

PUK-IMK War in 1993

The evidence on the brief Kurdish inter-rebel war between the PUK and the IMK in December 1993, which preceded the KDP-PUK war, is too limited to assess the fit of window theory with any confidence.[142] The IMK was one of various small Kurdish parties-cum-armed groups trying to carve out a space for themselves in the context of the KDP-PUK duopoly (the group had Kurdish membership and professed a blend of Kurdish nationalism and Islamism). Consistent with window theory, the PUK initially tolerated the activities of the IMK in Sorani areas (around Halabja, near the Iranian border) given the group's extreme weakness—it controlled five hundred armed men compared to at least PUK twelve thousand peshmerga.[143]

The fact that in 1992 the IMK started experiencing rapid growth in popular support, owing to significant financial aid from Iran, suggests that the late 1993 episode of infighting could be explained by window-of-vulnerability logic.[144] Thanks to external support, the IMK soared above what I called the threshold of extreme weakness, making it a potential threat for the PUK. The PUK then might have decided to nip the rival in the bud while it still enjoyed an overwhelming military advantage, even if the possibility that the KDP would intervene in the fight implied that the costs of inter-rebel war could be high. The broader window of vulnerability faced by the PUK produced by its decline relative to the KDP might have amplified the threat posed by a growing IMK: PUK leaders would see even a marginal loss of support in its stronghold to the Islamist organization as particularly ominous in a context in which the

PUK was already having trouble keeping up with its main competitor, the KDP.

I do not, however, have direct evidence of the PUK's decision making, and I cannot rule out that the weak but rising IMK initiated the fight, which would contradict window theory (an insurgent group experiencing growth should want to postpone inter-rebel war).[145] Thus I refrain from making claims about the fit of window theory to this specific instance of inter-rebel war.

Alternative Explanations and Endogeneity Concerns

It is time to discuss potential alternative explanations for inter-rebel war and address concerns about the endogeneity of windows of opportunity and vulnerability, that is, the possibility that the hypothesized causes of inter-rebel war are themselves the effects of some other, more fundamental cause.

According to Fotini Christia's minimum winning coalition (MWC) theory, inter-rebel war should occur only when at least one rebel group is sufficiently strong to take on both the government and the other rebels.[146] This explanation of inter-rebel war fares poorly in Iraqi Kurdistan. In the years 1962–1964, both the Barzani and the Ahmed-Talabani groups were much weaker than the government in terms of territorial control—Christia's preferred measure of the balance of power among civil war parties. As the two rebel groups jointly had full control over less than one-third of Kurdish territory in 1964,[147] MWC theory fails to predict the inter-rebel war that we actually observe in that year.[148] The balance of power was also skewed in favor of the government in terms of troop numbers and weaponry. By the summer of 1963 the government had deployed in Kurdistan at least forty thousand troops (twelve infantry brigades, supported by armor and airpower) and five to ten thousand police as well as large numbers of Kurdish and Arab counterinsurgent militia members. By contrast, the forces of the Barzani and the Ahmed-Talabani groups numbered twenty-five thousand overall, including both regular fighters and militias, and they possessed only small arms and light weapons.[149]

MWC theory does not shed light on the second episode of inter-rebel war, the 1978 PUK-KDP fight, either. In 1976–1978 the two groups did not control any territory and operated in small bands of guerrilla fighters, constantly on the move for fear of government attacks.[150] The balance of power in terms of troop numbers and weaponry was also unambiguously favorable to the government: Baghdad had at its disposal over 150,000 regular troops armed with modern heavy weapons, while the combined insurgent forces did not exceed a few thousand lightly armed individuals.[151] Thus MWC theory wrongly predicts a continuation of peaceful coexistence among rebel groups in the face of government's overwhelming superiority in 1978.

While MWC predicts correctly the absence of inter-rebel war in the years 1979–1982 and 1985–1988, it also leads us to expect, wrongly, that the insurgents would eschew infighting in 1983. Over the years 1979–1983, the military position of the rebel movement as a whole improved, as Iraq's forces were increasingly absorbed in the war against Iran. Yet the government's power still dwarfed the rebels' in terms of territorial control, troop numbers, and weaponry. Though the insurgents had more freedom of movement than in 1975–1978, they did not manage to establish "liberated areas" from which they could exclude government forces as before 1975.[152] In this period the Iraqi military underwent a major expansion, more than doubling the size of its regular ground forces to over 400,000 men and acquiring large numbers of heavy weapons, tanks, and aircraft,[153] while the insurgents had probably less than fifteen thousand lightly armed fighters.[154] Faced with a starkly more powerful government, according to Christia's argument, in 1983 the rebel groups should have remained at peace, as they had done in 1978–1982 and would do in 1985–1988, rather than clashing as they actually did.

If the balance of power is measured in terms of territorial control, the KDP-PUK fight in 1994–1998 would be consistent with MWC theory, as the rebels controlled most of Iraq's Kurdish-inhabited territories.[155] However, Christia's argument could not explain the absence of infighting in the previous three years, as the KDP and PUK were already in full control of the de facto autonomous region by late 1991.

Peter Krause's argument that infighting tends to be initiated by relatively weak organizations attempting to undermine a stronger coethnic rival finds only limited support. The first episode of inter-rebel war in

1964 is clearly a poor fit, given that the initiator was the dominant Bar-zani group; the weaker Ahmed-Talabani group, consistent with window theory, refrained from inter-rebel aggression. The other main episodes (in 1978, 1983, and 1994) can be thought of as consistent with the "spirit" of Krause's argument because they resulted from the actions of a group—the PUK—whose position in the inter-rebel balance of power was precarious. The evidence discussed in this chapter, however, suggests that window-of-vulnerability logic represents a more convincing explanation. In fact, in all these cases the PUK was not experiencing a condition of static weakness but rather an impending or ongoing steep decline in power relative to the KDP. Attacking a militarily stronger rival would not seem a sensible course of action under static conditions, due to the high chance that the initiator would be further weakened. By contrast, a gamble of resurrection in the face a window of vulnerability, with the corresponding high-risk, high-reward payoff, may make strategic sense, given that the alternative to infighting is inexorable decline.

Alternative explanations emphasizing the role of ideology are not empirically convincing. Ideological differences between the various Kurdish groups do not seem to be driving the overall pattern of inter-rebel war: the conservative Barzani group, the somewhat more leftist post-1975 KDP, and the Marxist-leaning PUK all resorted to force against their rivals at some point. Moreover, groups' relatively stable ideological positions cannot explain the alternation of inter-rebel war and peaceful coexistence within short time spans.[156] "Dyadic" forms of the ideological argument, positing that groups with similar ideologies are either more or less prone to inter-rebel war with one another, are not supported by the evidence either: at different moments, the leftist PUK fought and peacefully coexisted with all Kurdish groups, spanning a broad ideological range (including the Communist Party to the extreme left and the Islamist IMK to the extreme right).

A variant of the ideological explanation would trace the origins of inter-rebel war to diverging views between hard-liners and moderates about the acceptability of compromise with the government; this too has limited explanatory power. The fact that a ceasefire between the government and the Barzani group (which the Ahmed-Talabani group firmly opposed as "selling out") preceded the episode of inter-rebel war in 1964 would seem consistent with the argument. A closer look suggests otherwise. As soon as Barzani eliminated the rival group, he adopted the more hard-line position of Ahmed and Talabani, denouncing government guarantees of Kurdish rights as insufficient and demanding autonomy.[157] On its part, the supposedly hawkish Ahmed-Talabani group flipped to the government's side in 1966 after being defeated in the first round of inter-rebel fighting.[158] These two facts cast serious doubts on the hypothesis that inter-rebel war occurred because of a divergence of deeply held preferences between the two groups about the acceptability of compromise with the government.

Similarly, there is no indication of any appreciable ex-ante difference along the hard-line to moderate spectrum among the PUK, the KDP, and the other main Kurdish rebel groups in the years 1976–1988; in any case, whatever difference might have existed likely did not drastically change over time and thus cannot explain why the groups clashed early on but cooperated from 1985.[159] By contrast, in the 1992 elections the KDP adopted the slogan "autonomy for Kurdistan, democracy for Iraq," while the PUK called for "Kurdish self-determination within a federal Iraq," which hinted at a more radical aspiration to something closer to independence.[160] No source, however, suggests that this difference in long-term goals played any role in fueling the conflict between the KDP and the PUK.

The various Kurdish organizations displayed some problems of discipline and limited leadership's ability to control local units.[161] Yet, as with ideology, these organizational features cannot explain why some groups fought in some phases but not in others, as the moments in which violence erupted were not necessarily characterized by especially high levels of decentralization or lack of discipline. In addition, the evidence of rebel decision making presented earlier suggests that the intra-Kurdish wars occurred as a result of explicit decisions of the organizations' leaders, even if it is likely that skirmishes contributed to a climate of fear and distrust between rebel groups, which in turn factored into the leaders' calculations about the use of force.

For similar reasons, individual leaders' characteristics do not provide a powerful explanation for intra-Kurdish fighting: various leaders, with different personalities, backgrounds, and worldviews, opted for inter-rebel war in some moments but not in others, based on the strategic environment in which they operated. In addition, some important rebel decisions appear to have been the outcome of sustained debate within organizations rather than the manifestation of the whims of an individual leader. For example, the fateful decision of the PUK to embark on a major expedition to establish a supply route to Syria in 1978 resulted from a drawn-out deliberation process, as discussed earlier. Talabani, the PUK supreme leader, initially even opposed the idea of opening negotiations with Baghdad in late 1983, later acquiescing to the initiative out of respect for the opinion of the majority of the group's leadership council.[162]

Among my Kurdish interviewees and in the literature, a dyadic version of the leadership-level explanation of infighting is especially popular. According to this view (which incorporates elements of alternative explanations emphasizing ideology), intra-Kurdish violence in 1964 resulted from the clash between Barzani's tribal, authoritarian, and religious personality and the intellectual, urban, and secular sensibilities of Ahmed and Talabani, with similar tensions persisting when new organizations emerged after 1975.[163] However, leadership incompatibility, as a constant, cannot explain the variation of infighting, that is, its occurrence in some moments but not in others. Assessing the narrower claim that early leadership tensions constituted a necessary condition for infighting is more difficult, due to the lack of a counterfactual within the confines of the case (i.e., a parallel world where Barzani, Ahmed, and Talabani were not the early leaders of the Kurdish rebel movement).[164] Yet the occurrence of infighting in the other cases discussed in the next chapters of this book suggests that the kind of leadership incompatibility that characterized the Kurdish case does not constitute a necessary condition, although it may well have been an important contributing factor in Iraqi Kurdistan.

What about the actions of third-party states and the incumbent? The historical record clearly shows that neighboring countries and Iraqi government played an important role in bringing about inter-rebel war. Their influence, however, occurred through paths envisioned by window theory. Probably the clearest instance of a third party contributing to cause intra-Kurdish fighting occurred in 1983: consistent with window-of-vulnerability logic, the prospect of an invasion of Iraqi Kurdistan by Teheran, which was hostile to the PUK and supported its rival KDP, prompted the PUK to gamble for resurrection. Another clear instance of third-party influence is the window of vulnerability faced by the PUK in the 1990s, produced by Turkey's willingness to engage in oil smuggling through KDP-held territory. No evidence suggests that third parties managed to instigate inter-rebel war in Iraqi Kurdistan in the absence of windows or to deter it when windows were present.

Similarly, there is no indication that Baghdad influenced inter-rebel war independent of the presence of windows of opportunity and vulnerability. Unsurprisingly, fear that coethnic rivals would defect to the government figured in rebel groups' calculations; but they did not trigger inter-rebel war in the absence of windows. In particular, Barzani had feared that the Ahmed-Talabani group might collude with Baghdad during a government offensive at least since 1963.[165] Barzani launched his hegemonic bid, however, only when a window of opportunity opened up, following his 1964 ceasefire with the government.[166]

The episode of inter-rebel war that lends itself most easily to be interpreted as engineered by the government occurred in 1983: the PUK attacked the Socialists and Communists in May and reached a ceasefire agreement with Baghdad in December.[167] According to this interpretation, by attacking its rivals, the PUK either complied with a government request or tried to impress Baghdad with a display of military strength, thus signaling its worthiness as negotiating partner.[168] Conclusively disproving this explanation for the PUK's attack is difficult, as individuals with relevant decision-making information (i.e., PUK-related subjects) may have an incentive to deny any collusion with Baghdad in order to portray the PUK's actions in a positive light. (This is the case even for former PUK members who were in the Gorran Party at the time of the interviews. While this PUK splinter party has been critical of the PUK on a range of issues, its members may not have an incentive to be candid about the 1983 episode as the Gorran leader at the time of the interviews, Nawshirwan Mustafa, commanded the PUK forces in that attack.) A key piece of evidence, however, casts doubts on the specific hypothesis that the PUK's attack reflected some form of ongoing cooperation with the government, later formalized in a ceasefire agreement: the PUK was engaged in heavy fighting against the government as late as October 1983, that is, months *after* its attack against the other Kurdish groups.[169] Conversely, the available evidence does not allow me to rule out the possibility that the hope of reaching some form of understanding with Baghdad in the future may have contributed to shape the PUK's actions.

The literature on Iraq's Kurdish insurgencies suggests two additional alternative explanations. First, several scholars have argued that

intra-Kurdish fighting resulted from the weakness of Kurdish ethnonationalism, which could not overcome tribal and linguistic subethnic
loyalties.[170] Second, Theodore McLauchlin and Wendy Pearlman have
suggested that the existence of different institutional arrangements
within the rebel movement explains why inter-rebel clashes quickly followed the 1975 government victory, while inter-rebel cooperation prevailed for several years in the aftermath of government victory in 1988.[171]
In the mid-1970s the dissatisfaction of marginalized elements in the
movement with its erstwhile domination by Mullah Mustafa Barzani
caused the emergence of new rebel groups that intensely competed with
one another. By contrast, in the late 1980s the KDP and PUK were both
satisfied with the alliance they were part of (together with the other
smaller Kurdish organizations) and thus continued to cooperate for several years.

The first argument, pointing to a weak Kurdish identity as an explanation, verges on tautology, as it seems to infer a limited sense of com-
monality among Kurds from the observation of intra-Kurdish rebel
competition. The implied counterfactual—a Kurdish identity washing
away all subethnic distinctions that would deter inter-rebel war—flies in
the face of the dominant scholarly understanding of ethnic identities,
which emphasizes their frequently nested nature. In any case, as a constant, the purportedly underdeveloped Kurdish identity could at best
represent a permissive background condition, not a complete explanation, given that inter-rebel war varies over time. As the case studies in
the next chapters make clear, neither tribal nor linguistic subethnic
cleavages are necessary for the occurrence of war between coethnic rebel
organizations.

The institutional arrangement argument put forth by McLauchlin
and Pearlman is theoretically sound but has less explanatory power than
window theory. Inter-rebel war was not a constant feature of the Kurdish
rebel movement in the pre-1988 period, occurring instead only when
windows of opportunity or windows of vulnerability emerged. Moreover, it was the opening of a window of vulnerability that pulled the PUK
and the KDP back into inter-rebel war in the mid-1990s after their cooperation in the previous years.[172]

Finally, it is important to address explicitly concerns about the endogeneity of windows of opportunity and windows of vulnerability. The

fact that the hypothesized causes of inter-rebel war—windows of opportunity and windows of vulnerability—are themselves the effects of some other cause is not in itself problematic, as they are not supposed to be an "unmoved mover." My argument would be trivial, however, if the emergence of windows of opportunity and vulnerability were simply the last link in a more fundamental causal chain. One particular form of endogeneity would exist if rebel groups could typically create the conditions necessary to launch a hegemonic bid—a favorable imbalance of power relative to coethnic rivals and a limited government threat—whenever they wished to engage in inter-rebel war. Alternatively, the incumbent could trigger inter-rebel war when it pleased, by adopting a limited-threat stance, thus creating a window of opportunity for a powerful rebel group, or third-party states could induce infighting by manipulating the inter-rebel balance of power through selective support to some of the rebels. In all these scenarios, windows would be endogenous to the real cause—the decision of rebel groups, the incumbent, or a third party to unleash inter-rebel war.

General theoretical considerations and empirical evidence specific to the Kurdish insurgencies suggest that endogeneity is not a serious problem here. Theoretically, we should expect rebel groups to strive generally for more power, as helpful in their dealings with both competitors and the government. At the same time, rebel groups should not to be able to simply increase their power as they please. In the one instance of intra-Kurdish war driven by window-of-opportunity logic (in 1964), the Barzani group enjoyed a significant military edge over the rival Ahmed-Talabani group from the outset, due to Barzani's clout with Kurdish tribal fighters; the gap persisted despite the Ahmed-Talabani group's attempts to outgrow its rival. In the three instances of inter-rebel war onset caused by windows of vulnerability (in 1978, 1983, and 1994), the relative rise experienced by the KDP to the detriment of the PUK resulted from dynamics beyond the rebel groups' control.

Similarly, the incumbent, let alone rebel groups, may often be unable to engineer the condition of limited government threat necessary for the occurrence of hegemonic bids. In fact, we should expect rebel groups to assess government threat based on indicators and signals of government capabilities and intentions that are hard to fake (e.g., the state of readiness of the government forces or their deployment in other conflicts).

Moreover, governments may follow different strategies, rather than those implied by window theory, to provoke inter-rebel fighting, such as confrontational "wedge strategies" aiming at creating tensions among rebel groups through increased counterinsurgency pressure.[173] In any case, the decline in government threat that prompted the Barzani group's attack in 1964 did not result from Baghdad's clever posturing but from the widely understood fact that after the November 1963 coup the government needed respite from the fight against the rebels in order to consolidate its power in the capital and reorganize its armed forces.[174]

As noted above, Iran and Turkey played a key role in creating the windows of vulnerability prompting PUK's gambles for resurrection in 1983 and 1994, respectively. Though I cannot rule out that either government hoped to create tensions between the KDP and the PUK, it is clear that the main drivers of the actions of Tehran and Ankara were other factors, which do not amount to general explanations for third-party state behavior in the context of civil wars, thus placating endogeneity concerns. In 1983, revolutionary Iran was hostile to the PUK and supported its rival, the KDP, primarily due to the PUK's leftist ideology and its refusal to abandon its Iranian Kurdish allies. In the early 1990s, Ankara colluded with the KDP in smuggling Iraqi oil to reduce the severe impact on the Turkish economy of the international embargo imposed on Iraq.[175]

⸺ ⊛ ⸺

The evidence presented in this chapter shows that the ebb and flow of intra-Kurdish fighting in the years 1961–1998 was shaped by the opening and closing of windows of opportunity and vulnerability. Moreover, consistent with window theory, the Barzani group was able to extend its authority to areas formerly under its coethnic rival's control in 1964 without facing any resistance throughout the following decade. However, the fact that all the rebel groups in this case were coethnic does not allow me to fully assess whether a shared ethnic identity is indeed a powerful propellant of inter-rebel war. Would similar dynamics have been at play in relations between non-coethnic groups? To answer this question, I now turn to the cases of the insurgencies in Eritrea and Tigray, where rebel groups operated in close proximity to both coethnics and non-coethnics.

4

Parallel Paths to Ethnic Hegemony

Even dogs fight each other only after they deal with the hyena.
—ERITREAN SAYING

We are all nationalists, and we have one thing to do now—win our
independence.
The rest can be worked out later.
—MANNA BAHRE, ERITREAN LIBERATION FRONT'S
POLITICAL ORGANIZER (C. 1974)[1]

In May 1991 the tanks of the Tigray People's Liberation Front (TPLF) rolled into the streets of Ethiopia's capital, Addis Ababa, bringing the brutal Derg regime crashing down. Only a few days later the Eritrean People's Liberation Front (EPLF) entered Asmara, the Eritrean provincial capital, thus taking a decisive step in the thirty-year-long struggle for Eritrean independence.

The TPLF and the EPLF were not the only Eritrean and Tigrayan organizations to fight against the Ethiopian government. The TPLF had shared the Tigrayan field of battle with various groups, including the near homonymous Tigray Liberation Front (TLF) and Tigray People's Liberation Movement Coordinating Committee, better known as "Teranafit" (Tigrigna for "coordinating"), while the EPLF had emerged as a splinter of the Eritrean Liberation Front (ELF). Why did the TPLF and the EPLF, rather than their coethnic rivals, eventually emerge victorious?

Window theory provides powerful insight on this question. The EPLF and the TPLF rose as rebel hegemons in their respective ethnic camps through a process of violent selection, by which they wiped out weaker coethnic rivals during phases of limited government threat. Consistent with my argument, the bulk of the inter-rebel fighting took place within, rather than across, ethnic lines, even if the rebels in the two adjacent provinces had comparable opportunities for contact, and thus violent conflict, with coethnics and non-coethnics (see figure 4.1). Crucially, despite serious political and strategic disagreements, the EPLF and the

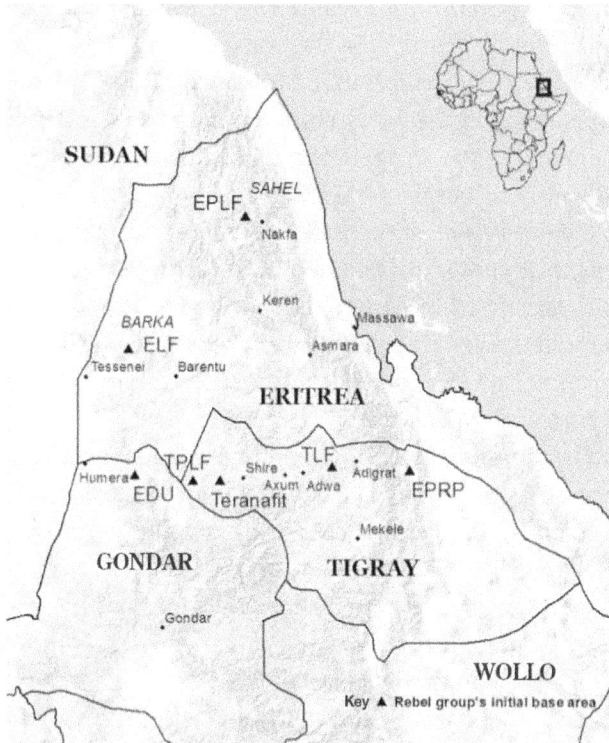

FIGURE 4.1 Map of northern Ethiopia

TPLF refrained from fighting each other and eventually jointly defeated the Ethiopian government—only to engage in an interstate war following Eritrean independence in 1998–2000.

In this chapter I first present an overview of relations among rebel groups active in the two Ethiopian provinces, followed by an assessment of the empirical fit of window theory with the observed pattern of inter-rebel war and peaceful coexistence. Then, toward the end of the chapter, I address alternative explanations and endogeneity concerns. I conclude by summarizing the main findings.

Tracing Trajectories of Rebel Relations in Northern Ethiopia

As the Ethiopian government maneuvered to revoke Eritrea's autonomy, in 1961 the ELF took up arms.[2] In the first decade of the national liberation struggle, the Eritrean Liberation Movement's (ELM) attempt to start military operations in the Sahel represented the only challenge to the ELF's hegemony in the struggle for Eritrean independence. The ELF responded by wiping out the ELM's contingent.[3]

In 1971 the emergence of three ELF splinters from a drawn-out process of organizational implosion heralded a more serious challenge to the ELF's dominance.[4] In early 1972, shortly after the splinter groups had announced their decision to merge into the EPLF, the ELF attacked them.[5] This time, however, a quick and decisive victory eluded the ELF.

The inter-rebel fight continued until 1974, when the fall of Ethiopia's emperor radically altered the political-military landscape. Amid strikes, student protests, and army mutinies, a group of left-leaning officials known as the Derg ("Committee" in Amharic) took control of the government.[6] In the following three years, the ELF and EPLF cooperated in wresting most of Eritrea's territory from government forces, weakened as they were by turmoil in the capital, rebellions throughout the country, and Somalia's attack in the Southeast of Ethiopia.[7]

In 1976 a third Eritrean insurgent group, the Eritrean Liberation Front–Popular Liberation Forces (ELF-PLF), emerged. This was the consequence of a fallout between the head of the EPLF's office for foreign relations, Osman Saleh Sabbe, and the EPLF leadership in the field. After initially allowing the fledgling group to operate in remote areas in western Eritrea, the ELF attacked the ELF-PLF's bases in the fall of 1978 and pushed the group into Sudan by the beginning of the following year.[8]

The cooperation between the other two Eritrean rebel groups—the ELF and the EPLF—continued in the face of a radical reversal of military fortunes in 1978. Having consolidated its hold on power in the capital and benefiting from massive Soviet military support, the Derg repelled the Somali invasion and then launched a major offensive in Eritrea. The ELF and the EPLF lost virtually all of their territory but managed to jointly defend their positions in the Sahel. After the final unsuccessful government offensive in 1980, the EPLF, in cooperation with the Tigrayan TPLF, attacked and defeated the ELF, thus establishing itself as the rebel hegemon in the Eritrean camp.[9]

In neighboring Tigray, several insurgent groups started operating in 1975–1976. Crucially, the fledgling Tigrayan organizations established their bases near the areas of operations of their Eritrean counterparts, in the hope of receiving support from them.[10] Though physical proximity created potential opportunities for violent interactions across ethnic lines, the bulk of inter-rebel fighting in Eritrea and Tigray took place among coethnics.

The TPLF easily crushed its coethnic rivals TLF and Teranafit. The subsequent fight against the Ethiopian Democratic Union (EDU)—a pan-Ethiopian, rather than Tigrayan, organization—proved more difficult, but the TPLF prevailed in 1978. The group was now in a position to deal with its last remaining coethnic competitor, the Ethiopian People's Revolutionary Party (EPRP), which it quickly defeated.[11]

Once the EPLF and the TPLF were firmly in control of their respective ethnic communities, they argued bitterly over the conduct of the struggle against the regime, yet they refrained from fighting each other. Following a renewal of their alliance, the EPLF and the TPLF inflicted a decisive blow on the government in 1991.[12] The TPLF then took power in Addis Ababa while the EPLF achieved its goal of Eritrean independence, formalized with a referendum in 1993.

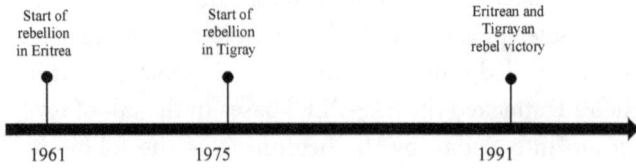

(a) Rebels vs. government

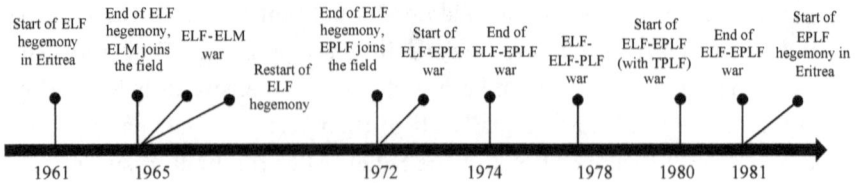

(b) Rebels vs. rebels in Eritrea

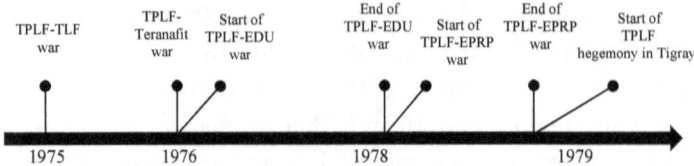

(c) Rebels vs. rebels in Tigray

FIGURE 4.2 Timeline of rebellions in northern Ethiopia, 1961–1991

Assessing the Fit of Window Theory

In this section I assess the empirical fit between the observed pattern of inter-rebel war and peaceful coexistence and the predictions of window theory (summarized in table 4.1). I first examine relations among Eritrean groups, then among Tigrayan groups, and finally across the ethnic cleavage.

Before I proceed, a note on Eritrean and Tigrayan ethnic identities is in order.[13] Both identities coexist with other nested and overlapping identities. The Eritrean identity, in particular, encompasses subethnic religious (Muslims vs. Christians), linguistic (Tigrigna speakers vs. speakers of

TABLE 4.1 Inter-rebel Relations in Eritrea and Tigray, 1965–1991

Observed Outcome (war/no war)	Type of Window	Correct Prediction?
War, ELF–ELM, 1965	Window of opportunity (coethnic, imbalance of power, low government threat, low opportunity cost)	✓
War, EPLF–ELF, 1972–1974	Window of opportunity (coethnic imbalance of power, low government threat, low opportunity cost)	✓
No war, EPLF–ELF, 1975–1979	No window (coethnic, balanced power, no power shift, high opportunity cost, 1975–1977; high government threat, 1978–1979)	✓
War, TPLF–TLF, 1975	Window of opportunity (coethnic, imbalance of power, low government threat, low opportunity cost)	✓
War, TPLF–Teranafit, 1976	Window of opportunity (coethnic, imbalance of power, low government threat, low opportunity cost)	✓
No war, TPLF–ELF, 1975–1978	No window (non-coethnic)	✓
No war, TPLF–EPRP, 1976–1977	No window (coethnic, no power shift, low government threat, but TPLF stretched thin fighting other groups)	✓
No war, ELF–Teranafit, 1976	No window (non-coethnic)	✓
War, TPLF–EDU, 1976–1978	No window (non-coethnic)	×
No war, ELF–EDU, 1976–1978	No window (non-coethnic)	✓
War, ELF–ELF–PLF, 1978	Window of opportunity (coethnic, imbalance of power, low government threat, low opportunity cost, EPLF forces pinned down by government offensives)	✓

(continued)

TABLE 4.1 (continued)

Observed Outcome (war/no war)	Type of Window	Correct Prediction?
War, TPLF–EPRP, 1978–1979	Window of opportunity (coethnic, imbalance of power, low government threat, low opportunity cost)	✓
War, TPLF–ELF, 1979–1981	No window (non-coethnic)	✗
War, EPLF–ELF, 1980–1981	Window of opportunity (coethnic, imbalance of power, low government threat, low opportunity cost)	✓
No war, TPLF–EPLF, 1981–1991	No window (non-coethnic)	✓

Note: Each row indicates an episode of inter-rebel war or inter-rebel peace involving rebel groups operating in adjacent areas (pairs whose members could not have fought each other, as they did not operate in adjacent areas or were not active at the same time, are not reported). The years 1961–1964 are not included as the only rebel group was the ELF.

other languages), and regional (highlanders vs. lowlanders) cleavages, while many of Eritrea's and Tigray's inhabitants share a Tigrigna-speaking identity.[14] As is common in civil wars, Ethiopia's rebel groups formed around subethnic social networks, along largely overlapping religious, linguistic, and regional lines in Eritrea, and along a primarily regional divide in Tigray. Based on the definition of coethnicity discussed in chapter 1, I consider rebel groups with distinct subethnic bases coethnic if their political goals relate to the fate of the ethnic group as a whole and if they recruit (or are willing to do so) across subethnic cleavages.

Intra-Eritrean Relations: E Pluribus Unum—the EPLF

Window theory provides a powerful explanation for the alternation of fighting and peaceful coexistence that characterized relations among Eritrean rebel groups. The ELM, the ELF, the EPLF, and the ELF-PLF were coethnic, as they all struggled for Eritrean independence and had exclusively Eritrean memberships.[15] In 1965 and 1972, in phases of low government threat, the ELF launched hegemonic bids against the weaker ELM and the EPLF, respectively. By contrast, the ELF and the EPLF, which had survived the rival's 1972 attack, cooperated in the years 1974–1979, when the costs of infighting were prohibitively high. The ELF attacked the much weaker but rapidly growing ELF-PLF in 1978, when the government did not pose a serious and immediate threat, following window-of-opportunity logic. Finally, in 1980, the EPLF took advantage of a fleeting moment of limited government threat to crush the weaker ELF and establish itself as the Eritrean hegemon.

The ELF-ELM War

The evidence on the May 1965 attack by the ELF on the ELM is consistent with window-of-opportunity logic: in a phase of the civil war in which the Ethiopian government did not pose a serious and immediate threat, the ELF attacked and defeated a weaker coethnic rival, which was trying to start military operations in the region, thus preserving its hegemonic position in the Eritrean rebel camp.[16]

The stark imbalance of power between the two groups nearly guaranteed that the fight would be short. The ELF had about a thousand troops at the time, while the contingent the ELM deployed in Eritrea consisted of only fifty fighters.[17] The ELM, however, represented a more significant threat than this puny force would suggest, because the organization had deeply infiltrated Eritrean society, with many thousands of underground cell members, and thus could have rapidly expanded its fighting power if it had gained a military foothold in Eritrea.[18] Given its immediate prospects of rapid growth, the ELM should be considered above what I termed the threshold of extreme weakness (despite the fact that it had much less than one-third the number of ELF fighters) and thus a meaningful threat to the ELF's hegemony in the armed struggle in Eritrea.

The government's initial feeble response to the insurgency created a permissive threat environment for the ELF's attack. As John Markakis notes, the "regime was characteristically slow to react to . . . the ELF. Local insurrections were nothing new, and the trouble in Eritrea did not worry officialdom in Addis Ababa unduly." Thus at first "the government seemed inclined to believe its own propaganda image of the Eritrean nationalists as a few bands of shifta [bandits]."[19]

In 1965, besides the local police, only one brigade of the Ethiopian army's Second Division (consisting of about three thousand troops) was tasked with dealing with the Eritrean insurgents; the troops were mostly deployed in static garrison duty in bases in Asmara, Keren, and smaller stations in other towns, with the rest of the province covered by occasional patrols.[20] The first major government offensive took place only two years later, in 1967.[21] The available evidence on the pattern of fighting between rebels and government forces paints a consistent picture of limited government threat: in 1964 and 1965 the bulk of clashes were initiated by the ELF, which suggests that the group could control the pace of its losses and thus faced a low risk of being wiped out by the government.[22]

The ELF's hegemonic ambition emerges clearly from the group's own accounts of the episode. According to Ahmed Nasser (ELF member from 1961), "The chief reason for the ELF attacking the ELM was its belief that the Field could support only one organization."[23] In my interview with him, Nasser elaborated on the ELF's calculus:

> We lost our independence [after Italian colonial rule] as a consequence of internal conflict, Ethiopian ambition, and international conspiracy. The obvious lesson of this was that the Eritrean revolution should avoid new divisions. . . . There must be one [rebel] leadership, one army, one program. . . . In 1965 the ELM gathered a group of fighters and infiltrated the Sahel. At that time the [ELF] supreme council decided not to give them the opportunity to develop in Eritrea. Some of the members of the ELM contingent were liquidated and some went back to Sudan.[24]

Consistent with window theory's expectation that the resources of the coethnic ELF and ELM would be cumulative, as the ELF expanded its guerrilla operations and the ELM started to crack under government pressure, even before the clash between the two groups a number of ELM cells (some of which had been infiltrated by the ELF) joined the rival organization, taking their recruits with them.[25]

The First ELF-EPLF War
Window-of-opportunity logic fits the ELF's early 1972 attack on the EPLF. The ELF acted in a moment of marked military superiority and

limited government threat, with the objective of reasserting its hegemony of the Eritrean liberation struggle.

The stark imbalance of power between the ELF and the three splinter
groups in the process of merging into the EPLF is beyond doubt. The
new organizations were initially very weak; they operated in remote
areas of Eritrea and suffered from little and inconsistent access to external supplies.[26] As EPLF senior commander Mesfin Hagos noted, "It was
a one-sided war at the start. The EPLF was at an infantile stage as an
organization . . . the balance of power was five to one."[27]

Despite the fact that the fledgling group had less than one-third the
manpower at the disposal of its more established rival, due to its significant growth potential the EPLF was far from a negligible threat for the
ELF (i.e., it was above the threshold of extreme weakness). The group was
well positioned to attract substantial foreign support and grow rapidly as
Osman Saleh Sabbe, one of three supreme leaders of the ELF and main
fundraiser abroad, had thrown in his lot with the EPLF.[28] Moreover, with
Christians in leadership positions, the EPLF was particularly well placed
to mobilize the Christian population in the Eritrean highlands, hitherto
only marginally involved in the rebellion.

It is also clear that the Ethiopian government posed a limited threat
when the ELF launched its hegemonic bid. The last major government
offensive had occurred in early 1971; and in the period June 1971–
June 1972, the insurgents initiated the vast majority of clashes.[29] In an
interview with the author, Gime Ahmed (then ELF counterintelligence
officer) noted that intercepted communications at the time revealed that
the government had no intention of escalating its limited military efforts
to take advantage of the infighting.[30] In fact, during the 1972–1974 inter-
rebel war, government forces kept a low profile.[31]

Decision-making evidence confirms that the ELF tried to eliminate
the splinter groups' challenge to its hegemonic position. In late 1971
the ELF passed a resolution authorizing the use of force to "preserve the
unity of the revolution" in case the groups refused to come back to the
fold, and then it tried to enforce it.[32]

ELF-EPLF Peaceful Coexistence

Despite its military superiority, the ELF fell short of crushing its competitor, probably because of tactical blunders and the interposition of the

Sudanese army between the two groups in a potentially decisive battle just across the Sudanese-Ethiopian border. By late 1974 a combination of pressure from the Eritrean population to stop the fratricide, the emergence of opportunities for major battlefield gains against the government, and the substantial strengthening of the EPLF had brought the inter-rebel war to an end.[33] Window theory correctly predicts the absence of a new burst of inter-rebel fighting in the following five years, given its prohibitively high costs—the opportunity cost of forgoing victory at first, and then the risk of outright defeat at the hands of the government.

In 1974, while the central government was in disarray, the leaderships of the EPLF and the ELF grasped the clear chance of strategic success they faced and understood that infighting could spoil it. ELF leader Ahmed Nasser noted: "We concluded that fighting [with the EPLF] must stop to exploit the new developments; the regime was weak, this was a moment of opportunity to achieve independence."[34] EPLF leader Osman Saleh Sabbe expressed his conviction that the liberation struggle had reached a key turning point, declaring that the separatist groups, now stronger than ever, would switch from hit-and-run attacks in the countryside to open offensives against army camps and in urban centers.[35] These expectations proved largely correct: by 1977 the ELF and the EPLF had gained control of 90 percent of Eritrea (with both controlling large swaths of territory) and all but three main urban centers.[36]

Window theory correctly predicts that two rebel groups would not fight each other under these circumstances lest they undermine their rapid military progress. Moreover, the power advantage that had prompted the ELF to attack in 1972 had all but vanished by late 1974: the EPLF had substantially grown in strength, and ELF leaders had concluded that its rival could not be easily defeated, making inter-rebel aggression too costly.[37]

The year 1978 saw a drastic reversal of battlefield trends. With massive Soviet aid, the Derg launched a major offensive in Eritrea. To survive, the EPLF and ELF had to withdraw to remote areas in the province's Northwest and North. The insurgents then jointly resisted a rapid succession of four additional large-scale offensives against their main remaining strongholds in the Sahel.[38] As window theory predicts, the rebel groups did not fight each other in 1978–1979 when confronting a serious and immediate government threat: inter-rebel war would have been suicidal in the face of "one of the biggest setbacks Eritrean independence fighters endured."[39]

The Second ELF-EPLF War

Window theory fits the EPLF's attack on the ELF in 1980, too. The EPLF exploited a fleeting window of opportunity to crush the ELF and become the Eritrean hegemon.

The EPLF enjoyed a clear edge over the ELF. As Awet Weldemichael puts it when referring to the first government offensive in 1978 and the EPLF's 1980 attack, the "ELF was an already collapsing edifice, waiting for an Ethiopian onslaught and a push from its domestic rival."[40] The imbalance of power between the two groups was primarily a function of the ELF's lack of internal cohesion, as several ELF interviewees stressed.[41] The EPLF leadership was fully aware of this situation. In the words of commander Mesfin Hagos, the "ELF was weak in organization more than in numbers. . . . By the time of the second civil war [between the Eritrean rebel groups], the EPLF was slightly bigger numerically. But the ELF organizationally was very weak" and the EPLF leaders knew full well that "the ELF did not have a comparable organization" to the EPLF.[42]

Although a marked imbalance of power between the EPLF and the ELF had existed for some time, the EPLF did not face a permissive threat environment until 1980. In late 1979 an EPLF counterattack at the end of the fifth government offensive disrupted preparations for a subsequent operation. The government continued to plan actively for a massive attack in the Sahel but would not be able to launch operations of comparable intensity in Eritrea until 1982.[43] EPLF sources suggest that the group's leadership understood the constraints preventing the government from launching a new all-out offensive and decided to exploit them to eliminate the ELF. In interviews with the author, Mesfin Hagos noted that the attack on the ELF was timed so that inter-rebel fighting would be over by the time the government threat intensified once again:

We needed to kick the ELF out before the new offensive. We were following the [government] propaganda, the military mobilization, troop movements. We knew we would not be able to sustain a war on two fronts. . . . The Ethiopians were saying: "The next offensive will be decisive." So, they were trying to organize a massive offensive, but their capacity had been weakened in the fifth offensive in July 1979. So, we knew we had a long time to solve our issues with the ELF.[44]

As window theory would lead one to expect, once it emerged victorious from the inter-rebel war, the EPLF did not experience any serious trouble in operating in areas previously under its coethnic counterpart's sway, and many ELF fighters joined the EPLF. As senior EPLF commander Adhanom Gebremariam recalls, "The Eritrean people were willing to support any organization that would have the upper hand. They thought that the government was the primary enemy and the EPLF was a formidable force, which could defeat the enemy."[45]

Peaceful Coexistence and War Between ELF and ELF-PLF

The evidence about the relations between the ELF and the ELF-PLF, while limited, is consistent with window theory. The ELF initially tolerated the ELF-PLF, which was so weak as not to pose a meaningful threat. However, when the ELF-PLF started expanding rapidly, the ELF launched an attack following window-of-opportunity logic.

In 1976 the ELF offered refuge to EPLF elements that remained loyal to Osman Saleh Sabbe after his expulsion from the EPLF, thus enabling the formation of ELF-PLF. The ELF appears to have thought that by supporting Sabbe it could further promote fragmentation in the EPLF.[46] As the new group operated near the ELF stronghold in the Eritrean lowlands and could marshal a force of only fifteen hundred, it represented no meaningful threat for the approximately eighteen-thousand-strong ELF (i.e., the ELF-PLF was well below the threshold of extreme weakness of less than one-third the size of its counterpart).[47]

The ELF's calculus changed, however, when the ELF-PLF started becoming more powerful. According to Tesfay Degiga (in the ELF leadership at the time), while the ELF-PLF forces were initially in a state of disarray, "then their numbers grew and with money [from donors in the Arab world] at his disposal Sabbe started creating a bigger military camp, while for the ELF it was meant to be a temporary refuge."[48] Of particular concern for the ELF leadership was the fact that Osman Saleh Sabbe was managing to attract to his organization ELF members and supporters.[49] In a context of tensions and skirmishes between fighters of the two groups, the ELF decided to use force when the balance of power was still favorable. As senior ELF cadre Tewolde Gebrselassie succinctly put it, "Sabbe's group was growing stronger and the attack was meant to prevent that."[50] By the time of their war in November 1978, though the ELF-PLF had expanded to three to five thousand fighters, the ELF retained a significant margin of superiority.[51] Thus the "ELF felt it would be easy to liquidate Sabbe."[52]

The government probably did not pose an immediate and serious threat for the ELF. While the Derg's offensive in the summer of 1978 reversed the previous wave of insurgent battlefield successes, its subsequent four offensives in 1978 and 1979 targeted EPLF positions, far from the remote areas near the Sudanese border where the bulk of ELF forces had withdrawn.[53] The fact that EPLF forces were pinned down by major government offensives on a distant front, coupled with the poor relations between the EPLF and the ELF-PLF, made it virtually impossible that the EPLF would intervene before the ELF finished the job. In sum, in 1978 the ELF launched a hegemonic bid, expecting a quick and cheap victory against a much weaker coethnic rival, whose unabated growth had come to pose a serious threat for the ELF.

Intra-Tigrayan Relations: The TPLF's March to Hegemony

Window theory is also an insightful guide to understanding rebel relations in Tigray. As one of the organization's leaders, Aregawi Berhe, noted in his book, the "TPLF saw it as imperative to claim and realize a *power monopoly* in Tigrai [sic]," which it achieved by sequentially crushing the weaker TLF, Teranafit, and EPRP in a period of limited government threat.[54]

The TPLF-TLF War

Although I lack incontrovertible decision-making evidence, the broad outlines of the November 1975 attack by the TPLF against the TLF are consistent with window-of-opportunity logic: the TPLF was stronger than its coethnic rival—both organizations had Tigrayan membership and ethnonational agendas—and the government posed a limited threat, which together implied the prospect of a cheap and quick victory for the TPLF.[55]

The TPLF launched a surprise attack on the TLF when the two were camped together for talks aimed at forming a united Tigrayan front. Many TLF members joined the TPLF's ranks after the defeat of their group.[56] While precise figures are lacking, TPLF interviewees unanimously point to the numerical inferiority of the TLF, which had also been experiencing problems of internal cohesion and a membership hemorrhage.[57]

The government did not pose a serious and immediate threat, because, as Aregawi Berhe noted about the Derg's activities at that time, "In the vast rural areas of Tigrai, there was no meaningful government hold or influence to deter the mobility of the TPLF."[58] It is important to note that this low level of government threat permitting inter-rebel war in Tigray and the situation of potentially high opportunity costs of infighting in Eritrea (lasting up to 1978) are two sides of the same coin: the deep disarray of the Ethiopian government in the aftermath of the Derg revolution. The crumbling of central government authority affected the two rebel movements differently because it caught them at different stages of development. On the one hand, the ELF and the EPLF could each marshal thousands of battle-hardened, relatively well-equipped troops, resulting in their ability to take control of much of the province and laying siege to its capital Asmara by early 1975.[59] On the other hand, organized rebellion in Tigray started from scratch in 1975, and the tiny insurgent groups there were incapable of holding significant territory, let alone confronting government forces in open battle.[60]

The TPLF-Teranafit War

In 1976 the TPLF faced a temporary window of opportunity, likely to turn into a window of vulnerability: the group was stronger than its coethnic rival, Teranafit, and the government still posed a limited threat, but the EDU—allied with Teranafit—was organizing a formidable force across the border in Sudan in preparation for an offensive into Tigray.

Consistent with my argument, the TPLF wiped out its weaker coethnic rival before EDU reinforcements could tilt the balance.

Teranafit was a loose coalition of Tigray's landlords and bandits at the head of a peasant army that took up arms against the government in 1976. It did not have an articulated ideological program, besides wanting to restore traditional Tigrayan authority in the wake of the Derg revolution. In particular, Teranafit professed allegiance to Ras Mengesha, a former provincial governor and symbol of Tigrayan nationalism (he was the heir in Tigray's royal line), who had fled to Sudan amid a roundup by the revolutionary regime of high-ranking officials and royal family members. As John Young notes, "The Derg's dismissal of Tigrayan governor Ras Mengesha appeared to herald an era of even more harsh Amhara rule. In such a climate, appeals to Tigrayan national sentiments were essential for any political group wanting peasant support."[61] Teranafit and the TPLF should thus be considered coethnic, as both had Tigrayan membership and leadership and professed some form of Tigrayan ethnonationalism (in the case of Teranafit, related to the restoration of Ras Mengesha). Local peasants saw both TPLF and Teranafit as "sons of Tigray" and urged them to cooperate against the Amhara-dominated Derg.[62]

In Sudan, Ras Mengesha joined other members of the old regime and set up the EDU, with the plan of launching a sweeping offensive across the border into Tigray and then overthrowing the Derg. Supporters of Ras Mengesha in Tigray started coalescing into Teranafit even before the announcement of the creation of the EDU in early 1976.[63] TPLF founding member Ghidey Zeratsion pointed out that the TPLF leadership "knew that Teranafit would grow stronger as it established relations with the EDU. We knew that the EDU was being organized in Sudan and was getting weapons. Its launch base would be Tigray."[64] While the threat gathered across the border, the TPLF enjoyed a margin of superiority over Teranafit. According to TPLF sources, the two organizations had a comparable number of fighters, but the TPLF possessed superior cohesion and discipline.[65] As a result, the TPLF expected to crush Teranafit when they eventually fought.[66]

The TPLF also believed that for some time it could grow at Teranafit's expense by attracting its peasant members with better mobilizing techniques and a political program that would resonate more with their class and national aspirations. As Ghidey Zeratsion put it, "Teranafit did not have a good political orientation; they were mostly made up of peasants and feudal lords. So, we thought we could attract their rank and file over time."[67] Thus two competing dynamics presented themselves to the TPLF: on the one hand, the creation of the EDU, which would strengthen Teranafit and directly intervene in Tigray eventually; on the other, the prospect of outsmarting Teranafit in mobilization and recruitment. Faced with this situation, the TPLF leadership initially opted for tactical cooperation with Teranafit, thus postponing the inevitable showdown. Negotiations led to the signing of a cooperative arrangement in June 1976.[68]

Shortly afterward, however, the killing of "Sihul," a TPLF leader, during one of the occasional skirmishes between TPLF and Teranafit fighters overturned the TPLF's calculus. As Sihul had served as Tigray's representative in the Parliament and enjoyed a reputation as the province's staunch defender, the TPLF had depended on him to start operating among the conservative peasantry. Aregawi Berhe observed, "[Tigrayans'] compliance [with TPLF's mobilization efforts] was granted not because they understood the objectives of the emerging front or because of the young revolutionary students, but simply because [of] Sihul . . . without him the unknown TPLF would have found it difficult to survive and expand."[69] Sihul's death undermined the TPLF's short-term strategy of growing larger than its rival while avoiding open confrontation. In an interview, Aregawi Berhe suggested as much: "For us Sihul was key, because he represented a link between the younger and older generations as well as between the rural and urban environments."[70] Not long after, the TPLF attacked and quickly defeated Teranafit, enabling the TPLF to tap into its rival's pool of resources. A large number of Teranafit rank and file joined the TPLF, which did not experience any organized resistance in areas where Teranafit previously held sway.[71]

The continued limited threat posed by the Derg at the time comes across from interviews with TPLF leaders. Ghidey Zeratsion recalled, "We knew that . . . the government was very weak at that time, so it would not launch a major campaign."[72]

From Peaceful Coexistence to War Between TPLF and EPRP
Window theory helps us make sense of the alternation of peaceful coexistence and inter-rebel war characterizing the TPLF-EPRP relationship.

The two groups should be considered coethnic, as the EPRP's program emphasized the need to end the oppression of ethnic groups, including Tigrayans, by the Amhara-dominated central government, and the bulk of its leadership was from Tigray.[73] From the moment the TPLF and the EPRP established a military presence in eastern Tigray in late 1975 until their armed conflict in 1978, ideological disagreements and competition for support of Tigray's peasants created tensions between them.[74] Until the spring of 1978, no window emerged and, consistent with my argument, no inter-rebel war occurred. Throughout this period, the government had very limited power projection in rural Tigray and the TPLF was stronger than the EPRP, but TPLF forces were stretched thin in fights against Teranafit and then the much stronger EDU in the western part of the province; opening another front against the EPRP would have put the TPLF's very existence at risk. (As the EDU was not a Tigrayan group—it had a pan-Ethiopian agenda and ethnically mixed composition—the TPLF-EDU fight represents a failed prediction for window theory.)[75]

The situation would change in the spring of 1978. By then, while EPRP forces in eastern Tigray had languished amid internal turmoil and lack of significant military engagement with the Derg, the TPLF had defeated its rivals in the West, acquiring in the process much valuable battlefield experience. At that point, the TPLF apparently took advantage of an opportunity to establish itself as Tigray's hegemon by attacking its weaker coethnic rival's base area in mid-March 1978. By 1979 the EPRP was relegated to an inconsequential role in the armed struggle and could operate only far from Tigray.[76]

Importantly, unlike for the infighting with TLF and Teranafit, TPLF sources do not acknowledge an explicit decision to wipe out the EPRP, suggesting instead that the rival's provocations forced the TPLF's hand. Yet the prevailing balance of power and the level of government threat were conducive to a TPLF's hegemonic bid. TPLF and EPRP sources agree that the TPLF was stronger than the EPRP when war broke out. Though the two organizations had roughly comparable numbers of fighters and levels of armaments, the TPLF possessed superior internal cohesion, discipline, and fighting skills.[77] Aregawi Berhe's words summarize the prevailing perception of the EPRP among TPLF leaders: "We considered them militarily ineffective. There was a lot of rhetoric on their part, but just that. They had no military experience, unlike us. We had fought against Teranafit and EDU for a long time. We had also fought the Derg, even if not in major battles. . . . We understood we were in a better position than the EPRP if war broke out."[78]

In addition to lacking significant battlefield experience, the TPLF leaders knew that the EPRP was riven with factionalism.[79] As with the other episodes of inter-rebel war in Tigray, the government posed a limited threat. Once again Aregawi Berhe's view is illuminating: "Our assessment was that the government was weak in Tigray. They could not penetrate rural areas; they had limited forces; they would not dare going to the countryside. . . . They had most of their forces there [Eritrea], and in Tigray they were mostly watching the fight between TPLF and EPRP, the way they had done with Teranafit."[80]

Tigray was thus safe for the final TPLF's hegemonic bid. Consistent with window theory, the TPLF was able to expand to areas previously under the EPRP's influence and intensify its mobilization efforts, regimenting Tigray's rural population into peasant, women, and youth associations to a degree that had been impossible in the presence of coethnic competitors.[81]

Rebel Interactions Across the Eritrea-Tigray Ethnic Divide

While both the Eritrean and Tigrayan insurgent movements experienced multiple episodes of infighting, there was remarkably little inter-rebel violence between Eritrean and Tigrayan rebel groups. In fact, the Eritrean fronts provided vital help to fledgling Tigrayan groups in 1975–1976. The EPLF trained and armed the TPLF and the EPRP, while the ELF provided similar support to the TLF and refrained from fighting Teranafit.[82] Relations between Eritrean and Tigrayan groups were not always harmonious: mutual suspicion, fear of exploitation and abandonment, and tough bargaining were pervasive, as the groups' interests were far from perfectly aligned.[83] Yet disputes did not tend to escalate to all-out fights, as the TPLF-EPLF relationship illustrates.

EPLF-TPLF Peaceful Coexistence
After the TPLF and the EPLF consolidated their hegemonic positions in the respective movements, relations between the two allies soured. The

main issue concerned the TPLF's war aims. The TPLF maintained an ambiguous position on whether its goals were limited to the liberation of Tigray or extended to overthrowing the Ethiopian government. By contrast, the EPLF opposed Tigray's independence, as it wanted a friendly TPLF-led central government to legitimize Eritrean independence after battlefield victory. Thus the EPLF insisted that Tigrayan insurgents should seek to rule a multiethnic Ethiopia (minus Eritrea) rather than a breakaway Tigrayan state.[84]

Tensions boiled over in 1985, with the two groups engaging in public recriminations through publications and radio broadcasts. After the TPLF labeled the EPLF an enemy, the EPLF severed all contacts and even denied its Tigrayan counterpart access to Sudan through Eritrean territory for the delivery of humanitarian aid to victims of the famine ravaging Tigray. Relations between the groups remained strained for three years, until an opportunity emerged in the spring of 1988 to inflict a decisive defeat on the Derg with a coordinated TPLF-EPLF effort. Then, in a nod to the EPLF's position, the TPLF publicly stated that regime change was a prerequisite for peace and for any act of national self-determination. The declaration led to the resumption of joint operations and ultimately rebel victory.[85]

Notwithstanding the acrimony between the TPLF and the EPLF in 1985–1988 and the opportunity for military confrontation provided by the physical proximity of their base areas, no large-scale fight ensued. Consistent with window theory, there is no indication that the EPLF leadership ever thought it could defeat the TPLF and then mobilize Tigray's population the way it had done with the ELF and the population under the latter's control. On the contrary, the EPLF continued to believe that the defeat of the Derg could be achieved only with a multiethnic rebel alliance. As EPLF commander Mesfin Hagos noted, "We were aware of our interdependence with the TPLF. We knew that the enemy wanted to destroy one [rebel group] at the time, and we would be the next target if it defeated the TPLF."[86] The TPLF followed a similar multiethnic approach to move beyond Tigrayan territory and take power in Addis Ababa: it groomed the Ethiopian People's Democratic Movement (EPDM) and the Oromo People's Democratic Movement (OPDM), with the objective of mobilizing the Amhara and Oromo populations, and then in 1989 brought them into an umbrella organization under its control.[87]

The TPLF-ELF War

By contrast, interactions between the Tigrayan TPLF and the Eritrean ELF do not fit window theory. Besides occasional skirmishes related to competing claims over the Eritrea-Tigray border, major clashes between the two occurred in 1979–1981. In the fall of 1979 and spring of 1980, the TPLF fought ELF contingents trying to escort EPRP elements to neighboring Gondar province through TPLF's areas of influence; then in 1980–1981 the TPLF took part (on the EPLF's side) in the intra-Eritrean war. A closer look at these episodes, however, reveals mechanisms that, albeit not part of window theory, are not at odds with it. The TPLF-ELF fight thus represents a less damaging falsification blow than if dynamics similar to those that characterize cases of intra-ethnic war, which are explicitly ruled out by window theory, were in evidence.

The first TPLF-ELF clashes occurred in the context of the intra-Tigrayan TPLF-EPRP fight. Bereft of allies in Tigray (as the TPLF had wiped out its local partner, the TLF, and had grown closer to the EPLF), the ELF tried to prop up the EPRP after its first defeat at the hands of the TPLF. Evidence on the ELF's decision making is limited, but it seems that the ELF intended to escort EPRP survivors to Gondar, where they would reunite with other EPRP units.[88] The TPLF was alarmed by the possibility of its rival's return to Tigray, and thus a battle ensued when its forces encountered the ELF-EPRP contingent in the fall of 1979. Similarly, in the spring of 1980 the TPLF clashed with an ELF contingent escorting EPRP elements expelled by the TPLF from Gondar. After these battles, in early 1981 the TPLF eagerly accepted the EPLF's proposal to join it in its ongoing all-out offensive against the ELF.[89] Gebru Asrat noted that there was "a transmission of the intra-Eritrean conflict in Ethiopia through this system of alliances"—a mirror image of the ELF's earlier entanglement in the TPLF-EPRP feud.[90] Though the TPLF wanted to eliminate an organization that had threatened its interests in Tigray, the ELF, there is no indication that the TPLF expected to take over the resources previously under the ELF's control, as in instances of intra-ethnic war. In fact, the concern driving the TPLF to help crush the ELF was the survival of its ally, the EPLF, rather than absorption of the ELF's resources. Having noted that the ELF could hinder the EPLF's defensive efforts against the massive Derg offensive then under preparation and thus bring about government victory, Tedros Hagos summed up the

TPLF's rationale for helping the EPLF against the ELF: "The collapse of the Eritrean revolution was not going to have a pleasant effect on our self-interests."[91]

The implied counterfactual is that the TPLF likely would not have launched a large-scale attack to expel the ELF from Eritrea had there not been another Eritrean organization (the EPLF) ready to fill the vacuum. Although providing supporting process evidence is exceedingly difficult, given that rebel decision makers tend not to indulge in counterfactual analysis, EPLF-TPLF relations after the ELF's defeat represent a helpful comparison: notwithstanding the tensions between the EPLF and the TPLF discussed earlier, the two groups refrained from fighting each other. Indeed, the TPLF continued to be deeply interested in the survival of its Eritrean counterpart, as the alternative would not have been the takeover by the TPLF of the insurgency in Eritrea, but rather an opportunity for the Derg to focus its full resources on the Tigrayan insurgents.[92]

Alternative Explanations and Endogeneity Concerns

In this section I show that alternative explanations of inter-rebel war perform poorly, focusing in particular on Fotini Christia's minimum winning coalition (MWC) theory, Peter Krause's argument about competition within national liberation movements, and group- and leader-level factors, as well as actions of third-party states and the Ethiopian government. In doing so, I also address key endogeneity concerns.

MWC theory suggests that infighting should occur when one rebel group (or coalition) is sufficiently strong to take on both the government and other rebels. Christia's theory, however, predicts inter-rebel cooperation in all instances in which inter-rebel war occurred in Eritrea and Tigray: the rebels were much weaker than the Ethiopian government in terms of troop numbers, armaments, and territorial control, so they should have refrained from infighting.

In Eritrea, when the ELF wiped out the ELM in 1965, the insurgents could operate in about half of the province but did not fully control any territory and were outgunned and outnumbered 3:1 by Ethiopian forces.[93]

In 1972, when the ELF attacked the EPLF, the government-rebel balance of power was roughly comparable.[94] As Michael Woldemariam comments on military conditions in Eritrea in 1972, "The position of the Ethiopian military in the province was simply too strong to be challenged. . . . The chance that the Ethiopian military would incur significant losses at the hands of an increasingly bold, but outgunned band of rebels was remote."[95] The government still controlled the bulk of Eritrean territory, and its forces outnumbered and outgunned the rebels by even wider margins in 1980, when the EPLF attacked the ELF. Like window theory, MCW logic correctly predicts the absence of inter-rebel war in Eritrea in 1978–1979, when a reinvigorated army launched a series of major offensives.[96] Moreover, Christia's theory correctly leads us to expect the EPLF and the TPLF not to fight each other after establishing their hegemonic positions in the respective rebel movements, given that the two groups were dwarfed by government forces. MWC theory cannot explain, however, why the rebels continued to cooperate past the point when they grew stronger than the government, before their eventual military victory.

MWC theory's explanatory power is comparably limited in Tigray. When the TPLF wiped out the TLF, the two combined had two hundred fighters and controlled no territory. Similarly, at the time of their fight, Teranafit and the TPLF were lightly armed, controlled no territory, and had roughly a thousand fighters each, compared to forty-five thousand government troops. An even more skewed balance of power prevailed in 1978, when the EPRP and the TPLF fought each other: each group had a thousand fighters, controlled little territory, and mostly executed hit-and-run attacks, while the government forces had significantly expanded in number and firepower with Soviet support.[97] In these three cases of infighting, MWC theory predicts inter-rebel cooperation.

Krause's argument about how the competitive dynamics of nonhegemonic national liberation movements undermine the effectiveness of the antigovernment struggle represents a powerful guide to understand the path leading to ultimate rebel victory in Ethiopia: only after the EPLF and the TPLF got rid of their respective ethnic competitors were they able to fully mobilize the resources of their communities and focus their undivided attention on the fight against the government.[98] Nonetheless, the argument sheds less light on the identity of the initiators and the timing of inter-rebel war in Ethiopia. Krause expects relatively weak groups to display a particular propensity to infighting, in the hope that internecine violence will propel them to a position of dominance in the movement. However, all episodes of inter-rebel war were initiated by a relatively strong (but not yet in a hegemonic position) group.[99] Moreover, Krause's argument does not make predictions about *when* we should expect infighting, given a certain hierarchy of power among coethnic groups.[100] By contrast, with its emphasis on trends in relative power and the level of government threat, window theory provides predictions about the timing of inter-rebel war onset, which hold up reasonably well to empirical scrutiny.

The character of rebel leaders could have significant influence on the risk of inter-rebel war. Accounts of the Eritrean independence struggle are often dominated by the figure of EPLF leader Isaias Afewerki, variously described as power-hungry, ruthless against opponents, and farsighted as a military strategist.[101] One could therefore hypothesize that his ambition and aggressiveness set the EPLF on a collision course with its Eritrean rival or that inter-rebel war resulted from his peculiar ability to grasp the kind of strategic logic envisioned by window theory. Isaias Afewerki's characteristics, however, are an unconvincing explanation for the overall pattern of inter-rebel fighting in Eritrea, as the EPLF initiated only one of the episodes of intra-Eritrean rebel war. The ELF, whose leadership changed over time and was less tightly dominated by a single individual, initiated multiple attacks. Moreover, EPLF interviewees suggest that the decision in 1980 to eliminate the ELF once and for all was driven by widely understood situational factors (i.e., the favorable balance of power and the limited government threat) rather than Afewerki's individual initiatives. In addition, the same ELF leaders who vowed to destroy the splinter groups in 1971 opted for peaceful coexistence from late 1974. Similarly, the EPLF leaders who decided to wipe out the ELF in 1980 refrained from this course of action in previous years and avoided throughout military confrontation with the TPLF.

As some accounts of the TPLF's military struggle stress the ambition and cunning of Meles Zenawi—the late TPLF leader and subsequently Ethiopian prime minister—one could conceive of similar leadership-level explanations of the TPLF's behavior toward other rebel groups.[102] Yet Zenawi's character cannot explain the episodes of inter-rebel war in which the TPLF was involved, as they occurred when the organization had a collective leadership (Zenawi consolidated his hold on power in the mid-1980s).

Given the range of political views espoused by Ethiopia's rebel groups, it is particularly important to probe the influence of ideology as an alternative explanation for the observed pattern of infighting. Ideological differences and similarities are a function not only of groups' positions on the leftist-conservative spectrum but also of the scope of their nationalist claims (i.e., autonomy vs. independence) and their willingness to compromise with the government. Yet ideology appears to have limited explanatory power in this case. In Eritrea, the EPLF had a more straightforward Marxist-Leninist orientation than the ELF, where a communist core competed with conservative elements. These marginal ideological differences, however, cannot explain the pattern of alternating cooperation and violence between the two main Eritrean groups, given that their ideologies were relatively stable features of the organizations. Moreover, despite these differences, the ELF and the EPLF resorted to force only when facing windows of opportunity or windows of vulnerability, and the ELF attacked both the Marxist EPLF and the conservative ELF-PLF. Also, the ELF, the EPLF, and the ELF-PLF all advocated Eritrean independence, and there is no indication of any one of them being more willing to compromise with the government. In Tigray, the TPLF fought the conservative Teranafit as well as groups with which it shared a Marxist-Leninist outlook (EPRP) and similar hopes for self-determination (TLF). The groups' different agendas for the province did not result in any of them trying to reach a separate settlement with the government.

The degree of cohesion and decentralization of rebel organizations could also affect the risk of infighting. As with ideology, however, organizational features cannot explain variation over time, as the phases of inter-rebel fighting were not characterized by especially high levels of decentralization or indiscipline. Moreover, both relatively cohesive and disciplined organizations (EPLF and TPLF) and low-cohesion and undisciplined ones (ELF) launched attacks against their rivals. Also, the evidence about rebel decision making presented earlier shows that inter-rebel war typically resulted from explicit decisions to use force, even if skirmishes may have influenced those decisions, by intensifying threat perception, or operated as immediate triggers for war.

A thoughtful reader might wonder whether the observed association between coethnicity and inter-rebel war is a reflection of preexisting tensions correlated with, but causally unrelated to, ethnicity. In particular, antagonism among their respective leaderships could cause coethnic rebel groups to fight one another. The available evidence suggests this is unlikely to be the case. Whether a rebel group emerged as a splinter from another can be used as a proxy for preexisting tension between organizations' leaders; but in Ethiopia, both groups with a common "parent" organization (ELF and EPLF) and others with separate origins (TPLF, TLF, Teranafit, and EPPR) fought one another. Conversely, while there were tensions between EPLF and TPLF leaders, these did not erupt in violence (at least not until the Ethiopia-Eritrea interstate war, years after rebel victory).

A final set of alternative explanations emphasizes the role of foreign governments and the incumbent in inciting or restraining inter-rebel war (beyond their impact on the balance of power and the threat environment, as envisioned by window theory). Third parties could induce infighting or cooperation with positive and negative incentives, e.g., offers of aid and threats of abandonment. The incumbent could pit groups against one another by stirring up fears that a rival was cooperating with the government or by cajoling one organization to attack another.

The available evidence for the Eritrea case does not indicate any attempt on the part of insurgents' foreign patrons to ignite inter-rebel violence. On the contrary, they repeatedly tried to promote cooperation against the Ethiopian government. For example, the former EPLF foreign emissary Osman Saleh Sabbe reported mediation attempts by Sudan in 1975–1977 to create a joint Eritrean rebel front.[103] A skeptic could argue that Eritrea is a peculiar case of exceptionally limited foreign involvement and leverage, in which the insurgents could follow window logics given the absence of constraints to their behavior imposed by outside actors.[104] Indeed, some observers of the Eritrean insurgency depict a herculean, autarkic effort that brought about independence despite the world's neglect or even hostility.[105] Although Eritrea represents an exception to the cold war pattern of superpower confrontation by proxy (the Soviet Union provided military aid to the Derg, but the United States did not support the insurgents), this interpretation is overstated. Both the ELF and the EPLF received vital support from various Arab countries,

Somalia, and, in particular, Sudan.[106] As Weldemichael notes, "Sudan provided what any rebellion needs for survival and success: cross-border sanctuaries, secure and reliable supply routes beyond Ethiopian reach, and shelter to waves of Eritrean refugees who, among other things, replenished the guerrillas' ranks."[107] Khartoum provided similar support to rebel groups in Tigray, and there is no indication that the Sudanese government departed from its approach in Eritrea of promoting cooperation among opponents of the Ethiopian government.[108]

What about the role of the incumbent? Fears that one group might reach a deal with the government at another's expense were pervasive in Eritrea. The Derg probably played up these fears to drive a wedge between its opponents. For example, in 1976 it did not include the EPLF on its list of public enemies, and it held meetings with representatives of the organization. Moreover, in subsequent years the government maintained separate contacts with both the ELF and the EPLF.[109] The fact that fear of defection to the government may affect rebel threat perception and thus contribute to motivate inter-rebel war is fully consistent with window theory. The argument would be falsified only if fear of defection were sufficient to cause infighting, regardless of the presence of windows of opportunity and vulnerability. The evidence presented in this chapter suggests that this was not the case: inter-rebel war did not occur without windows of opportunity or windows of vulnerability. The ELF and the EPLF may have been alarmed by news of contacts between their rival and the Derg, but infighting occurred only when an opportunity for the EPLF to launch a hegemonic bid materialized in 1980. Analogously, in the mid-1980s the TPLF feared that the EPLF might reach a separate agreement with the government, but this did not lead to inter-rebel war in the absence of a window of opportunity or a window of vulnerability. On the other hand, TPLF sources do not reveal specific fears of defection driving the group's actions toward other organizations operating in Tigray. In fact, TPLF leaders thought that the Derg saw their group as less threatening than others and thus would not provide support to its rivals in Tigray.[110]

This observation points to the potential endogeneity of government threat. The fact that threat levels are influenced by other factors is not problematic in itself. However, if strategic decisions by the government systematically shape the rebels' threat environment, then a satisfying account of inter-rebel war would require theorizing about the incumbent's calculus. A different endogeneity problem would arise if some factor that the government, but not the researcher, can observe influenced both the level of government threat and the risk of infighting: if the government had intelligence indicating that infighting between two rebel groups was imminent, it might decide to withdraw forces from the area to redeploy them in locations where other insurgent groups were likely to be actively engaged in antigovernment operations; in this scenario, the subsequent infighting would be causally unrelated to the change in government threat.

Empirically, however, these endogeneity concerns are assuaged by the fact that the changes in the level of threat posed by the Ethiopian government over time were not the result of its strategic manipulations or anticipation of infighting. In particular, the collapse of central authority in 1974–1977, the series of government offensives in 1978–1979, and the subsequent lull in 1980–1981 all reflected the tightening and untightening of exogenous resource constraints faced by the incumbent for counterinsurgency operations. When the government had fewer resources at its disposal, it adopted a defensive stance; when more weapons and disciplined soldiers were available, it went on the offensive.

The insurgencies in Eritrea and Tigray provide strong support for window theory. A clear majority of instances of inter-rebel war in the two provinces were driven by window-of-opportunity logic. In the Eritrean camp, the EPLF emerged on top by launching a hegemonic bid against the ELF (1980–1981), which had previously wiped out the ELM (1965) and the ELF-PLF (1978), in addition to unsuccessfully trying to nip in the bud the EPLF (1972–1974). Similarly, the TPLF achieved hegemony of the Tigrayan insurgent movement by sequentially crushing the weaker TLF (1975), Teranafit (1976), and the EPRP (1978–1979). Window theory generally predicts correctly the absence of inter-rebel war in moments in which its costs would be prohibitively high (1974–1979, in relations between the ELF and EPLF, and 1976–1977, in relations between the TPLF and the EPRP) or its benefits too low due to the lack of common ethnic constituencies (most notably, the peaceful relationship between the two ethnic hegemons, the EPLF and the TPLF).

The wars between the EDU and TPLF and between the TPLF and ELF represent exceptions to the pattern of rebel groups abstaining from infighting across ethnic lines. The available evidence, however, does not reveal causal processes at odds with window theory, and thus these two failed predictions are not especially damaging for it. In the next two chapters I present ancillary case studies and statistical analysis to assess the validity of window theory beyond Iraq and Ethiopia.

5

Inter-rebel War in Lebanon, Sri Lanka, and Syria

oes window theory of inter-rebel war travel outside the rebellions in Iraqi Kurdistan and northern Ethiopia? To answer this
question, this chapter presents ancillary case studies of the civil
wars in Lebanon (1975–1990) and Sri Lanka (1983–1990), as well as ISIS's
initial relations with other rebel groups fighting in Syria (2013–2014).

Besides constituting instances of multiparty civil wars, each of these
cases presents peculiar advantages for additional tests of window theory.
The Lebanese civil war is especially useful as it features both coethnic
and non-coethnic armed groups operating in close proximity and thus
with opportunities to fight one another, which allows me to test the
expectation that coethnic rebel groups should be distinctively prone to
infighting. Moreover, prima facie this is not an easy case for window
theory, as Lebanon's civil war is infamously described as a uniquely complex conflict devoid of clearly identifiable patterns of fighting among its
participants—"a war-of-all-against-all" where "the number of opponents
was beyond strategy" and by the end of which all "had fought one another
in a full schedule of round-robin matches."[1]

The case of the Islamic State of Iraq and Syria allows me to assess the
relevance of window theory to Jihadist rebel groups, increasingly important actors in civil wars and world politics more generally.[2] In addition,
ISIS is inherently interesting as it has been a major focus of U.S. foreign
policy since 2014; this fact, in my view, more than offsets an inevitable

drawback of studying an extremely recent case—the limited quality and patchiness of the available evidence. Finally, the Tamil insurgency in Sri Lanka allows me to probe the explanatory power of window theory beyond Africa and the Middle East, the world regions where all other cases I examine are located.

The Lebanese Civil War

The domestic element of the Lebanese civil war—a dispute over the distribution of political power among the country's ethnosectarian groups—overlapped and interacted with the Arab-Israeli conflict, intra-Arab rivalries, and U.S.-Soviet competition for influence in the Middle East, as reflected in the Palestine Liberation Organization's (PLO) involvement in the fight, Syria's and Israel's occupations, as well as the deployment of a Western multinational peacekeeping force. This resulted in a kaleidoscopic battlefield with a multitude of armed actors, frequently shifting sides and even fighting their erstwhile allies.

Window theory proves a useful key to make sense of much (but by no means all) of the pattern of inter-rebel fighting and performs better than alternative arguments. In particular, the opening of windows of opportunity and vulnerability can explain infighting among Lebanon's Christian armed groups in 1980 and 1989–1990 and some key aspects of the intra-Shia fight in 1988, as well as the absence of inter-rebel war among the ethnically diverse rebel coalition that challenged the Lebanese government in 1976 and 1983–1984. Window theory, however, cannot explain the clashes between rebel groups across ethnic lines that occurred in 1985–1988.

As discussed in the first chapter, in keeping with much of the literature on ethnic politics, this book adopts a broad definition of ethnicity—a subjectively experienced sense of ascriptive shared identity based on skin color, language, religion, or other markers of common culture and descent. In Lebanon, religious sect has long been the most salient marker of ethnicity, as political notables and parties have vied for influence and representation at different levels of government for their religious communities since before the country's independence in 1943.[3] Thus, for instance, two rebel groups recruiting from and making claims on behalf of the Shia population would be considered coethnic, while a Sunni and a Druze organization would be considered non-coethnic.

To facilitate the reader's journey through the case, I divide it into six phases, based on major changes in the intensity of fighting between the opposing civil war camps or the degree of external intervention. For each phase, I discuss my argument's fit with the available historical data (summarized in table 5.1). I then address alternative explanations.

The First Round of Civil War, 1975–1976

At the outbreak of large-scale violence in 1975, the Lebanese Front, which was an alliance of Christian Maronite militias, faced off against the coalition of organizations forming the National Movement, which enjoyed the military support of PLO forces deployed in Lebanon. The Lebanese Front consisted of two main militias—the Phalanges and the Tigers—and several other smaller ones, including the Guardians of the Cedars, the Tanzim, and the Marada Brigade.[4]

The National Movement was a collection of ethnically and ideologically diverse organizations: the Druze-dominated but secularly oriented Progressive Socialist Party (PSP), Sunni Mourabitoun, the multiethnic Lebanese Communist Party, and various Arab nationalist formations, such as the Syrian Social Nationalist Party as well as the Syrian and Iraqi branches of the Baath Socialist Party. The National Movement's glue was a profound disaffection with the Christians' dominant position in Lebanon's ethnosectarian power-sharing system, which the members of the National Movement perceived as especially unfair considering the decline of the Christian share of the population since the establishment of the system in 1943. The Lebanese army became an active belligerent on the side of the Christian militias only in 1976, after primarily Muslim units defected and joined the National Movement, which I thus consider a rebel coalition from then on.[5]

With limited help from the Syrian government, in the course of 1976 the rebels gained the upper hand on the battlefield; by the summer the Lebanese government appeared on the verge of defeat. The Syrian government then reversed course, launching a large-scale intervention in

TABLE 5.1 Inter-rebel Relations in Lebanon, 1976–1990

Observed Outcome (war/no war)	Type of Window	Correct Prediction?
No war between members of the National Movement, 1976	No window (non-coethnic)	✓
No war, Phalanges–Tigers, 1977–1979	No window (coethnic, imbalanced power, but high Syrian threat, no power shift)	✓
War, Phalanges–Tigers, 1980	Window of opportunity (coethnic, imbalanced power, low Syrian threat, low opportunity cost)	✓
No war between PSP, Amal, and Mourabitoun, 1982–1984	No window (non-coethnic)	✓
War, Amal and PSP–Mourabitoun, 1985	No window (non-coethnic)	✗
War, Amal–PSP, 1985–1988	No window (non-coethnic)	✗
No war Amal–Hezbollah Front (1985–1987)	Window of opportunity (coethnic, imbalanced power, low government threat, low opportunity cost)	✗
War, Amal–Hezbollah 1988–1990	Window of opportunity (coethnic, imbalanced power, low government threat, low opportunity cost)	✓
War, Aoun's forces–Lebanese Forces, 1989	Window of opportunity (coethnic, imbalanced power, low Syrian threat, low opportunity cost)	✓
War, Aoun's forces–Lebanese Forces, 1990	Window of vulnerability (coethnic, balanced power, high Syrian threat, but power shift)	✓

Note: Each row indicates an episode of inter-rebel war or inter-rebel peace involving rebel groups in Lebanon. The table does not include the year 1975, as I consider the National Movement an alliance of rebel groups only from the moment when the Lebanese army entered the civil war on the side of the Christian militias in 1976.

Lebanon to forestall rebel victory. While the Syrian leadership had previously supported the National Movement in the face of advances by Christian militias, notes Theodor Hanf, Damascus was "not prepared to countenance a victory of the Palestinian-National Movement coalition," as this "would raise the spectre of Israeli intervention—or the emergence of a militant politico-military bastion of completely independent Palestinian organizations and Lebanese like Jumblatt [the National Movement's leader], whom the Syrians regarded as a political buccaneer."[6] The newly formed alliance among the Lebanese army, the Christian militias, and Damascus inflicted heavy losses on the National Movement until Syria imposed a ceasefire on the two civil war camps and deployed a twenty-five-thousand-strong contingent in central and northern Lebanon to enforce it in October.[7]

Window theory correctly predicts the absence of inter-rebel fighting in this initial phase of the Lebanese civil war, given that the main members of the National Movement were not coethnic, and thus the rebels faced neither windows of opportunity nor windows of vulnerability: in the absence of a shared ethnic identity, inter-rebel war did not promise meaningful gains in terms of an improved threat environment or a broader pool of resources.[8]

"Pax" Syriana and Its Discontents, 1977–78

The two main Christian militias—the Phalanges and the Tigers—welcomed Syrian help against the National Movement–PLO alliance and only grudgingly accepted the deployment of Syrian forces in much of the country in late 1976. Yet the Christian leaders soon started dreading the prospect of permanent Syrian suzerainty and thus established close ties with Israel as a potential counterweight to the Syrians. On its part, Damascus mended fences with the PLO.[9] The seeds of a new round of armed conflict were being sown.

Skirmishes between the Syrian forces, on the one hand, and the Phalanges and the Tigers, on the other, escalated into all-out fighting in the summer of 1978. Heavy clashes in Beirut and in the Christian heartland north of the capital continued into the fall.[10] In this phase I consider the Syrian occupier as the incumbent and the Christian militias pitted against its forces as rebel groups. (These included the Tanzim and the Guardians of the Cedars, besides the Phalanges and the Tigers; the Marada Brigade, by contrast, remained a staunch ally of Syria throughout.) Lebanese sovereignty existed in form only, as the government did not control fully any portion of the country. While Lebanon's president, Elias Sarkis, had nominal command of the Syrian peacekeeping contingent, the fight between Christian militias and Syrian forces left no doubt that Damascus was in charge: when Sarkis ordered a halt to the Syrian bombardment of Christian areas, the Syrians simply ignored the order.[11]

Consistent with window theory, despite the fact they were clearly stronger than the other Christian organizations, the Phalanges did not launch a hegemonic bid, given that with their superior numbers and firepower around Christian-populated areas the Syrian forces posed an immediate and serious threat.[12] In the course of their fight against the Christian armed groups, the Syrians cut off all land routes out of eastern Beirut and subjected it to massive bombing. The Phalanges and the Tigers repelled large-scale Syrian ground assaults at a high cost in human lives and launched a series of ultimately unsuccessful counterattacks to break their encirclement. An intra-Christian fight under these dire circumstances would have been tantamount to handing over victory to the Syrians. Moreover, no source indicates a shift in the inter-rebel balance of power that might have prompted a gamble for resurrection by one of the Christian groups.

Damascus's Partial Disengagement, 1979–1981

At last, in October 1978 Damascus decided to end its inconclusive offensive in the face of strenuous resistance by the Christian militias. In the words of Antoine Abraham, "Syria had committed most of its forces in the northern half of Lebanon into battle, and reinforcements continued to pour into Lebanon, tapping Syria's reserves." This attempt to bring the Christian militias to heel "had proven too costly for the Syrian regime. Syrian hospitals were filled to capacity with the dying and the wounded. Not since the last Arab-Israeli war had Syria seen its forces return home so badly mauled."[13]

The end of the Syrian offensive marked the beginning of a period of a gradually receding incumbent threat for the Christian rebels. As domestic unrest back in Syria and international isolation added to the costs of the fight against the Christian rebels, Syrian troops started withdrawing from positions in and around east Beirut at the end of 1978 and then in early 1980 redeployed from the entire Beirut area to the Beqaa valley in the east of Lebanon.[14] Damascus's lack of an appetite for a new offensive against the Christian militias was unmistakable.[15] As Yair Evron notes in discussing Syria's position in late 1979:

> The difficulties faced by Asad [sic; Syria's president, Hafez al-Assad] both in the Arab world and at home would not have been sufficient to force a change in the Syrian posture in Lebanon. But combined with Syria's continued inability to impose its will in Lebanon, they obliged Damascus to search for ways to diminish the Syrian presence, and so reduce the costs involved in staying there. In January 1980, Syria announced a plan for a limited withdrawal from the Beirut area.[16]

At home, the Syrian government was facing an escalating rebellion by the Muslim Brotherhood.[17] Internationally, the September 1978 Camp David Accords and the March 1979 peace treaty between Egypt and Israel left Syria increasingly isolated in the region and dangerously exposed to Tel Aviv's military might. The redeployment to the Bekaa valley "was a statement of priorities" for Damascus, as Itamar Rabinovich puts it, given that the area was the main defense line against a possible Israeli attack on Syria, which had already invaded southern Lebanon in 1978 to try to crush PLO forces. Damascus's conciliatory feelers toward the Phalanges in the spring and summer of 1980 were additional signs of the limited Syrian threat. While ultimately unsuccessful, "Phalangists leaders, aware of Syria's weak bargaining position, tried to extract concessions that Syria had refused in the past."[18]

As window theory predicts, only when Syria no longer posed a serious and immediate threat did the Phalanges launch a hegemonic bid against the weaker Tigers. In July 1980 the Phalanges conducted a series of coordinated attacks against offices, barracks, and strongpoints of the Tigers: with "a quick, extremely brutal and successful operation," the Phalanges defeated their rivals.[19] Faced with no alternatives, the Tigers' leadership surrendered and handed over the group's weapons and ammunitions, while its fighters were absorbed in a unified Christian militia—the Lebanese Forces—under the control of Bashir Gemayel, the head of the Phalanges.[20]

The balance of power among Christian militias was favorable to the Phalanges, which Hanf describes as "the strongest by far."[21] The second-ranked group, the Tigers, was "smaller and less organized."[22] (By contrast, there is no indication of any difference between the two militias in terms of access to weapons and battlefield proficiency.[23]) Unfortunately no figures about the size of the organizations are available for 1980, but a Lebanese army intelligence report estimated the Phalanges and the Tigers at eight thousand and four thousand militants, respectively, at the beginning of their fight against the National Movement. Moreover, no source indicates a shift in relative power over time.[24]

According to window theory, we should not expect the Phalanges to attack the other two anti-Syrian Christian militias, the Guardians of the Cedars and the Tanzim, as they could not pose a meaningful challenge to the ethnic hegemon owing to their extreme weakness—their fighting forces were in the hundreds rather than thousands—combined with the absence of immediate prospects of rapid growth, given that they operated in territory under the control of the Phalanges and had no independent access to external support.[25] After the showdown with the Tigers, the Guardians and the Tanzim acquiesced to their incorporation in Bashir Gemayel's organization.

The secondary literature paints a picture of the Phalangist leadership's calculus consistent with the theoretical expectation that coethnicity prompts rebel groups to resort to force to eliminate coethnic rivals and harness their resources in the fight against the incumbent. According to Hanf, as early as 1976 Bashir Gemayel had concluded that the Lebanese Front (the alliance of Christian armed groups) would be more effective as a "tightly disciplined, properly led, unified commando" and thus "resolved to use violence" to achieve that objective when the opportunity arose.[26] As Rabinovich observes, the "Phalangist drive was more than the pursuit of power and domination; it was rooted in a concept in which the unification of the Maronite and Christian communities' resources was a crucial interim strategic goal in the struggle over Lebanon's future."[27]

The Phalanges did benefit handsomely from their hegemonic bid, as my argument predicts. Besides acquiring Tigers' cadres and weapons, they gained unrivaled access to the recruitment pool and tax base of the Christian community of central Lebanon. Under Bashir Gemayel's leadership, the ongoing process of building an embryonic Christian state within the Lebanese state accelerated; the Lebanese Forces introduced conscription and levied direct taxes on businesses and homeowners as well as sales taxes and custom duties in the Christian heartland extending along the coast from East Beirut to Batroun in the North.[28] In the absence of coethnic competitors, the Christian population docilely complied. In the words of Jonathan Randal, after the Phalangist victory over the Tigers, "with rare—almost personal—exceptions, the Marounistan [the Maronite-dominated area in central-western Lebanon] Christians now fell into line behind their most militant, radical leader," Bashir Gemayel.[29]

Israeli and Multinational Interventions, 1981–1984

Emboldened by the consolidation of the rebel movement under their control, Syria's persistent weakness, and Israel's support, in 1981 the Lebanese Forces set out to expand their territory and drag Tel Aviv into their fight against Damascus so as to negotiate a peace settlement from a position of strength.[30] In June 1982 the Lebanese Forces' hopes appeared close to fulfilment when Israeli forces crossed into Lebanon and rapidly swept away PLO units in the South and Syrian forces encountered on their way to Beirut. In August the PLO fighters in refugee camps in West Beirut capitulated to Israel's siege and heavy bombing, accepting to relocate to Tunis under the supervision of a U.S., French, and Italian multinational force (MNF).[31]

The Christian leaders saw the deployment of the Israeli army over much of Lebanon as a clear opportunity for establishing Christian supremacy.[32] Thus in late 1982 the Lebanese Forces (with some support from the Christian-dominated units of the Lebanese army) launched an attack on the Druze stronghold (known as the Chouf) south of Beirut.[33] At around the same time, with the help of the MNF, the Lebanese government reasserted its control of West Beirut—an event marking its reemergence as the incumbent for our purposes (albeit a particularly weak one, as its writ did not extend beyond the capital).[34]

Yet the Christians' fortunes were soon to plummet. Amid a domestic political storm over the occurrence of massacres of Palestinian refugees under its forces' watch, Israel signaled its intention to disengage from Lebanon.[35] As Israeli forces started withdrawing from the country in August 1983, Damascus regained the initiative. With Syrian support, the Druze PSP, the Shia Amal movement, and Sunni Mourabitoun militia launched an offensive to take back Muslim-inhabited West Beirut, which succeeded in February 1984, after months of fighting. The MNF withdrew from Lebanon shortly afterward. Facing a tightening encirclement of enemy forces and bereft of external support, the Lebanese government capitulated to the rebels' demand of abrogation of the recent peace treaty with Israel and agreed to form a national reconciliation cabinet including Damascus's allies.[36]

The various rebel groups pitted against the Lebanese Forces and the Christian-dominated Lebanese army in 1982–1984 did not fight one another. Window theory correctly predicts this outcome, given that the ethnic heterogeneity of the rebels implied the absence of windows of opportunity and windows of vulnerability, as in the first phase of the civil war in 1976.

No War, No Peace, 1985–1989

The formation of a national reconciliation government with the participation of both the Lebanese Forces and the opposition in 1984 marked the suspension of major fighting between the two main civil war camps.[37] Yet the following three years were far from peaceful, as erstwhile allies in the antigovernment camp clashed with one another: in 1985 Amal and the PSP ganged up against Mourabitoun; after wiping out the latter, Amal turned on the PSP, while also engaging in the infamous "war of the camps" against PLO forces attempting to regain a foothold in West Beirut. Then in 1988 Amal attacked Hezbollah, the newest entry in Lebanon's landscape of armed actors and a direct challenger for control of Lebanon's Shia population. Finally, an intra-Christian fight occurred in 1989 as the segment of the Lebanese army under the control of interim prime minister General Michel Aoun resorted to force to rein in the Lebanese Forces. Window theory provides useful insights on the intra-Shia and the intra-Christian fights but not on the other episodes of inter-rebel war, as they occurred across ethnic lines.

Amal and PSP vs. Mourabitoun; Amal vs. PSP

The Shia Amal's attack on Sunni Mourabitoun in 1985 appears to have been motivated by a desire to forestall the return of PLO forces in West Beirut, as Mourabitoun was closely associated with the Palestinians.[38] The Druze PSP's motives for joining the fight against Mourabitoun are harder to divine.[39] Syria supported (and may have even incited) the Amal-PSP offensive, owing to its concern about the prospect of renewed PLO's influence in Lebanon.[40]

After Mourabitoun's demise in April 1985, Amal attacked the Palestinian camps in Beirut, where the PLO had reestablished a military presence. Some Palestinian positions fell quickly, but others withstood ruthless siege tactics. The PSP provided support to the Palestinians and thus ended up fighting against Amal. After intermittent clashes, Amal took a beating at the hands of the joint forces of the PSP and smaller Sunni-dominated groups and had to be rescued from the brink of defeat by Damascus, which redeployed in strength in West Beirut in late 1987.[41]

Window theory cannot explain these two instances of inter-rebel war (Amal and PSP vs. Mourabitoun; Amal vs. PSP), given that they pitted non-coethnic rebel groups, which should have limited motives for resorting to force, against one another. How can we make sense of these anomalies? My speculative answer is that the suspension in the fight between the two civil war camps in the years 1985–1989 created a situation in which neither side had a reasonable prospect of making significant gains on the battlefield, let alone achieving outright military victory. Under these circumstances, the structural forces envisioned by my theory might be relatively weak, and thus we should be more likely to observe episodes of inter-rebel war caused by other factors.

The interruption of the fight against the government and the Christian militias, on the one hand, and the Syrian-supported rebels, on the other, was not a mere tactical break for recuperation and reorganization of the competing forces. Rather, it reflected the widely understood fact that a stalemate had set in: a violent process of ethno-sectarian unmixing early in the war had created demographically homogeneous and easily defensible enclaves in urban and mountainous terrain. As Hanf observes, "After all fronts were established, the enclaves overrun and the respective minorities expelled, there was a military stalemate between the Lebanese adversaries."[42] After the withdrawal of Israeli forces from central Lebanon, the Syrians were the only actor with the power to try to bring about a decisive outcome to the war. By the spring of 1984 there was little doubt, however, about the fact that Damascus preferred a negotiated settlement to an outright rebel victory. In 1976 Syrian forces had saved the Christian militias and the Lebanese government from defeat at the hands of the National Movement and the PLO; similarly, in 1984, after the Lebanese president accepted its demands (most crucially, the abrogation of the peace treaty with Israel), Damascus extended its support to him, and Syria's allies toed the line by withdrawing their request for resignation and joining a national unity cabinet. In Hanf's summary, "The Syrian government had again demonstrated that after the correction in foreign policy [by the Lebanese government] they had little interest in the ascendancy of one of the parties to the civil war. For the time being, there was a military stalemate. Neither the Druze-Shi'a coalition nor the Christians, nor the different parts of the army had any prospect of victory."[43]

When the constraints on infighting envisioned by window theory are softened—that is, when we are no longer in a "normal" civil war environment, characterized by a concrete possibility that the government will crush the rebel movement or that the insurgents will make major gains against the incumbent—window theory may be a less helpful guide to understand rebel groups' relations.[44] In this context, other factors, like the prospect of marginal territorial expansion, personality clashes, ideological disputes, score settling or instigation by third parties, may be sufficiently powerful to prompt infighting.

Amal vs. Hezbollah

Shortly after Amal's siege of the Palestinian camps came to an end, in the spring of 1988 the group launched an all-out attack against Hezbollah.[45] The evidence at my disposal, while limited, is largely consistent with window theory: Amal appears to have launched a hegemonic bid to stem the rise of its coethnic rival while it enjoyed a clear margin of superiority and the government did not pose a meaningful threat. The one aspect inconsistent with theoretical expectations is timing: Hezbollah emerged as a potential Shia rival around 1985, but Amal's hegemonic bid took place only in 1988. In the absence of evidence about Amal's decision making, the fact that the group was engaged in several other fights is the most plausible explanation for the delay, but this begs the question of why Amal would not prioritize cementing its dominant position in the Shia community.

The "Party of God" had emerged as a coherent organization in the mid-1980s from the amalgamation of several pro-Iranian Islamist groups.[46] With its efforts to mobilize Lebanon's Shia community by combining a radical religious-ideological message, provision of social services, and daring attacks against Israeli and Western forces in the country, Hezbollah had started "gnawing at the support base of its main adversary, the Amal movement."[47]

Several factors appear to have contributed to shield the fledgling organization from Amal's wrath until 1988. In 1982 and 1983 Syria and Iran enabled the groups that would later form Hezbollah to start organizing undisturbed in the Bekaa valley.[48] Then, from 1983 to 1987, Amal had its plate full fighting the Lebanese army (1983–1984), the Israeli occupying force (1983–1985), Mourabitoun (1985), and the PSP and PLO (1985–1988). As Eitan Azani notes, after the 1984 rebel takeover of west Beirut, "Hezbollah still did not constitute a concrete threat for Amal" as the latter was at "the peak of its power."[49] However, the subsequent long fight against the PSP and the PLO weakened Amal politically and militarily vis-à-vis its coethnic rival: many cadres left the group in disgust with the assault on the Palestinian camps, while others were being enticed by Hezbollah's Iran-financed deep pockets.[50]

When Amal eventually attacked, it still enjoyed clear numerical superiority over Hezbollah.[51] Moreover, as discussed earlier, the Lebanese government did not pose a serious threat. However, the fight proved more difficult than Amal might have anticipated.[52] Though the group had the upper hand in the initial battles in southern Lebanon, its forces were bested by Hezbollah in the southern suburbs of Beirut. After almost two years of inconclusive fighting punctuated by several ceasefires, the two organizations reached an agreement with the mediation of Syria and Iran, permitting Hezbollah to return to the South to continue its struggle against Israel, while Amal demobilized in the context of the broader settlement of the Lebanese civil war with the Ta'if Accord (see next phase).[53]

Aoun's Forces vs. Lebanese Forces

While the Amal-Hezbollah war raged, in 1989 the Christian heartland too was rocked by intra-ethnic fighting. As the Parliament failed to elect a new president, Lebanon found itself with two governments (and two armies) in late 1988: one was led by General Michel Aoun, nominated as interim prime minister by the outgoing president on the eve of the expiration of his term, and held sway in the Christian stronghold in central Lebanon; the other, headed by Sunni former prime minister Salim al-Hoss, extended its authority over areas under Syrian control. Rather than arbitrarily deciding which side should be considered the incumbent, I assess whether window theory sheds light on relations among armed actors on both sides from this point to the end of the civil war in 1990.

In February 1989 Aoun's forces attacked the Lebanese Forces to subdue the armed group and take over control of lucrative custom posts. After heavy fighting, the Lebanese Forces conceded the custom posts, but overall Aoun's offensive stalled.[54] While I do not have decision-making evidence, key features of this episode of infighting are consistent with window-of-opportunity logic. First, the two entities should be considered coethnic. The ranks of both consisted overwhelmingly of Christians: the Lebanese Forces had an explicit Christian agenda, while Aoun's government—his Lebanese nationalist rather than ethnosectarian rhetoric notwithstanding—was widely perceived as pro-Christian. They thus found themselves locked in a "competition . . . for the hearts of the Christian population."[55]

Second, the battle lines between the two civil war camps had largely been inactive since 1985, and there was no indication that Syria—the only actor with enough potential power to break the stalemate—intended to alter unilaterally an equilibrium that suited it well; under these circumstances, infighting should carry relatively low risks.[56] Third, Aoun's forces may have had a large enough numerical superiority— fifteen thousand troops, compared to the ten-thousand-strong Lebanese Forces—to achieve a quick and cheap victory.[57]

The Last Bout of Civil War Fighting, 1989–1990

Emboldened by major arms shipments from Iraq, in March 1989 Aoun decided to reestablish the authority of the state by trying to seize the ports (and the corresponding major sources of revenues) under the control of the militias allied with Damascus, thus provoking a resumption of the long-dormant civil war.[58] Syrian and PSP forces responded to Aoun's actions with a blockade of the Christian heartland and an artillery barrage.

Battles between the two sides (with the Lebanese Forces supporting Aoun) raged until September 1989. Then an Arab League–mediated ceasefire heralded a meeting of the members of the Lebanese Parliament in the Saudi city of Ta'if, where they voted a document of national reconciliation, envisioning constitutional reform rebalancing the distribution of power among the country's ethnic groups in favor of Muslim sects and legalizing the Syrian presence (on terms dictated from Damascus). In November the Parliament also elected a new president, Elias Hrawi, whose cabinet was hailed as the legitimate executive by Syria and all local actors, except Aoun.[59]

As a violent showdown between the two governments laying rival claims on Lebanon—Aoun's and Hrawi's—was in the offing, the last episode of infighting took place. In January 1990 Aoun's army attacked the Lebanese Forces in a renewed effort to obtain full control of the Christian heartland. The fight continued until May without the emergence of a clear winner; its main result was solidifying of the Lebanese Forces' support for Hrawi's government, rather than strengthening Aoun's hand. After various offers to Aoun to join his government, in October Hrawi authorized an all-out attack by his army and Syrian forces against Aoun's stronghold; the Lebanese Forces joined in the offensive with artillery fire. In the face of Syria's overwhelming firepower, Aoun's defiance quickly came to an end, as he surrendered and sought asylum in the French Embassy. Thus fifteen years of almost uninterrupted violence came to a conclusion; the national unity government and its Syrian foreign protector, whose forces would remain in Lebanon until 2005, could now focus their attention on the difficult tasks of disarming the various militias and implementing the new power-sharing deal struck at Ta'if.[60]

The absence of infighting among Syria's allies in this final phase is consistent with window theory, given that the most significant actors on this side of the civil war, namely, the Druze PSP and Shia Amal, were non-coethnic.[61] Inasmuch as we can treat Aoun's troops and the Lebanese Forces (before the latter flipped sides and joined in the final Syrian offensive) as rebel groups (i.e., on the opposite civil war side as the pro-Syria camp), window-of-vulnerability logic could explain Aoun's January 1990 attack on the coethnic rival.

The threat environment faced by Aoun and the Lebanese Forces was certainly not a permissive one: Syria and the PSP had shelled the Christian heartland up to September 1989, and the newly elected president, Hrawi, "was determined to deal quickly with Aoun, if necessary with the help of the Syrian army."[62] Moreover, while enjoying an advantage over the Lebanese Forces in terms of numbers of fighters and heavy weapons, most of Aoun's forces were deployed on the border of the Christian enclaves facing a beefed-up contingent of forty thousand Syrian troops and thus were not available for the fight against the Christian militias.[63]

Although a hegemonic bid was therefore out of the question, the sudden prospect of a rapid deterioration of his army's power relative to the Lebanese Forces may have created a window of vulnerability for Aoun. In November 1989, upon Hrawi's request, Lebanon's Central Bank stopped all payments to the civil servants and soldiers under Aoun. As a result, Aoun could no longer finance the long-standing budget deficit of his government and risked losing recruits to the Lebanese Forces, which could pay much higher salaries. "This situation," Hanf observes, "had long been a thorn in Aoun's side. When the Central Bank stopped payment it became a matter of necessity to change it."[64] Thus the attempt by Aoun's forces to take government property from the Lebanese Forces, which set off this episode of infighting, could be seen as a gamble for resurrection: faced with intense competition from a coethnic rival and dwindling financial resources, Aoun embarked on the risky path of trying to increase his revenues by subduing the Lebanese Forces.

Alternative Explanations

The available evidence does not provide much support for alternative explanations of inter-rebel war in the Lebanese civil war. Christia's minimum winning coalition theory predicts infighting to occur only when one rebel group (or a rebel coalition) is sufficiently strong to take on both the government and another rebel group (or other groups).[65] However, no rebel organization was that powerful at any point during the war. The Phalanges, which launched a hegemonic bid in 1980, may have been the strongest nonstate armed actor at the time, but they controlled only a small portion of Lebanon's territory (i.e., the Christian heartland). Moreover, they were outnumbered by the combined forces of the opposing militias, which were comparably well-armed (not to mention the thirty thousand heavily armed Syrian troops in Lebanon on the side of National Movement from 1977).[66] MWC theory does not shed light on the intra-Christian fights in 1989–1990 either, as the Christian heartland was surrounded by the overwhelming forces of Syria and its allied militias. Analogously, MWC theory fails to explain the onset of the two episodes of inter-rebel war across ethnic lines in 1985 and the intra-Shia fight in 1988 because none of the rebel groups involved was nearly as strong as to be able to single-handedly take on the Lebanese government and the Lebanese Forces.

Peter Krause's argument about competitive dynamics among coethnic organizations based on their relative power seems to have little traction in explaining inter-rebel war in this case.[67] In particular, contrary to Krause's expectation that a relatively weak rebel group will tend to initiate infighting, in all instances of inter-rebel war among coethnics in Lebanon, a strong (but in some cases declining) group was the initiator.

Armed groups' ideologies, organizational cohesion and centralization as well as leaders' personalities fall short as alternative explanations. The first episode of intra-Christian fighting in 1980 occurred between organizations with virtually identical political platforms and ideological outlooks. By contrast, the second and third (in 1989–1990) pitted the

Lebanese Forces, which aspired to a de facto partition of Lebanon into ethnosectarian cantons, against Aoun, who intended to rule a united Lebanon after freeing it from foreign encroachments.[68] On their part, the ideologically heterogeneous members of the National Movement (espousing a broad range of Pan-Arab and leftist views) did not engage in infighting in 1976, while the intra-Shia war pitted the Islamist Hezbollah against the secularly oriented Amal. Thus no clear pattern of association between ideological similarity and inter-rebel war emerges. Indiscipline and decentralization as an explanation of inter-rebel war also finds little support. There is no evidence suggesting that any of the episodes of infighting resulted from the escalation of skirmishes initiated by soldiers or local commanders without leadership endorsement.

The fact that the Phalangist leader Bashir Gemayel and General Aoun are often described as particularly ambitious and ruthless suggests that their personalities may have caused inter-rebel war. However, it is hard to tell the extent to which these personality descriptions are post hoc attempts at making sense of observed behavior, i.e., given that these leaders fought even against their coethnics, they *must* have been especially power-hungry and aggressive. In the case of the hegemonic bid in 1980, Bashir Gemayel's personality could at best represent a necessary but insufficient condition, given that he opted for an attack against the Tigers only when the Syrian threat had clearly receded. Moreover, both armed groups that emerged as separate entities from the outset (Phalanges and Tigers) and groups that resulted from a process of fragmentation (Hezbollah was formed as merger of several groups, including a splinter from Amal, known as Islamic-Amal) fought one another, casting doubt on the hypothesis that pre-existing interpersonal or intra-organizational tensions primarily drive inter-rebel war.

A highly relevant set of alternative explanations for this case concerns the role of external interveners. Syria is of particular interest as it had an imposing military presence in Lebanon throughout the war. In theory, Damascus could have provoked infighting indirectly, by manipulating the armed groups' threat environment and thus creating windows of opportunity, or directly, by cajoling armed groups to attack their rivals. The available evidence, however, suggests that only one episode of infighting could be explained plausibly as a result of Damascus' machinations—Amal against and PSP. Like Amal, Syria was deeply concerned with the risk of the PLO reestablishing a military presence in Beirut and thus might have incited Amal's attacks on the PLO camps and their ally, the PSP.[69]

By contrast, the windows of opportunity and the window of vulnerability that caused intra-Christian fighting were not cleverly orchestrated by Damascus. The window of opportunity for the Phalanges in 1980 resulted from the redeployment of Syrian forces from the Beirut area, in turn prompted by international isolation and domestic unrest plaguing Syria; the continuing limited threat posed by Damascus then enabled the 1989 hegemonic bid by Aoun's forces. The window of vulnerability faced by Aoun in 1990 was caused by the Hrawi government's attempt to assert control of the Christian stronghold by cutting off the financial lifeline of the Aoun government; the deployment of Syrian forces to the doorstep of the Christian heartland may have actually reduced the incentives for Christian infighting by increasing its expected costs. Syria also appears to have opposed the fight between Amal and Hezbollah, as it was heavily engaged in mediation efforts from the beginning of their clashes and threw its weight around to impose multiple ceasefires.[70]

Summary

Window theory sheds much light on the complex relationships between Lebanon's rebel groups. My argument explains the logic and timing of the Phalanges' hegemonic bid in 1980: the group attacked its weaker Christian rival, the Tigers, only once Syria did not pose an immediate and serious threat but eschewed such a course of action earlier, when the risks of infighting would have been much higher. As window theory predicts, the ethnically heterogeneous opposing coalition of pro-Syrian forces did not experience infighting in 1976 and 1984. Moreover, while the evidence is admittedly limited, the intra-Christian and intra-Shia fights toward the end of the civil war are largely consistent with window theory. To be sure, the fit of my argument is far from perfect, as it cannot explain two episodes of inter-rebel war occurring across ethnic lines and runs into difficulty in making sense of the timing of the Amal-Hezbollah fight. Nonetheless, window theory proves a more helpful guide for understanding inter-rebel fighting in Lebanon than alternative explanations.

Sri Lanka's Tamil Insurgency

In 1983 a long-simmering Tamil rebellion in the North and East of Sri Lanka erupted into full-scale civil war, setting the Sinhala-dominated government against five main Tamil insurgent groups: the Eelam People's Revolutionary Liberation Front (EPRLF), the People's Liberation Organization of Tamil Eelam (PLOT), the Eelam Revolutionary Organization of Students (EROS), the Tamil Eelam Liberation Organization (TELO), and the Liberation Tigers of Tamil Eelam (LTTE, henceforth alternatively referred to as Tigers). All groups appealed to Tamil nationalism, with the first three also espousing a leftist agenda, while the LTTE and TELO had a more straightforward nationalist focus.[71]

By 1990 the LTTE emerged as the undisputed rebel hegemon, having eliminated any potential challenger. Over the years the Tigers gained a reputation as "one the world's foremost paramilitary groups," establishing exclusive control of large swaths of Sri Lankan territory, holding their own against Indian peacekeepers-turned-counterinsurgents deployed in Sri Lanka in 1987–1990, and fighting the much larger government forces to a military stalemate until late 2006.[72] Then a much reinvigorated Sri Lankan army launched a major offensive and in the course of three years managed to annihilate the LTTE (in addition to massacring thousands of Tamil civilians), which had been significantly weakened by an international crackdown on diaspora fundraising and a major organizational split.[73]

The pattern of inter-rebel war in Sri Lanka closely fits the predictions of window theory. As Rohan Gunaratna observes, "Gradually, the LTTE attempted to eliminate all the other groups as they were competing with the LTTE for a common pool of resources."[74] The LTTE took advantage of windows of opportunity by attacking and dispensing of coethnic rivals in moments in which they were weak and the government posed a limited threat. By contrast, the group refrained from launching hegemonic bids early in the civil war, when it did not enjoy a clear military advantage over its rivals.

I break down the years of multiparty civil war in Sri Lanka (1983–1990) into three phases, based on window theory's predictions about the occurrence of inter-rebel war (summarized in table 5.2). In the first phase

TABLE 5.2 Inter-rebel Relations Among Sri Lanka's
Tamil Rebel Groups, 1983–1990

Observed Outcome (war/no war)	Type of Window	Correct Prediction?
No war between LTTE, TELO, PLOT, EROS, EPRLF, 1983–1985	No window (coethnic, balanced power, low government threat, no power shift)	✓
War, LTTE–TELO, 1986	Window of opportunity (coethnic, imbalanced power, low government threat, low opportunity cost)	✓
No war, LTTE–PLOT, 1986	Window of opportunity (coethnic, imbalanced power, low government threat, low opportunity cost)	×
War, LTTE–EPRLF, 1986–1987	Window of opportunity (coethnic, imbalanced power, low government threat, low opportunity cost)	✓
War, LTTE–EPRLF, 1989-1990	Window of opportunity (coethnic, imbalanced power, low government threat, low opportunity cost)	✓

Note: Each row indicates an episode of inter-rebel war or inter-rebel peace involving Tamil rebel groups in Sri Lanka. The table does not include the year 1988 as the LTTE was the only rebel group at the time (the EPRLF served as counterinsurgency militia for the Indian forces).

(1983–1985), a roughly balanced distribution of power among the Tamil groups prevailed, which did not warrant a hegemonic bid, the limited threat posed by the government notwithstanding. Consistent with window theory, inter-rebel peace prevailed. In the second phase (1986), the LTTE took advantage of its newly acquired military superiority and continuing limited government threat to sequentially wipe out or expel its rivals. In the third phase (1987–1990), after resisting a large-scale government offensive and then the Indian army's counterinsurgency efforts, the Tigers managed to establish their hegemony of the Tamil movement by crushing their last remaining rival, the EPRLF, before the resumption of all-out war against Colombo.

Early Insurgency and Inter-rebel Cooperation, 1983–1985

Sri Lanka's ethnic civil war began in earnest in the summer of 1983, after over ten years of low-level militancy by several Tamil organizations.[75] The catalyst was the July ambush by the LTTE against an army convoy in the North. The attack sparked anti-Tamil pogroms throughout Sri Lanka, which in turn drove thousands of young Tamils into the rebels' arms and prompted India to provide the militants with training, weapons, and safe havens in the state of Tamil Nadu across the Palk Strait separating the two countries.[76] At long last, the Tamil rebels had the resources to launch a full-blown rebellion. "By the end of 1984, Jaffna [the northern insurgent stronghold] had become a war zone," John Richardson observes; "at night, life came to a halt and the militants were in control."[77] The influx of young men and Indian military support had dramatic effects: in the words of Narayan Swamy, "Training had changed all equations in Jaffna. Groups which had been virtually dormant or shown no special caliber for military operations were getting bloated."[78]

The rebels held the military initiative in the first years of the war. They would launch hit-and-run attacks on government forces (while not eschewing violence against Sinhala noncombatants); the government would engage in reprisal killings of Tamil civilians, pushing more young men and women into the insurgent camp.[79] The rebels "were harassing the Sri Lanka forces almost throughout the length and breadth of the sprawling northeast."[80] This pattern of fighting suggests a limited government threat in 1983–1985. However, the other ingredient of a window of opportunity—a marked inter-rebel imbalance of power—had not yet appeared.

In this phase, the LTTE and TELO, with roughly equal strength, towered over all other Tamil groups. TELO "alone could match the LTTE's cadres and firepower."[81] The other groups suffered from a lack of weapons, poor internal cohesion, or limited battlefield experience. As Swamy observes, "Numerically, the PLOT, TELO, and LTTE had the maximum number of members, although the last two were better armed."[82] PLOT's lack of weapons was largely a function of its leadership's inability to establish close relations with India.[83] Two additional difficulties bedeviled PLOT: limited battlefield experience (probably to some extent due to the lack of weaponry at its disposal) and serious problems of internal cohesion.[84] The other two armed groups—EROS and EPRLF—could marshal much smaller numbers of fighters and engaged in very limited military operations.[85] Consistent with window theory, in the context of a rough balance of power between the LTTE and TELO *and* in the absence of a clear shift in relative power that might have prompted a gamble for resurrection, no inter-rebel war occurred: the LTTE responded with uncharacteristic moderation (at least if one relies on the hindsight of its subsequent ruthless liquidation of rivals) to low-level clashes and accidents in which other Tamil organizations killed Tigers cadres, limiting itself to retaliation in kind rather than unleashing the all-out attacks that would characterize the following phase.[86]

The Tigers Bite, 1986

As Colombo continued to pose a limited threat to the insurgents, the internal crisis of TELO—the only organization that could match the Tigers' power up to then—marked the opening of a window of opportunity for the LTTE. In March 1986 tensions within TELO exploded into open factional violence, bringing about "major upheaval" in the group.[87] Two factions, led by strongmen Das and Bobby, clashed with each other, Bobby's eventually having the upper hand.[88] The LTTE took advantage of its rival's moment of weakness by launching devastating attacks on TELO's camps throughout Sri Lanka's Northeast in late April: it took the Tigers about a week to liquidate TELO.[89] "With the demise of TELO," as Swamy points out, "the bulk of the money raised by Sri Lankan Tamils abroad began flowing to the LTTE kitty. Recruits rushed to Tiger ranks, attracted by its awesome military operations, its army-like discipline and the aura of Prabhakaran [the late LTTE leader]."[90]

The Tigers then turned their sight on PLOT. An all-out attack proved unnecessary as after the LTTE disarmed or killed several of its members (including the group's military commander in Jaffna) in a show of force, PLOT complied with the Tigers' ultimatum to leave Jaffna in October.[91] The organization essentially imploded and ceased all military activities.[92] The EPRLF's turn came shortly afterward. The group had started to gain significant battlefield experience in 1986 by conducting a number of operations against government forces but was still outclassed by the Tigers in terms of overall military experience, manpower, and cohesion (the EPRLF experienced an episode of internal fragmentation in that year).[93] In December the LTTE overran all EPRLF camps in Jaffna with a lightening attack; the EPRLF, however, managed to mount an effective resistance in the East, where it was relatively strong, and then turned for protection to the Indian peacekeepers after their deployment in the spring of 1987.[94] The EPRLF obtained only temporary respite from the LTTE's wrath, as the Tigers would finish it off when the Indian forces departed in late 1989–early 1990. As it sidelined its rivals, the "LTTE leaders began issuing public statements arrogating to their organisation sole authority to represent the Tamil people."[95]

In contrast with the treatment reserved to all other Tamil groups, the LTTE tolerated EROS, by now an extremely weak organization that quietly accepted the Tigers' hegemony. As Staniland puts it, EROS's "lack of large-scale activity or presence made its survival more acceptable to the LTTE since it could pose no real challenge."[96] Though I do not have estimates of EROS's size, all available evidence suggests that the group was below what I termed the threshold of extreme weakness and had no hope of growing to become a meaningful threat to the LTTE. EROS is reported as the smallest and least militarily experienced among the Tamil outfits,[97] and in 1987 LTTE spokesman Anton Balasingham observed that the Tigers had established "a very cordial relation" with "tiny groups, like EROS" that had accepted the LTTE's hegemony of the Tamil movement.[98] By the time of the Tigers' attack on the EPRLF, EROS "acted more like an appendage" to the LTTE than an autonomous organization.[99] Subsequently, during the Indian peacekeeping mission, EROS did not engage in military operations but essentially functioned as an unofficial political front for the Tigers, by running for elections and making sympathetic public statements. Eventually EROS experienced a major split, leading to the absorption of its main faction into the LTTE, while the other EROS members left the country.[100]

The pre-existing condition of limited government threat continued to hold in this second phase of the Tamil insurgency. By 1986 Jaffna was a "liberated zone," where government forces were bottled up in fortified bases and could move around only at the cost of provoking a major battle;[101] the "initiative lay with the militants" on the battlefield, until Colombo launched its first major offensive in early 1987.[102] Moreover, in the course of 1986 the prospect of a sudden, radical escalation of the government's military effort likely appeared a remote possibility to LTTE leaders, as Colombo, under increasing diplomatic pressure from India, signaled willingness to find some form of negotiated solution addressing Tamil demands short of secession. In particular, each LTTE attack against its Tamil rivals coincided with Indian diplomatic initiatives that the Sri Lanka government appeared willing to accept but that the Tigers ultimately resisted. The LTTE's attack against TELO occurred during a high-level meeting between Indian envoys and the Sri Lankan president on the Tamil issue, which had been announced a few weeks earlier.[103] The Tigers expelled PLOT from Jaffna during militant-government initial talks and in a context in which the chief minister of Tamil Nadu was pressuring (ultimately unsuccessfully) the LTTE leadership to meet Sri Lanka's president during a South Asian Association for Regional Cooperation summit in November 1986.[104] Finally, in the period leading to the attack on the EPRLF, the "L.T.T.E. and the government gave the impression that a move for a negotiated settlement was on," and a set of proposals, drafted with India's help, were announced by the government less than ten days after the Tigers' onslaught.[105]

In sum, as window of opportunity logic would suggest, "the LTTE always struck at the other organizations when they were weakened and preoccupied with internal rivalries," while the government did not pose a serious and imminent threat.[106] The one feature of this phase of Sri Lanka's civil war that does not fit my argument relates to the way in which the Tigers got rid of PLOT—a limited show of force, including the killing of PLOT's commander in Jaffna, followed by the group's decision to abandon the battlefield. The LTTE's behavior is not surprising, as we should expect strong rebel groups to prefer to achieve hegemony without paying the cost of inter-rebel war if at all possible. My argument, however, suggests that rebel groups typically will not find a peaceful bargain that both sides prefer to war in the presence of windows due to pervasive commitment problems: the weaker group, as long as it is strong enough to put up meaningful resistance, would generally prefer to fight against long odds to accepting complete submission to the hegemon.

From India's Peacekeeping to LTTE's Hegemony, 1987–1990

In the third phase, the Tigers managed to withstand a large-scale government offensive and then an intense counterinsurgency campaign by the Indian army after its peacekeeping mission floundered in the face of LTTE recalcitrance. Eventually, in the spring of 1990 the Tigers crushed their last remaining rival, the EPRLF, after the departure of its Indian protectors and before the resumption of the fight against Colombo, thus fully consolidating their dominance of Sri Lanka's Tamil movement.

The circumstances leading to the first major government offensive in 1987 suggest that the LTTE may have miscalculated Colombo's ability or willingness to escalate its hitherto limited military effort. In early 1987, as it was still fighting the EPRLF in the East of the country following the late 1986 attack, the LTTE declared that it was taking over Jaffna's civil administration in the North and deployed uniformed policemen on the streets. The government responded to what it perceived as a blatant challenge to its sovereignty with an embargo on Jaffna and then a massive offensive. For the first time since the beginning of the war, the LTTE was under unrelenting government military pressure in the North, while continuing to clash with the EPRLF in the East. Loathe to see the Tamil insurgency crushed, New Delhi imposed the India–Sri Lanka Accord on the belligerents in the summer of 1987, which envisioned the deployment of an Indian peacekeeping contingent to facilitate the disarmament of the insurgents as Colombo devolved power to the Tamil areas.[107]

The Tigers paid lip service to the agreement but took advantage of the respite in the fight against Colombo to reorganize and launch a surprise offensive against the EPRLF in September 1987. As the LTTE kept dragging its feet on the implementation of the agreement, New Delhi decided to use force to bring the group to heel.[108] The Indian army's belief that "the LTTE could be driven into a corner in 72 hours," as Swami puts it, however, turned out to be ill-founded. The Tigers had to yield ground in the face of the Indian juggernaut's advance, but in doing so they denied a decisive battle to the counterinsurgent forces, while inflicting heavy losses on them with skillful use of hit-and-run attacks and improvised explosive devices (IEDs).[109] The EPRLF, which had taken refuge in the Indian contingent's camps after the LTTE's September attack, served as an auxiliary force in New Delhi's counterinsurgency campaign.[110]

In time, a combination of LTTE's guerrilla warfare, Colombo's diplomatic pressure (spurred by a rebellion against India's presence among Sinhala nationalists in the South), and a change of government in New Delhi prompted the withdrawal of the Indian contingent from Sri Lanka's Northeast in late 1989. Seizing the advantage, the Tigers wiped out the EPRLF and rapidly consolidated their hold on the Tamil community. "The LTTE was in total control of northeastern Sri Lanka," Gunaratna observes, "within a week of the departure of the Indian forces."[111]

At that time, Colombo did not represent a threat for the Tigers, as it had been engaged in peace talks with them since the spring of 1989 and was waging a counterinsurgency campaign against the Sinhala nationalist JVP in the South while the Indian forces—which Sri Lanka's government had come to perceive as a major infringement on its sovereignty—were still present on Sri Lankan soil, though on their way out. Having subdued all its Tamil competitors, the Tigers resumed their antigovernment struggle in June 1990, much to Colombo's dismay, initiating what came to be known as Eelam War II.[112]

In sum, the LTTE fought its weaker coethnic rival EPRLF in moments of limited government threat: in September 1987, after the deployment of Indian peacekeeping force (before it turned on the Tigers), and in late 1989, as the Indians were withdrawing. (The fighting between EPRLF and LTTE during the Indian campaign against the Tigers does not amount to inter-rebel war as the EPRLF operated as a counterinsurgent militia force rather than a rebel group.)

Consistent with my theoretical expectations, the LTTE did not experience any difficulty in exerting control on and mobilizing Sri Lanka's Tamil population after dealing with its competitors. As Staniland puts it, "Once rival organizations were broken, the civilian population faced fewer outside options and the Tigers were able to consolidate their hegemonic hold."[113] The Tigers absorbed some members of the defeated rivals in their rank and file but also killed many others considered irreconcilable.[114]

Alternative Explanations

The evidence presented provides much support for window theory of inter-rebel war. Alternative explanations do not fare as well. Christia's

MWC logic predicts inter-rebel war only when at least one rebel group is stronger than the government. However, when it launched its hegemonic bid in 1986, the LTTE was certainly weaker than Colombo in terms of territorial control and manpower. The Tamil groups had almost complete control over only the Jaffna peninsula, which is but a small part of Tamil-inhabited areas of Sri Lanka. Moreover, in this phase the Tigers shared control of Jaffna with the other major rebel outfits.[115] In 1987 the LTTE had an estimated three thousand fighters at its disposal, while the Sri Lankan armed forces were at least several times as large.[116]

The fact that the Tamils experienced their phase of greatest power vis-à-vis the Sri Lanka government after the LTTE became the ethnic hegemon is a testament to the importance of Krause's argument about the deleterious effects of internally competitive national liberation movements.[117] Contrary to that argument, however, the initiator of infighting was a relatively strong group interested in consolidating its dominance, the LTTE, rather than rivals trailing behind and hoping to induce a shift in the power hierarchy.

Analysts of the LTTE often hint at the personality of its leader, Velupillai Prabhakaran, as a key to understanding the group's behavior. Swamy notes that "Prabhakaran orchestrated deadly action with ruthless efficiency," which was "his trademark."[118] As Prabhakaran's group was the initiator of all episodes of inter-rebel war in Sri Lanka, it is not possible to rule out that his personality or military acumen may have played an important causal role. However, the fact that across the cases examined in this book inter-rebel aggression occurred under a variety of leadership types casts doubt on the general validity of this kind of individual-level argument. In any case, leader characteristics may at best provide a partial explanation for the LTTE's behavior, as Prabhakaran's "ruthlessness" manifested itself only when his group was stronger than the rivals. In the same vein, the widely noted high cohesion and discipline of the LTTE may only offer a partial explanation of the pattern of inter-rebel war, as this was a constant feature of the group while infighting varied, that is, occurred only in some phases.[119]

A different set of alternative explanations would focus on India's involvement in Sri Lanka's civil war. New Delhi played a crucial role in getting the Tamil insurgency off the ground by supporting several fledgling rebel groups; but India does not appear to have instigated inter-rebel war, which occurred despite New Delhi's efforts to induce inter-rebel cooperation.[120] Indian intervention may have contributed to inter-rebel fighting in indirect and unintended ways. Stephen Hopgood, for example, contends that Indian support for Tamil insurgents ended up fueling inter-rebel competition for outside aid and thus conflict;[121] others suggest that the Tigers attacked TELO because they perceived the latter as an Indian stooge.[122] These arguments about how India's intervention may have contributed to inter-rebel war are not necessarily implausible (although I did not come across any concrete supporting evidence) but do not constitute genuine alternative explanations. The idea that external support for a coethnic rival could affect rebel groups' threat perception and factor in their decisions to use force is fully consistent with window theory. The theory would be contradicted only if external intervention tended to spur inter-rebel war in the absence of windows of opportunity and vulnerability or if windows of opportunity and vulnerability did not typically lead to inter-rebel war in the absence of external intervention. Neither was the case in Sri Lanka. The Tigers targeted TELO in 1986, when the latter was engulfed in internecine strife, but abstained from large-scale violence against it earlier, when the balance of power was not favorable. Moreover, after crushing TELO, the LTTE expelled PLOT from Jaffna, even if the group had not managed to attract Indian support.[123]

The final set of alternative explanations concerns the role of the Sri Lankan government in provoking inter-rebel war. There is little evidence that the Tamil insurgent groups feared that their rivals may reach a separate deal with Colombo at their expense or that the government tried to drive a wedge between its opponents by playing up these kinds of fears.[124] It is plausible that concerns that the EPRLF would continue to serve as an auxiliary force for Colombo's counterinsurgency campaign after the departure of the Indian contingent affected the LTTE's decision to wipe out the rival in 1989. But fear of EPRLF defection hardly constitutes a complete explanation for the LTTE's actions: the Tigers had already attacked the EPRLF in 1986, before India's deployment in Sri Lanka was a concrete possibility, and the EPLRF's decision to side with India was largely due to its desperate need for protection from the LTTE.[125]

Moreover, the available evidence does not suggest that Colombo manipulated the insurgents' threat environment to spur the Tigers to attack their rivals. The government's initial limited response to the Tamil insurgency was largely a function of "severe structural and organizational problems in the military," as documented by Ahmed Hashim, which took time for Colombo to overcome.[126] What the government did do was opportunistically refrain from any action that might prompt an interruption of inter-rebel war once it had started, so that the insurgents would continue to bleed each other white, while it organized its forces for an eventual intensification of the counterinsurgency campaign.[127]

Summary

Window-of-opportunity logic offers a powerful explanation for infighting among Sri Lanka's Tamil insurgent groups. The Tigers attacked their coethnic rival organizations when a favorable imbalance of power prevailed and neither government forces nor the Indian military posed an imminent threat to the group. From its hegemonic position, the LTTE managed to rally the Tamil population to its side and pose an even more serious challenge to Colombo's authority than in the previous years.

The Islamic State in the Syrian Civil War

ISIS represents a difficult case for window theory, given the prevalent view of the group as driven by ideological zeal and religious fervor rather than strategic calculations. Observers have stressed the centrality of apocalyptic thinking in ISIS's worldview and the organization's enormous bloodlust, expressed in its frequent atrocities toward combatants and civilians alike.[128] Others have pointed to ISIS's "self-defeating military strategy," irrationally bent on multiplying the number of its enemies rather than focusing on one at the time.[129] Regarding inter-rebel relations in particular, Mohammed Hafez has argued that the group's aggressive behavior toward other rebels pitted against the Syrian government was a direct result of ISIS's extremism: similarly to earlier Jihadist groups in Algeria and Iraq, ISIS's puritanical and uncompromising positions inexorably pushed it to "attack fellow rebels of all stripes."[130]

The following analysis of the onset of infighting between ISIS and the rest of Syria's Sunni insurgent movement reveals a mixed record for window theory.[131] On the one hand, my argument fails to predict ISIS's initiation of several episodes of infighting in 2013. On the other, window theory helps us make sense of the early 2014 attack by a broad rebel coalition against ISIS, as the organization's rapid growth opened a window of vulnerability for the rest of the insurgent movement (see table 5.3). After presenting some background information on the Syrian civil war, I assess in two sections the degree to which window theory can explain infighting in 2013 and 2014, respectively.

TABLE 5.3 Inter-rebel War Between ISIS and Other Syrian
Rebel Groups, 2013–2014

Observed Outcome (war/no war)	Type of Window	Correct Prediction?
War, ISIS–Ahfad al-Rasul Brigades, 2013	No window (coethnic, balanced power, power shift in favor of attacker)	×
War, ISIS–Liwa al-Nasr and Al-Farouq Brigades, 2013	No window (coethnic, balanced power, power shift in favor of attacker)	×
War, ISIS–Northern Storm Brigade, 2013	No window (coethnic, balanced power, power shift in favor of attacker)	×
War, ISIS–Suqur al-Sham, 2013	No window (coethnic, balanced power, power shift in favor of attacker)	×
War, ISIS–anti-ISIS coalition (30 groups), 2014	Window of vulnerability (coethnic, balanced power, high government threat, but power shift that previous nonviolent efforts failed to address)	✓

Note: Each row indicates an episode of inter-rebel war between ISIS and other rebel groups active in the Syrian civil war in 2013–2014.

Background

The Syrian civil war started in the summer of 2011, as peaceful protests turned into armed resistance in the face of brutal government repression. An overwhelmingly Sunni Arab rebel movement was pitted against the Alawite-dominated regime of President Bashar al-Assad's Alawite regime, which would soon start receiving battlefield support from Iraqi and Iranian Shia militias as well as the Lebanese Hezbollah, and eventually from Russia.[132]

The first groups to take up arms against the government consisted mostly of local volunteers and army deserters, operating under the loosely knit umbrella of the Free Syrian Army (FSA). Shortly afterward, the Islamic State of Iraq (ISI, the "successor" of al-Qaeda in Iraq) dispatched operatives to Syria to create a new Jihadist organization—the al-Nusra Front. Al-Nusra and a host of moderate Islamist and Salafist organizations began military operations in early 2012.[133] Following my definition, I consider these organizations as coethnic: they had predominantly Syrian Sunni Arab membership and their goals directly related to the fate of the Sunni Arab community. Even the moderates' goal of a democratic system with equality before the law for all ethno-sectarian groups inevitably entailed the end of Alawite domination and the empowerment of the hitherto politically excluded Sunni majority. Moreover, groups affiliated with the FSA, while adopting a nationally inclusive, rather than ethnosectarian, discourse, often emphasized their Sunni nature, for example by naming themselves after Sunni historical figures.[134]

ISI joined the fray in April 2013 by crossing into Syria from its areas of operations in Iraq. The group's leader, Abu Bakr al-Baghdadi, publicly revealed its role in setting up the al-Nusra Front and announced the merger of the two organizations into the Islamic State of Iraq and Syria. Al-Nusra's leadership rejected the initiative, thus asserting its independence from ISIS.[135] Like the rest of the armed opposition, ISIS was a Sunni Arab rebel group. Despite its activities in Iraq and the presence of a large number of foreign fighters in its ranks, the majority of ISIS fighters in Syria were Sunni Arab Syrians, and the group styled itself as the defender of Syria's Sunni community from the Alawite regime and its Shia allies.[136]

The disagreement between ISIS and al-Nusra gave rise to a broader rift within the transnational Jihadist community when al-Qaeda's leader,

Ayman al-Zawahiri, backing al-Nusra, ordered al-Baghdadi's group to restrict its operations to Iraq; ISIS responded by openly challenging al-Qaeda's authority. Jihadist ideologists, grassroots activists, and insurgents around the world pledged support to one of the two sides, often bitterly criticizing the other.[137] Yet ISIS and al-Nusra did not engage in large-scale fighting against each other. Rather, from August till the end of 2013 ISIS cooperated with al-Nusra as well as various FSA affiliates and Islamist organizations, like Ahrar al-Sham, in several major offensive and defensive operations against government forces near Aleppo and in Latakia province.[138]

Importantly, I do not consider the Kurdish Democratic Union Party (PYD) as a rebel group in the period 2013–2014, and thus its fights against ISIS and various other Sunni rebel groups, including al-Nusra and Ahrar al-Sham, as well as affiliates of the Free Syrian Army, are beyond the scope of window theory, which aims at explaining interactions among rebel groups.[139] As an International Crisis Group report points out, since the summer of 2012 the Kurdish organization had been in a "de facto alliance with the regime, which handed territories [mostly in Kurdish-inhabited areas of Aleppo and Hasaka governorates] over to it while continuing to give material support to those territories," in order to free government forces to fight the Sunni insurgents. Though denying rebels' accusations of collusion with the regime, "PYD officials acknowledge they have made a strategic decision not to confront Damascus."[140] As a result, PYD and Syrian forces did not engage in sustained fighting in the period of interest, establishing instead "a modus vivendi that closely resembles a nonbelligerency pact."[141] Thus my argument's expectation that rebel groups generally would refrain from fighting against non-coethnic rebels due to the limited prospects of major gains and the costs involved in diverting resources from the struggle against the common enemy does not apply to relations between Sunni insurgents and the PYD: the insurgents understood that the de facto cooperative relationship between the PYD and Damascus freed regime forces for counterinsurgency operations, so defeating the Kurdish group had the potential of undermining the government's plan (besides being appealing on ideological grounds); on its part, the PYD saw the Sunni insurgency as the biggest threat to the Kurdish community, while it considered the prospect of the collapse of the regime as a "disaster."[142]

ISIS's Inter-rebel Wars, 2013

Notwithstanding ISIS's key contribution to battles against the regime in 2013, its behavior toward the rest of the Sunni rebel movement was far from uniformly cooperative. The group would often resort to violence short of inter-rebel war, harassing and sometimes even kidnapping or killing members of other organizations at checkpoints or engaging in skirmishes with them.[143] More crucial for our purposes, ISIS launched at least four large-scale attacks against other rebel groups. In August ISIS targeted the Ahfad al-Rasul Brigades headquarters in Raqqa with four suicide attacks, expelling the group from the city and then attacking it again in September in Deir ez Zour. In that month ISIS also repeatedly clashed with Liwa al-Nasr and the Al-Farouq Brigades near Aleppo as well as violently taking over the headquarters of the Northern Storm Brigade in the border town of Azaz. Then in November ISIS overran the headquarters of the Suqur al-Sham Brigades in Atmeh in Idlib province.[144]

Window theory cannot explain ISIS's behavior because the group faced neither a window of opportunity nor a window of vulnerability. In the course of 2013 ISIS was in no position to launch a hegemonic bid, as it was not the strongest organization in a crowded rebel camp.[145] With an estimated number of fighters in Syria ranging from three thousand to eight thousand, ISIS was of comparable size as al-Nusra (five to eight thousand) and smaller than Ahrar al-Sham (ten to twenty thousand), "Syria's then dominant insurgent faction."[146] Though ISIS had displayed impressive cohesion, firepower, and battlefield effectiveness against government forces in the previous months, Ahrar al-Sham and al-Nusra were also widely praised for those very reasons.[147] No window of vulnerability for ISIS existed either, given that the group was experiencing rapid relative growth, rather than decline, as I discuss below.

Syria's Sunni Insurgents Take on a Rising ISIS, 2014

In early 2014 the bulk of the Sunni opposition attacked ISIS. The rebel alliances Jaysh al-Mujahidin (eight groups) and the FSA-affiliated Syrian Revolutionaries Front (fourteen groups) launched coordinated attacks against ISIS's positions in Aleppo and Idlib governorates on January 4. Only days later the Islamic Front coalition (seven groups, led by Ahrar al-Sham) and al-Nusra joined the battle against ISIS raging across northern Syria.[148]

In less than two weeks, inter-rebel fighting broke out in over sixty municipalities in eight of Syria's fourteen governorates, causing about 1,000 deaths (primarily combatants).[149] After intense fighting, the rebel offensive succeeded in dislodging ISIS from northwestern Syria. ISIS, however, managed to regroup and consolidate its dominance on Raqqa, which allowed it to "fight back from the brink of defeat," as an International Crisis Group report puts it.[150] Then in summer 2014, massively reinvigorated by its takeover of Mosul, the acquisition of four infantry divisions worth of weapons, vehicles, and equipment given by the United States to the Iraqi government, and rapid conquest of swaths of Iraqi territory, ISIS would go on the offensive against Syria's rebels, which had their forces stretched thin in a two-front fight against ISIS and the Assad regime.[151] Much better armed and financed as well as with at least three times as many fighters as before, ISIS could now take on the other rebel groups from a clear position of strength.[152]

Window-of-vulnerability logic is a useful guide to making sense of the anti-ISIS attacks, as the rest of the armed opposition reluctantly resorted to force in the face of ISIS's "meteoric rise," as Charles Lister describes it: between its debut on the Syrian battlefield and early 2014, the group had gained full control or significant influence in at least thirty-five Syrian municipalities and conducted operations in ten out of fourteen governorates, thanks to "a combination of strategic guile, military proficiency and sheer brutality."[153] ISIS's governance model, mixing the provision of badly needed basic goods and services with consistent and impartial, if draconian, law enforcement in areas under its control, may have helped it too, by providing the group with an important source of legitimacy with the Syrian population.[154] ISIS had also been expanding its resource pool by increasing its activities in Anbar province across the border with Iraq. As a report by the International Crisis Group summarizes, "Due to superior planning, organising, funding and combat capacities in large part provided by its core of seasoned non-Syrian Jihadis and base in Iraq," by the end of 2013 ISIS "had grown to become one of the most powerful factions in rebel-held areas."[155]

The rest of the rebel movement could hardly miss ISIS's steep upward trajectory. As Brian Jenkins notes, the group's "rapid growth threatened the other rebel groups who became increasingly concerned that it would come to dominate the rebellion."[156] The other insurgent organizations debated (both among one another and within themselves) the trade-off between the long-term risk posed by a growing ISIS and the short-term benefits of its significant contribution to the difficult fight against the Assad regime.[157] For example, in November 2013 an Ahrar al-Sham fighter observed: "We need to fight them [ISIS] now, because if we don't, then by the time the regime falls they will have taken over."[158] But he also admitted that Ahrar al-Sham continued to significantly benefit from coordinating antigovernment operations with ISIS, given the group's competence on the battlefield. Moreover, Ahrar al-Sham and five other powerful Islamist groups tried to reverse or at least slow down ISIS's growth by jointly issuing a formal demand that the organization relinquish its hold on the border town of Azaz, which ISIS had wrested from the Northern Storm Brigade in September, and the corresponding revenues deriving from control of access to Turkey. ISIS did not budge.[159] A general agreement about the need to use force to deal with the rise of ISIS emerged only gradually in the insurgent movement, allowing the group's growth to continue unabated until the end of 2013.[160]

The insurgents' initial reluctance to attack ISIS is consistent with window-of-vulnerability logic, given the high level of threat posed by Damascus in late 2013 and early 2014; even if victory against ISIS could be achieved quickly, the intensity of government military operations in northern Syria all but guaranteed that inter-rebel war would be costly. The Assad regime had launched a massive offensive in Aleppo city and surrounding areas in late 2013, forcing the insurgents there to bring in reinforcements from other provinces; government operations were in full-swing as inter-rebel war erupted.[161] As it turned out, the government did benefit from insurgent infighting: the "Syrian army and allied militias made significant gains on the city's eastern edge, slowly progressing toward their goal of encircling rebel-held neighbourhoods," as the International Crisis Group reports, given that the "rebels lost great human and material resources and diverted men, weapons and ammunition from the Aleppo front at a time when pro-Assad forces were pushing to retake the city."[162]

Alternative Explanations

Given ISIS's oft-noted fanaticism, ideology deserves careful consideration as an alternative explanation for the pattern of inter-rebel war in Syria. Infighting may be more likely among ideologically distant organizations or ideologically extreme groups may be particularly prone to inter-rebel aggression.[163] Ideology does appear to shed significant light on the pattern of inter-rebel war; yet it works, at least in part, as a complement rather than an outright alternative to window theory. Moreover, one formulation of the ideological explanation—positing a distinctive proclivity to infighting for Jihadist groups—displays important blind spots.

One way to think about ideology in the context of Syria's war is as a continuum, featuring global Jihadists (e.g., al-Nusra and ISIS) on one end of the spectrum and FSA-affiliated moderate Islamists and secularly oriented groups on the other, with Syria-focused Salafists (e.g., Ahrar al-Sham) in the middle. Ideology thus conceptualized appears to explain the fact that in 2013 the extremist ISIS targeted moderate Islamist groups, rather than the more hard-line al-Nusra and Ahrar al-Sham. This approach, however, faces two problems. First, fellow Jihadist al-Nusra generally cooperated with a broad range of insurgent groups throughout this period, which raises doubts about claims that Jihadist groups are generally prone to inter-rebel fighting.[164] Second, the organizations that attacked ISIS in 2014 spanned the rebellion's ideological spectrum, including al-Nusra.[165]

An alternative conceptualization of ideology emphasizes ISIS's highly distinctive brand of Jihadism, whose inflexibility and uncompromising approach were reflected in all spheres of action—from the group's treatment of Sunni civilians and ethnosectarian minorities to its application of Sharia law and its dealings with other rebel organizations.[166] A comparison with al-Nusra suggests that ISIS's "Jihadism on steroids" is a plausible explanation for the 2013 infighting, which window theory instead cannot explain: al-Nusra, a group of similar strength but embracing a less extreme form of Jihadism, refrained from inter-rebel aggression.[167] ISIS's ideologically-driven assertiveness likely also contributed to motivate the anti-ISIS attacks in 2014.

This observation points to the potential role of organization-level factors like ideology as amplifiers of windows of opportunity and vulnerability: in this case, the threat represented by the rapid growth of a coethnic rival, which would normally be significant, was probably enhanced by ISIS's behavior before its power peaked. As ISIS bullied, harassed, and even outright attacked other organizations when it was relatively weak, there was little left to imagination about how the group would behave once dominant. The existence of this amplifier effect in the 2014 infighting is beyond window theory but does not contradict it.[168] By contrast, window theory would be falsified by evidence that the bulk of Syria's rebels would have attacked ISIS even in the absence of a power shift, due to its perceived assertiveness. Disentangling the effects of ISIS's rise in power and its behavior is difficult, as the two went hand in hand. While we currently lack fine-grained evidence of rebel decision making to advance any firm conclusion, the argument that the attack on ISIS was a response to its assertive nature as opposed to its growth runs into difficulties in explaining timing. In the absence of ISIS's growth, the rest of the insurgent movement would have had compelling reasons to postpone inter-rebel war. As noted earlier, the Assad regime had launched a major offensive in Aleppo in late 2013, which intensified in early 2014. Why would the rebels not wait until they had repelled the government offensive and consolidated control of Syria's largest city to deal with the troublemaker? Window-of-vulnerability logic provides a tenable answer: because postponing the showdown would mean an even lower probability of success against ISIS, given its rapid growth.

Another organization-level factor—the occurrence of splintering processes—is not a convincing explanation for ISIS's relations with other rebel groups. Al-Nusra emerged as a splinter of the Islamic State, following a bitter argument between al-Qaeda's leader al-Zawahiri and ISIS's al-Baghdadi. Yet in 2013 the Islamic State targeted moderate rebel groups, not al-Nusra. Moreover, in 2014 al-Nusra joined the anti-ISIS fight that several other rebel organizations had started.

I now turn to alternative explanations focused on the actions of external interveners and the Syrian government. As several observers have suggested, the existence of multiple sources of external funding for the Syrian rebellion, with foreign sponsors often competing for influence on the ground by supporting different groups, may have contributed to the proliferation of rebel organizations.[169] The available evidence, however, does not suggest important influence of third-party states on infighting.[170] Reportedly, in late 2013 Qatar, Saudi Arabia, and the United States encouraged Jaysh al-Mujahidin and the FSA-affiliated Syrian Revolutionaries Front to attack ISIS.[171] Yet even if this encouragement affected the calculus of these groups—and there is no evidence to that effect—it could not explain the participation of the Islamic Front and al-Nusra in the fight against ISIS (al-Nusra, in particular, is reported as not receiving significant outside state support). Moreover, there are reasons to be skeptical of the notion that third-party states' leverage was so strong as to prompt rebels to start a fight that they would have rather avoided. After the U.S. designation of al-Nusra as a foreign terrorist organization in December 2012, several FSA affiliates and likely candidates as recipients for Western military support—a potential "game changer" at the time—refused to distance themselves from the organization and instead continued to conduct joint military operations.[172]

Moving to the Assad's regime, thus far no evidence indicates that the government tried to drive a wedge between rebel groups (let alone succeeded at it) by offering to negotiate a settlement with some organizations at the expense of others or by providing positive inducements for some groups to attack their rivals. Damascus, however, may have contributed to creating a window of vulnerability in 2013 by focusing the bulk of its firepower against the rest of the opposition and leaving ISIS forces relatively undisturbed, which facilitated the group's growth.[173] It is unclear whether the Syrian regime calculated that the rise of ISIS would benefit it by showing to the outside world that Jihadists were a dominant force in the rebellion (thus reducing the probability of a more direct U.S. intervention), that inter-rebel war would ensue owing to the opening of a window of vulnerability for the rest of the opposition, or both. Regardless of the specific calculus pursued by Damascus, the fact that the posture of the Syrian forces may have contributed to the power shift in favor of ISIS, as we saw in other cases, does not in itself contradict window theory.

Of the two general alternative explanations assessed throughout this book—Christia's MWC theory and Krause's argument about competition in national liberation movements—the latter offers more traction in making sense of the observer pattern in Syria.[174] MWC logic incorrectly predicts continued inter-rebel cooperation well into 2014, as the Syrian government was the single strongest belligerent. At the time of anti-ISIS rebel attacks in early 2014, Damascus could count on a larger number of fighters than the opposition as a whole and controlled a comparable amount of territory (as well as a larger share of the population).[175] By contrast, although Krause's argument would correctly predict that ISIS, as a relatively weak rebel group, would initiate infighting in 2013, it cannot explain (without appealing to ISIS's ideology) why many other relatively weak rebel groups did not initiate infighting. Whether Krause's theory could explain the attacks against ISIS in 2014 hinges on how far the rise of ISIS had gone by the time the fighting broke out in January. If ISIS had become the dominant rebel actor, then Krause's argument would be vindicated. Yet there is no indication that by early 2014 ISIS had overtaken Ahrar al-Sham, which could boast a larger membership and a comparable record of cohesion and battlefield competence.[176]

Summary

Window theory helps us make some sense of the rebel anti-ISIS attack in early 2014. ISIS's rapid growth in the course of 2013, combined with its domineering and heavy-handed behavior toward civilians and rebels alike, raised acute fears among the Syrian opposition; after initial hesitation, a broad-based rebel coalition attacked ISIS, in a pattern of behavior consistent with window-of-vulnerability logic. Window theory, however, clearly fails to predict ISIS's attacks against other rebel groups in 2013, which may be more plausibly explained by ISIS's extreme ideology.

The three case studies presented in this chapter provide preliminary evidence of the external validity of my argument. Windows of opportunity and windows of vulnerability drive rebel groups' behavior in a variety of political and geographical settings beyond Iraq and Ethiopia. The cases, however, also reveal important variation that window theory cannot explain: it fits best in Sri Lanka and worst in Syria, with Lebanon somewhere in the middle.

The obvious limit of these additional case studies is that they do not inform us about the broader validity of window theory in the universe of multiparty civil wars. A skeptical reader may not help but wonder whether chance or, much worse, cherry picking can explain the fit between the argument and the evidence. To address this concern, in the next chapter I present statistical analysis to test a key observable implication of window theory—that coethnic rebel groups should be more likely to fight one another—using a dataset of all multiparty civil wars in the post–cold war era.

6

Are Coethnic Rebel Groups More Likely to Fight Each Other?

A STATISTICAL TEST

The previous chapter demonstrated the explanatory power of window theory in various civil wars beyond the two main case studies of this book, the Kurdish rebellion in Iraq and the insurgencies in northern Ethiopia. This chapter further probes the generalizability of the argument with a statistical analysis of all pairs of rebel groups pitted against the same government in the years 1989–2015 across the globe. The fine-grained data required for a full statistical test—time-varying measures of the inter-rebel balance of power and the level of government threat for a large number of rebel groups, besides information on their ethnic affiliation—simply does not exist. The threat environment faced by rebel groups can change rapidly, for example, as a result of a government's decision to launch a major offensive or the outbreak of unrest in the armed forces—developments that would not be reflected in slow-moving indicators of government strength like gross domestic product (GDP) and the size of the security forces. Similarly, the relative strength of rebel groups can sharply vary as they experience problems of internal cohesion or gain battlefield experience, but this change in the inter-rebel balance of power would not be necessarily captured by existing data on insurgent strength.

The available data does allow me to test a key observable implication of window theory: given that a shared ethnic identity is a constitutive component of both windows of opportunity and windows of vulnerability, pairs of coethnic rebel groups should be more likely to experience infighting than pairs of non-coethnic rebels, all things being equal; in other words, coethnic rebel groups should be more likely to fight each other.

After describing my dataset and statistical approach, I present the analysis. Consistent with theoretical expectations, coethnic rebel groups appear to be significantly and substantially more likely to clash.

The Dataset

My dataset includes all pairs of rebel groups engaged in armed conflict against the same government in a given year in the period 1989–2015, as listed in the Uppsala Conflict Data Program (UCDP) Dyadic Dataset (version 17.1).[1] The data includes 1,473 rebel pairs-years—523 distinct pairs of rebel groups active in 47 countries.[2] Just over 40 percent of the rebel pairs appear in the dataset in one year only (meaning that the two rebel groups were fighting the government at the same time just in one year), while the maximum number of years of presence for a pair is 25.

Key Variables

My dependent variable is *inter-rebel war*. This variable, based on data from the UCDP Non-State Conflict Dataset, takes on 1 in the first year in which the members of a rebel pair engaged in armed conflict against each other resulting in at least twenty-five battle-related deaths.[3] (I drop from the analysis all years of ongoing inter-rebel fighting, as they cannot experience a new onset.) The analysis is confined to the years 1989–2015 owing to the fact the Non-State Conflict Dataset coverage starts in 1989. This operationalization of inter-rebel war for statistical analysis differs from the one used in the rest of this book—leadership-endorsed, large-scale combat between distinct rebel organizations, involving repeated battles in a year, a major battle, or an all-out attack on the main headquarters of one of the rebel groups. Identifying instances of inter-rebel war by using a death threshold criterion is not ideal as it carries the risk of false positives. If rebel organizations are large and have multiple opportunities for contact, skirmishes initiated by foot soldiers may generate enough casualties for inclusion in the dataset, even if these episodes do not fit my conceptualization of inter-rebel war as large-scale combat endorsed by rebel leaders. This concern notwithstanding, I adopt the fatality threshold approach to measure inter-rebel war in the absence of more nuanced, systematic data on inter-rebel fighting.

The key independent variable is *coethnic*, which takes on 1 if both rebel organizations are "affiliated" with the same ethnic group and 0 otherwise. The variable is based on data from the Armed Conflict Database-2-Ethnic Power Relations (ACD2EPR, version 2018.1).[4] As for inter-rebel war, I operationalize rebel organizations' association with ethnic groups somewhat differently than in the rest of the book because of data constraints. Nonetheless, the measure I use captures the two key elements of my definition—rebel organizations' ethnic claims and recruitment along ethnic lines: I consider a rebel organization as affiliated with an ethnic group if it claims to fight on behalf of that ethnic group *and* "a significant number of the group members actively participate in the organization's combat operations."[5]

TABLE 6.1 Descriptive Statistics

Variable	Mean	Standard Deviation	Min.	Max.
Inter-rebel war	0.03	0.18	0	1
Coethnic	0.26	0.44	0	1
Splinter	0.03	0.18	0	1
Rebel asymmetry	0.15	0.35	0	1
Preponderance	0.64	0.48	0	1
Troop ratio	42.55	43.47	0.19	363.33
Weak leadership	0.40	0.49	1	1
Common supporter	0.19	0.39	0	1
Common ideology	0.25	0.43	0	1
Territorial control	0.51	0.5	1	1
Natural resources	0.43	0.5	0	1

Control Variables

I include in the analysis a series of control variables corresponding to factors, besides shared ethnicity, that could affect the probability of inter-rebel war as a way to assess alternative arguments amenable to statistical testing, and also to reduce the risk of spuriousness in the association between coethnicity and rebel infighting.

Splinters and the organization they separated from may be prone to infighting, as tensions leading to the fragmentation or emerging in the process could continue to plague relations among the groups. Taking into account the splintering process is particularly important, given that rebel pairs consisting of a splinter and the original organization may tend to be coethnic, thus potentially giving rise to a spurious correlation between inter-rebel war and shared ethnic identity. The variable *splinter* takes on 1 if one group in the rebel pair is a splinter of the other and 0 otherwise.[6]

As pointed out in previous chapters, Fotini Christia argues that civil war alliances follow a minimum winning coalition logic. Using data on the number of fighters at the disposal of the various belligerents, Christia conducts a statistical test of one implication of her argument: civil wars with a distribution of power particularly skewed in favor of one warring party should experience relatively few changes in alliances, while civil wars with a roughly balanced distribution of power should display more volatile alliances, as even small shifts in the balance of power could lead to the emergence of new minimum winning coalitions.[7] I include a dummy (i.e., binary) variable—*preponderance*—taking on 1 in cases in which one warring party controls more than half of the total number of civil war combatants (including rebels and the government) and 0 otherwise, based on Christia's own data.[8] Given that in all cases in my dataset with a warring party enjoying military preponderance the government is the strongest belligerent, Christia's theory makes the clear prediction that *preponderance* should have a negative effect on inter-rebel war: facing a particularly powerful government should provide incentives for rebels to ally with one another and thus refrain from infighting.

I also control for a continuous measure of government power relative to the rebel movement, as the stronger the incumbent, the warier insurgent groups may be of engaging in inter-rebel war, lest they are crushed when weakened by the infighting. I use the ratio of government forces and the total number of rebel fighters across all insurgent organizations pitted against the incumbent in a given year (*troop ratio*) as a proxy for government relative power.[9]

Rebel groups with weak leadership control may be particularly prone to inter-rebel war, as low-level clashes initiated by rank and file may end up escalating into large-scale fighting among rebel organizations. Thus I include as a control *weak leadership*, which is equal to 1 if the leadership of at least one member of the rebel pair exercises only limited control on the organization and 0 otherwise.[10]

External supporters of rebel groups could also influence the risk of inter-rebel war. In particular, third-party states may deter inter-rebel war by conditioning continued support on peaceful relations among rebel groups. Thus I control for *common supporter*, a dummy variable flagging rebel pairs in which both organizations receive support from the same country or from members of the same major international alliance, namely, NATO and the Warsaw Pact.[11]

I also control for rebel groups' shared ideology to assess whether constituencies defined on the basis of political ideology have comparable effects on inter-rebel relations as coethnicity. I measure shared ideology with the variable *common ideology*, taking on 1 if the groups in a rebel pair are both Islamist or both socialist/communist, and 0 otherwise.[12] I consider rebel groups as Islamist if they advance political goals inspired by their interpretation of Sunni Islam and/or aim to establish a separate state or autonomous region ruled by Sharia law. I code rebel groups as socialist/communist if they profess adherence to Marxism and/or aim at socialist revolution.

Hanne Fjelde and Desirée Nilsson find that rebel groups controlling territory and operating in areas with oil, diamonds, or drug production as well as relatively weak and strong groups are more likely to engage in inter-rebel war.[13] Rebel territorial control may reduce vulnerability to incumbent attacks and thus spur inter-rebel war. I measure rebel control with the dummy variable *territorial control*, taking on 1 if at least one of the two groups in the rebel pair controls some territory and 0 otherwise.[14] Rebel groups benefiting from natural resources may represent particularly attractive targets for inter-rebel aggression motivated by a desire to capture such resources, as an end in itself or as a means to obtain more and better weapons and to recruit and retain more fighters. My proxy for natural resources is a dummy variable, *natural resources*, taking on 1 if at least one group in the rebel pair earned income through extortion, theft, booty futures, or smuggling of oil, gold, diamonds, coca, or opium, and 0 otherwise.[15] Military superiority could reduce the costs of inter-rebel aggression for the stronger group in a rebel pair and thus increase the probability of infighting. While existing data does not allow for a nuanced measurement of the inter-rebel balance of power, following Fjelde and Nilsson I use a rough proxy, *rebel asymmetry*, which equals 1 if one member of a pair has at least two-thirds of the total number of rebel fighters across all pairs pitted against the government in a country-year, and 0 otherwise.[16]

Finally, to test the argument that the intensity of competition within self-determination movements, and thus the risk of infighting, is a function of the number of active organizations, I use three dummy variables, indicating, respectively, whether the members of a coethnic pair represent the only coethnic insurgent groups active in a given country and year (*bipolar*), a third coethnic group exists (*tripolar*), or there are more than three (*multipolar*).[17]

The Analysis

I use rare-event logit for my analysis as there are only forty-six onsets of inter-rebel war in my data.[18] I report robust standard errors clustered by pair of rebel groups. In all specifications, I include the variable *duration* (measuring the amount of time the rebel pair has been in existence) to account for the impact of time and duration dependence.[19] The sample size varies across the specifications reported in tables 6.2 and 6.3 owing to missing values, as different variables are available for different periods. The data on external support, for example, is available only up to 2009. My findings about coethnicity are substantively unaltered when I rerun the analysis with a restricted sample including only observations for which no variable has a missing value.[20]

I introduce sequentially one new control variable at a time, retaining only those variables that reach statistical significance in at least one specification. In column 1 in table 6.2 *coethnic* is the only explanatory variable (besides *duration*). A shared ethnic constituency has the expected positive sign and is significant at the 99 percent level. Column 2 adds the variable indicating that one organization in the dyad splintered off from the other. *Splinter* has the expected positive effect on inter-rebel war, significant at the 95 percent level, while the effect of coethnicity remains unaltered.

Column 3 includes the dummy variable *preponderance*, indicating whether the government enjoyed clear superiority in terms of troop numbers compared to all the rebel groups pitted against it. This variable, based on Christia's own data, allows me to conduct a test of minimum winning coalition theory as applied to inter-rebel war. The fact that *preponderance* does not reach statistical significance indicates that rebel

TABLE 6.2 Coethnicity and Inter-rebel War (I)

	(1)	(2)	(3)	(4)	(5)	(6)
Coethnic	1.013***	0.978***	1.715***	1.685***	1.349**	1.827***
	(3.23)	(3.13)	(3.16)	(2.98)	(2.24)	(3.10)
Splinter		0.985**	1.457**	1.493**	1.679**	1.477**
		(2.01)	(2.02)	(2.15)	(2.41)	(1.98)
Preponderance			0.201			
			(0.39)			
Troop ratio				−0.015		
				(−1.49)		
Weak leadership					0.069	
					(0.11)	
Territorial control						0.126
						(0.21)
Duration	−0.064	−0.059	−0.009	−0.001	−0.009	−0.018
	(−1.45)	(−1.34)	(−0.14)	(−0.01)	(−0.13)	(−0.26)
N	1444	1444	952	993	824	1013

Note: Rare-event logit models, standard errors clustered by rebel pair.

* $= p < 0.90$, ** $= p < 0.95$, *** $= p < 0.99$

pairs facing a particularly powerful government are neither more nor less likely to experience infighting compared to other pairs.[21] The analysis therefore does not provide support for Christia's argument, which predicts less inter-rebel war in the face of a preponderant incumbent. In column 4 I include another measure of government strength, the ratio of government troops and rebel fighters across all groups active in a given year. *Troop ratio* does not reach statistical significance either, while *coethnic* retains its positive effect in both specifications.

In columns 5 and 6 of table 6.2 and columns 1–4 in table 6.3, I include measures of rebel groups' weak central leadership, territorial control, an imbalance of power within the rebel pair, access to natural resources, a common third-party state supporter, and shared ideology. Except for the imbalance of power, none of the new variables is significant. The fact that pairs of rebel groups sharing an Islamist or socialist/communist ideology are not particularly prone to inter-rebel war is consistent with my claim about the distinctive effect of shared ethnic identity. Asymmetrically powerful rebel pairs are significantly more likely to experience infighting. Coethnicity continues to display a significant (at 95 percent level or above), positive effect in all specifications, while the inclusion of *rebel asymmetry* causes *splinter* to lose significance.

Column 5 in table 6.3 reports the effects of the number of coethnic rebel groups on the risk of inter-rebel war. Coethnic rebel pairs are more likely than non-coethnic pairs to experience infighting regardless of whether there are other coethnic rebel groups active in the country at the same time, casting doubts on this alterative explanation.[22]

Owing to the tendency of ethnic communities to be geographically concentrated, the observed positive association between rebel coethnicity and probability of inter-rebel war might be spurious, resulting from coethnic organizations' physical access to one another rather than their shared base of support. In other words, coethnic rebel groups may be prone to fight one another because of their physical proximity, itself a function of the clustering of the ethnic population in a certain location, rather than because of the competitive dynamics specific to coethnicity envisioned by window theory. To address this concern, I restrict my analysis to rebel pairs whose members operated in the same first-order subnational district (in the United States, this would be one of the fifty

TABLE 6.3 Coethnicity and Inter-rebel War (II)

	(1)	(2)	(3)	(4)	(5)	(6)
Coethnic	1.708***	1.826***	2.070***	1.693***		1.424**
	(3.03)	(3.07)	(2.64)	(2.99)		(2.50)
Splinter	0.918	0.911	1.654	0.883	0.839	0.887
	(1.08)	(1.02)	(1.61)	(1.00)	(0.88)	(1.08)
Asymmetry	1.377**	1.429**	1.349**	1.419**	1.388**	1.170*
	(2.19)	(2.21)	(2.22)	(2.05)	(2.07)	(1.86)
Common supporter		0.270				
		(0.39)				
Natural resources			1.070			
			(1.23)			
Common ideology				0.301		
				(0.41)		
Bipolar					2.039***	
					(3.36)	
Tripolar					1.097	
					(0.95)	
Multipolar					2.867***	
					(2.77)	
Duration	0.013	0.005	0.017	0.005	0.015	0.016
	(0.16)	(0.06)	(0.19)	(0.06)	(0.20)	(0.21)
N	893	819	793	893	893	647

Note: Rare-event logit models, standard errors clustered by rebel pair. Column 6 replicates the specification in column 1 using the restricted sample of physically proximate rebel groups.

* = $p < 0.90$, ** = $p < 0.95$, *** = $p < 0.99$

states; in France one of the eighteen regions) or, if active in adjacent districts (i.e., sharing an administrative border), within a radius of two hundred miles, making it thus plausible that the rebel groups *could* fight each other.[23] Column 6 in table 6.3 replicates the specification with all variables reaching statistical significance (column 1) using the restricted sample. As to be expected given the positive correlation between physical proximity and coethnicity, the positive coefficient of shared ethnic identity is smaller, if only marginally; however, the variable remains significant at the 95 percent level.

As logit coefficients cannot be easily interpreted, it is helpful to look at predicted probabilities to get a sense of the magnitude of the effect of coethnicity on the risk of inter-rebel war. Based on model 2 in table 6.2, holding *splinter* at 1 and *duration* at its means, the predicted probability of inter-rebel war for a rebel pair-year goes up from 0.5 percent for a non-coethnic rebel pair to 1.2 percent for a coethnic pair, an increase of nearly 2.5 times.[24]

In sum, the statistical analysis confirms that coethnic rebel organizations are significantly and substantively more likely to fight one another than non-coethnic organizations. This finding holds when controlling for a number of factors that could influence the risk of inter-rebel war, including whether a rebel pair consists of groups that splintered off from one another. The analysis also supports the notion that the effects of coethnicity are distinct from those of shared constituency defined on the basis of political ideology.

Additional Checks

To ensure the robustness of the main finding about coethnicity, I rerun the analysis with alternative measures of government strength and the balance of power between rebel groups, as well as with a restricted sample excluding Syria. Results are reported in the table A5 in the online appendix.

GDP per capita, an oft-used proxy for state capacity to effectively deploy substantial amounts of resources to repress challengers, may be negatively associated with the risk of inter-rebel war—rebel groups may be particularly reluctant to engage in infighting when facing a strong government.[25] I also use an alternative measure of inter-rebel balance of power, *rebel asymmetry2*, which equals 1 if the Non-State Actors Dataset codes one of the groups in a rebel pair as "much weaker" than the government while the other group is coded as "weaker," "at parity," "stronger" or "much stronger" than the government, and 0 otherwise.[26] Neither control variable reaches statistical significance, while the finding about coethnicity remains unaltered.

Finally, given that many episodes of inter-rebel war in my dataset took place in the context of the ongoing civil war in Syria, I check the robustness of my findings to dropping all Syrian rebel pairs. Once again, *coethnicity* retains its significant positive sign.

The statistical analysis presented in this chapter suggests that the explanatory power of window theory extends beyond the civil wars in Iraq, Ethiopia, Sri Lanka, Lebanon, and Syria. Consistent with the argument, in the post–cold war era coethnic rebel groups have been more likely to fight one another than non-coethnic groups. By contrast, shared political ideology does not affect the risk of inter-rebel war, which confirms the distinctiveness of rebel groups' shared constituencies defined along ethnic lines posited by window theory.

The analysis also indicates that an imbalance of power between rebel groups, roughly measured with the number of fighters, may positively affect the risk of inter-rebel war. Moreover, there is some evidence (though not fully robust) that splintering processes are positively associated with the probability of infighting. By contrast, the analysis does not lend support to minimum winning coalition logic, as facing a particularly powerful government does not appear to discourage rebel groups from engaging in internecine fights.

Conclusions

I nter-rebel war generally entails significant costs and risks for rebel groups. It diverts scarce resources from the fight against the government, which is often the strongest belligerent. More important, infighting risks to fatally weaken insurgent groups, thus handing over to the incumbent opportunities to make major military gains and, in the worst-case scenario, achieve outright victory. There are, however, moments when rebel groups expect the costs and risks of inter-rebel war to be more than compensated by the resulting benefits, namely, windows of opportunity and windows of vulnerability.

Windows of opportunity are situations in which a rebel group faces weaker coethnic rivals and a government that, while not on the brink of defeat, does not pose an immediate and serious threat. The strong group would thus be tempted to use force to eliminate its rivals, i.e., launch a hegemonic bid. The favorable balance of power and the limited threat posed by the government ensure that the risks and costs of infighting would be kept at acceptably low levels. Coethnicity entails significant benefits: the group that emerges on top can typically absorb the social resources previously under the control of the defeated rivals and extend its hold on the ethnic community. Infighting can thus strengthen the victor, which would then be in a better position to face the government. Further, eliminating coethnic rivals holds the promise of improving the threat environment of the would-be hegemon, as the other groups at some point down the road could have undermined its struggle against the government or engaged in outright inter-rebel aggression.

Windows of vulnerability are situations in which a rebel group faces the prospect of a drastic decline in strength relative to coethnic rivals, while the government poses an immediate and serious threat and/or the group does not occupy an especially favorable position in the inter-rebel balance of power. In this scenario, if no other solution appears feasible, the rebel group will be tempted to resort to force or initiate a course of action likely to lead to war in a desperate attempt to overcome its predicament, i.e., to gamble for resurrection.

The next section of this chapter provides an overview of window theory's fit with the evidence presented in this book. The following section discusses the book's contribution to the study of political violence and international relations theory. The final section draws policy implications for counterinsurgents, external interveners in civil wars, and rebels.

Window Theory's Empirical Record

Overall, the empirical evidence presented in chapters 3–6 provides strong, if still preliminary, support for window theory of inter-rebel war. In contexts as diverse as those of the civil wars in Iraq, Ethiopia, Lebanon, Sri Lanka, and Syria, rebel groups tend to fight one another when windows of opportunity or vulnerability are open, while eschewing infighting in the absence of windows. The available decision-making evidence (in particular for the Iraq and Ethiopia cases, for which I had access to former rebel leaders) indicates that rebel groups perceive the incentives provided by the environment in which they operate in ways consistent with window theory: they pay close attention to the inter-rebel balance of power and its trends as well as to the government's military strength, resolve, and strategy; they instrumentally use force to eliminate coethnic competitors in the rebel movement; they bide their time when weak but growing; and they diligently search for alternatives to the use of force to deal with decline in relative power in situations in which infighting would be very costly or risky. Moreover, my statistical analysis of all rebel dyads in the post–cold war era corroborates window theory's observable implication that, other things being equal, coethnic rebel groups should be more likely to clash. Case study evidence also confirms that rebel groups tend to be able to operate easily in areas previously controlled by coethnic rivals, they can recruit and extract resources from the local population, and they usually attract large segments of the defeated coethnic group's rank and file.

As table C.1 shows, windows of opportunity seem to be the most common path to inter-rebel war: thirteen instances of infighting in my case studies are hegemonic bids driven by window-of-opportunity logic while only five are gambles for resurrection prompted by windows of vulnerability. The relative prevalence of hegemonic bids makes intuitive sense. If we assume that the sets of circumstances giving rise to the two types of windows exogenously materialize and disappear with comparable frequency, we would expect to see more hegemonic bids: rebel groups should exploit eagerly temporary advantages in the balance of power and reductions in government threat to expand the resources at their disposal and to get rid of coethnic rivals on the cheap, that is, they should "jump" through windows of opportunity. By contrast, window theory suggests that rebel groups would embark on gambles for resurrection reluctantly, only after making sure that no alternative solution to their relative decline exists—to paraphrase Otto von Bismarck, insurgents are loath to commit suicide for fear of death. In some cases, rebel groups' efforts to address a looming decline in relative power may prevent the very opening of a window of vulnerability or ensure its quick closure, so that the historical record may contain little to no trace of such a window.

As expected, hegemonic bids tend to be successful, with the initiator of the inter-rebel war falling short of eliminating a weaker rival only in three cases out of thirteen. In other words, in the vast majority of cases, hegemonic bids helped rebel groups cement their dominant positions. On the other hand, four out five gambles for resurrection were failures, as the initiating group did not forestall its relative decline. Only one instance— the PUK's attack on the National Democratic Front in 1983—can be considered successful in addressing relative decline. The PUK expelled its rivals from its stronghold in northeastern Iraq, thus reducing the impact of increasing Iranian support for the KDP; the PUK, however, continued

TABLE C.1 Summary of Inter-rebel Wars by Type and Outcome

Hegemonic Bids	Outcome of War (from point of view of initiator)
Barzani vs. Ahmed-Talabani, 1964	Success
ELF vs. ELM, 1965	Success
ELF vs. EPLF, 1972–1974	Failure
ELF vs. ELF-PLF, 1978	Success
EPLF vs. ELF, 1980–1981	Success
TPLF vs. TLF, 1975	Success
TPLF vs. Teranafit, 1976	Success
TPLF vs. EPRP, 1978–1979	Success
Phalanges vs. Tigers, 1980	Success
Amal vs. Hezbollah, 1988–1990	Failure
Aoun's forces vs. Lebanese Forces, 1989	Failure
LTTE vs. TELO, 1986	Success
LTTE vs. EPRLF, 1986–1987, 1989–1990	Success

Resurrection Gambles	Outcome of War (from point of view of initiator)
PUK vs. KDP, 1978	Failure
PUK vs. National Democratic Front, 1983	Success
PUK vs. KDP, 1994–1998	Failure
Anti-ISIS rebel coalition (thirty groups) vs. ISIS, 2014	Failure
Aoun's forces vs. Lebanese Forces, 1990	Failure

Inter-rebel Wars Not Predicted by Window Theory	Outcome of War (from point of view of initiator)
TPLF vs. EDU, 1976–1978	Failure
TPLF vs. ELF, 1979–1981	Success
Amal and PSP vs. Mourabitoun, 1985	Success
Amal vs. PSP, 1985–1988	Failure
ISIS vs. four Syrian rebel groups, 2013 (four separate onsets)	Success

TABLE C.1 (continued)

Not Enough Evidence to Make a Call	Outcome of War (from point of view of initiator)
PUK vs. IMK, 1993	? (Uncertainty about identity of initiator)

Notes: The table reports instances of inter-rebel war encountered in the case studies presented in chapters 3–5, divided based on their type (hegemonic war and gamble for resurrection) and whether window theory can explain them. "Outcome" refers to the observed result of inter-rebel war. For hegemonic bids "success" means that the attacker defeated its target. For resurrection gambles, "failure" indicates cases in which the initiator did not forestall its relative decline; "success" is a situation in which the initiator was able to do so. For episodes of inter-rebel war not predicted by window theory, "success" indicates instances in which the initiator defeated or at least weakened the target(s), while "failure" corresponds to instances in which neither result was attained.

The table purposefully selects on the dependent variable, by reporting instances in which inter-rebel war occurred. This is because the table is not intended to provide information on the extent to which the theory makes correct predictions (the case studies do trace the presence of windows of opportunity and windows of vulnerability both when inter-rebel war occurs and when inter-rebel peace prevails).

to be in such a vulnerable position due to the impending Iranian invasion of Iraqi Kurdistan that shortly afterward it had to seek an accommodation with Baghdad. The low success rate of gambles for resurrection does not indicate that they are doomed to fail but rather that, as the very concept of gamble for resurrection implies, the odds are not favorable to the gambler.[1]

Failed Predictions

The case studies identify eight instances of inter-rebel war that window theory predicts should *not* have taken place, one instance in which a predicted inter-rebel war did not occur, and one episode of infighting that took place inexplicably late. Four of the episodes of inter-rebel war that according to my argument should not have taken place occurred across ethnic lines rather than within, while the other four saw ISIS attack Syrian coethnic rebel groups in a context in which the Islamic State was growing stronger but did not have enough power vis-à-vis the rest of the rebel movement to launch a hegemonic bid.

These failed predictions are important reminders of both the probabilistic nature of my claims and the need for future work aimed at identifying additional hypotheses and refining scope conditions.[2] Here I briefly discuss each of these failed predictions. None of them reveals causal dynamics specifically ruled out by window theory, which thus increases our confidence in the overall validity of the argument.

TPLF vs. EDU

The fight between the Ethiopian Democratic Union and the Tigray People's Liberation Front is anomalous as it involved two non-coethnic groups: the EDU had an ethnically mixed membership and its political agenda was not explicitly focused on Tigray, unlike the TPLF. Both groups, however, successfully recruited Tigrayan peasants in their ranks and thus effectively competed over the same population. It thus seems plausible that, in the specific political context of Tigray in the wake of the collapse of Ethiopia's imperial authority, the EDU had enough of a Tigrayan character (due its connection to the iconic Tigrayan figure of Ras Mengesha) to trigger the kinds of competitive dynamics with the TPLF that I expect to characterize relations between coethnic groups. Generating some predictions that are "wrong for the right reasons" may well be an inevitable drawback of adopting sufficiently abstract and general coding criteria to sooth concerns about reliability of coding and falsifiability.

TPLF vs. ELF

The other episode of inter-rebel war between non-coethnics in Ethiopia pitted the Tigrayan TPLF against the Eritrean Liberation Front. The two groups clashed first in Tigray, when the TPLF intercepted an ELF contingent escorting Ethiopian People's Revolutionary Party survivors from an earlier encounter with the TPLF, and then in Eritrea, when the TPLF helped its Eritrean ally, the Eritrean People's Liberation Front, in the final round of intra-Eritrean fighting. Without a doubt, this is an instance of inter-rebel war taking place across ethnic lines. The dynamics of the case, however, suggest the existence of a mechanism that, while not envisioned by window theory, does not contradict it: the transmission of intra-ethnic disputes to non-coethnic dyads through a network of interethnic alliances (a variant of the logic of "the friend of my enemy is my enemy").

Both the TPLF and the ELF had cooperative relations with rebel groups across the Tigray-Eritrea ethnic divide: the TPLF had long cooperated with the EPLF, while the ELF, left without other alliance options in Tigray (due to the TPLF's elimination of the other Tigrayan groups), eventually provided help to the EPRP. As tensions between coethnic rebel groups (expected by window theory) escalated, the ELF and the TPLF found themselves dragged into a fight across ethnic lines on the side of their respective allies.

Amal and PSP vs. Mourabitoun; Amal vs. PSP

The wars pitting, first, Amal and the Progressive Socialist Party against Mourabitoun in 1985 and then Amal against the PSP in 1985–1988 are inconsistent with window theory, given that they occurred among non-coethnic organizations. As discussed in chapter 5, the fact that by 1985 the fight between the two civil wars camps in Lebanon—the Christian-dominated government and the Lebanese Forces, on the one hand, and the opposition, supported by Syria, on the other—had virtually ended represents a plausible way to make sense of these anomalies. Given that the only actor with potentially enough power to break the long-standing stalemate, Damascus, had endorsed the formation of a government of national unity with the participation of the opposition, neither side of the Lebanese civil war faced a serious risk of inviting its own destruction or forgoing opportunities to make significant strides toward victory by engaging in infighting.

Under these peculiar circumstances, the prospect of even modest marginal territorial gains, incitement by third-party states, ideological disputes, score settling, or personality clashes may be sufficient to motivate infighting, given its very low costs. To put it differently, the conditions prevailing in Lebanon from 1985 to 1988 reduced radically the degree of "compulsion" of the environment faced by civil war belligerents; the less a civil war setting resembles a "house on fire," the more variability in the behavior of its inhabitants/warring parties we should observe.[3]

Amal vs. Hezbollah

Contrary to the predictions of window theory, Amal did not exploit promptly the window of opportunity to crush the coethnic Hezbollah. While the "Party of God" had probably emerged as a meaningful threat to Amal's dominant position in the Shia community by 1985, Amal launched its hegemonic bid only in 1988. The episodes of inter-rebel war involving Amal mentioned earlier may help us make sense of the delay, as Amal might have wanted to bring its fight against the PSP and the PLO to a satisfactory conclusion before turning on Hezbollah. However, even in the context of the stalemated battlefield that arguably contributed to prompt Amal to fight non-coethnic groups, the fact that the dominant Shia organization decided not to prioritize squashing an emerging coethnic rival remains a puzzle for window theory. Access to evidence of Amal's calculus (in particular concerning precisely when it came to perceive Hezbollah as a meaningful competitor and the reasons behind the decision to fight—and keep fighting after a quick victory failed to materialize—against non-coethnic groups) would be particularly useful to shed light on this episode.

ISIS vs. Syrian rebels, 2013

When ISIS attacked four coethnic rivals in Syria in the summer and fall of 2013, the group was facing neither a window of opportunity nor a window of vulnerability. In all likelihood, the Islamic State was not strong enough to launch a hegemonic bid against the rest of Syria's rebel movement, though its power was rapidly growing. Under these circumstances, window theory predicts the absence of inter-rebel war. It seems plausible that ISIS's aggression reflected its distinctively violent and domineering outlook, a factor beyond window theory. Yet my argument sheds significant light on the multiple episodes of inter-rebel war involving ISIS the following year. These episodes were initiated by other rebel groups feeling threatened by the Islamic State's rapid growth (in addition to its assertiveness), which is consistent with window-of-vulnerability logic.

LTTE vs. PLOT

In 1986 the Liberation Tigers of Tamil Eelam faced a window of opportunity to wipe out the People's Liberation Organization of Tamil Eelam.

Instead of an all-out fight, however, we saw a limited attack by the Tigers followed by an ultimatum that PLOT leave Jaffna, with which the group complied, before completely losing organizational cohesion and ceasing military operations. The puzzling aspect of this nonevent is not the Tigers' behavior—there was no reason for them not to want to achieve hegemony without paying even the low costs of a quick and decisive fight—but the fact that PLOT quietly accepted its demise. Although I do not have access to evidence on PLOT's internal deliberations, it seems plausible that the Tigers' limited use of force may have sufficed to intensify PLOT's already pervasive problems of inner cohesion leading to its implosion, which made the group incapable of any organized resistance to the Tigers, hence its acceptance of the ultimatum and subsequent demise. In particular, it is possible that the killing by the LTTE of PLOT's commander in Jaffna effectively decapitated the organization. This suggests the possibility (worth exploring in future research) of a different pathway to rebel hegemony involving leadership targeting rather than outright inter-rebel war.[4]

Contributions to the Study of Political Violence and International Relations Theory

Contrary to influential research positing a negligible impact of ethnic affiliations on civil war dynamics, this book shows that shared ethnic identity can powerfully shape the risk of inter-rebel war.[5] This finding is in line with several recent studies reasserting the causal importance of ethnic identities for different aspects of civil wars, ranging from the onset and duration of armed conflict to the effectiveness of counterinsurgency operations and the provision of intelligence by civilians to the warring parties.[6]

While alerting us not to dismiss ethnic identities as epiphenomenal in the civil war context, this book also highlights that their influence is far from straightforward: the cooperation-inducing effect of coethnicity at the individual level leads to intense competition between organizations mobilizing and recruiting from the same ethnic communities. Coethnic rebel groups tend to have conflictual relations *because* they can reasonably expect to be able to elicit the cooperation of the same ethnic community.

Analyses of the internal dynamics of self-determination and national liberation movements posit, sometimes implicitly, that a shared ethnic identity fuels interorganizational competition.[7] However, they cannot fully show this effect, as they focus only on coethnic organizations.[8] I address this limitation by studying inter-rebel relations both within and across ethnic boundaries. Moreover, this book suggests that, unlike other manifestations of competition in self-determination movements (e.g., outbidding, spoiling of peace negotiations, and a cacophony of conflicting coercive messages), infighting does not necessarily serve only the narrow organizational interests of the initiator but can also further the strategic goals of the movement as a whole.[9] Rebel groups launch hegemonic bids in the pursuit of their interest, as they hope to get rid of coethnic competitors on the cheap. Yet once hegemony is achieved, the movement is likely to be more effective in its fight against the incumbent, as the dominant group will enjoy unhindered access to its ethnic constituency and will be able to focus all its resources on a coherent antigovernment strategy. By contrast, the potential benefits of a gamble for resurrection for the initiator of inter-rebel war tend to come at a cost for the movement as a whole. A successful gamble for resurrection is less likely to result in the emergence of a rebel hegemon, given that the initiator is a group in a difficult position trying to forestall a deterioration of its relative power.

Critics may see window theory's emphasis on nuanced and dynamic measures of the inter-rebel balance of power and the level of government threat as a loss of parsimony compared to arguments focusing only on power. As the case analyses have shown, however, this cost is more than compensated by gains in explanatory power: window theory generally sheds more light on inter-rebel war across the various cases studied in this book than its competitors. Moreover, the case studies of insurgencies in Iraq and Ethiopia, in particular, indicate that it is possible to collect information on rebel leaders' perception of the relevant causal factors and strategic calculus to test this kind of multifaceted argument. It is my hope that this book may serve as inspiration for scholars interested in rebel organizations' strategic decision making to pursue historically grounded, in-depth analyses based on interviews with rebel leaders and other primary sources.

Moving from the field of political violence to international relations theory, it is clear that my argument belongs to the realist paradigm, given its depiction of inter-rebel relations as an intense competition for power and security in an anarchic environment.[10] It is nonetheless helpful to discuss similarities and differences between window theory and various arguments in the realist family.

Like Kenneth Waltz's and John Mearsheimer's, window theory is a structural or systemic argument, explaining the behavior of rebel groups as a function of the incentives provided by the environment (the "system") to "units" that, at a minimum, are interested in their survival and in the advance of their political-military struggle against the government.[11] The structure in which rebel groups are immersed, however, is made up not of material factors alone but also of ideational ones, namely, a set of intersubjective identities possessed by the warring parties and local civilians. Identities are typically multidimensional and socially constructed, but these facts do not make their effects less real. Complex political processes, with violence across ethnic lines playing a paramount role, make certain identities highly salient, so that they become "sticky" during civil wars and powerfully shape the behavior of individuals and rebel groups: "They confront actors as objective social facts with real, objective 'material' effects," as Alexander Wendt puts it.[12]

Shared ethnic identity both whets rebel groups' expansionary appetites and fuels their security concerns. The existence of a shared ethnic constituency means that inter-rebel aggression can succeed on the cheap and enable the victor's acquisition of more resources. In this context, even rebel groups that for some reason were not particularly interested in expansion may opt for the use of force against a coethnic rival when a window of opportunity opens, lest they be victimized down the road under changed circumstances. Disentangling predatory and security-seeking motives is made even more complicated by the presence of the other civil war side—the government. Inter-rebel aggression motivated by a group's desire to expand, rather than preventive self-defense from a rival, may be deeply rooted in the fear induced by the incumbent's overwhelming power and the ensuing realization that more resources are needed to confront it.

The fact that window theory envisions rebel groups as harboring mixed motives does not place it in either camp in the debate between offensive and defensive realists. As Jack Snyder observes:

> Both offensive and defensive realists believe that states are motivated
> by both expansionist and security goals. To some extent it is a debate

about the incentives that international anarchy creates for states. Offensive realists tend to believe that offensive action is more necessary for self-defense than defensive realists believe it is, but the two schools' divergence on this point should not be exaggerated. . . . This is a dispute not about theoretical principles but about empirical probabilities. It is as if defensive realists think the offensive glass is 20 percent full and the offensive realists think it is 30 percent full.[13]

Thus, following Snyder, if we take the extent to which offensive action is necessary for self-defense as a key distinguishing feature between the two variants of structural realism, window theory depicts a world that more closely resembles the one envisioned by offensive realists when it comes to relations among coethnic rebel groups. In this world, security is scarce, calculated aggression often pays off, and thus even insurgents that are mostly motivated by fear and security concerns tend to behave as expansionists. The conflict of interest between coethnic groups is real and does not result merely from interactions fraught with misperceptions (i.e., the so-called spiral dynamic): the combination of anarchy, intense conflict of interest, and cumulative resources provides rebel groups with strong incentives to take offensive actions against coethnic organizations. Negative interactions (like the skirmishes that so often characterize relations between coethnic rebel groups not engaged in all-out war against each other) can certainly make things worse by enhancing threat perception; but to an important extent they represent the mechanisms through which rebel groups concretely grasp structural imperatives (i.e., they understand the logic of the situation) and reveal, rather than cause, underlying conflict.

Some interactions among coethnic rebel groups encountered in the previous chapters do more closely resemble defensive realists' spiral dynamic. In particular, when weak rebel groups form a defensive alliance to balance against a stronger coethnic organization, the latter may not help but perceive a worsening of its situation. This sort of hostile encirclement can contribute to the emergence of windows of vulnerability and inter-rebel war, as in the case of the PUK's attack on the National Democratic Front in 1983 in Iraq. It should be noted, however, that this is a "deep" security dilemma, a situation in which hardly any attempt by A at showing goodwill can convince B without exposing A to serious risks, and which is thus extremely difficult to escape.[14]

At least since 1945, relations among states have been typically less conflictual than those among the coethnic rebel groups studied in this book. Economic changes making territorial expansion less profitable, the emergence of a powerful norm against territorial conquest, the further strengthening of nationalism, and the associated tendency of populations to violently resist foreign occupation, as well as the deterrent effect of nuclear weapons, probably have contributed to the relative peacefulness of international relations over the past decades.[15] The key point for our purposes is that all these factors have reduced the cumulativity (i.e., the ease of absorption) of states' national resources, thus subduing both defensive and offensive motives for interstate war. My argument thus indirectly suggests that defensive realism is likely to represent a more helpful lens to understand relations among great powers in contemporary world politics, while offensive realism should have had relatively more purchasing power in past eras, when current obstacles to the cumulativity of states' resources were weaker or inexistent.

Implications for Counterinsurgents, External Interveners, and Rebels

Inter-rebel war represents a mixed blessing for governments facing an insurgency. On the one hand, infighting entails the allocation of rebel resources that could have been employed against the government to killing insurgents instead. Moreover, inter-rebel war could trigger insurgent side-switching, as a rebel group that is being defeated by a rival turns to the government for help and offers its services as a counterinsurgent militia in return. On the other hand, a decisive inter-rebel war can give rise to an insurgent hegemon, which would then be able to fight the government more effectively by pulling together resources that previously had been dispersed across several organizations.

Thus when inter-rebel war is ongoing, it is in the interest of counterinsurgents not to increase military pressure on the rebels lest they stop squabbling against one other due to the threat posed by government forces. However, if a rebel group seems to have a good shot at achieving hegemony, intensified government operations and even efforts to provide timely support to the rebel groups at risk of being wiped out may be warranted. Therefore it is crucial for counterinsurgents—and external interveners interested in preventing the emergence of a rebel hegemon—to have access to real-time, detailed intelligence on the internal dynamics of the rebel movement. By contrast, external supporters of the insurgency should look favorably on short and decisive inter-rebel wars heralding the rise of a hegemon, while for some counterinsurgents and external interveners the objective of containing a particularly unpalatable group (ISIS, for example) may be worth the cost of allowing the consolidation of power into the hands of some other group. Besides, though a hegemonic movement would pose a serious challenge to the incumbent, from the point of view of conflict resolution and peacebuilding, the concentration of rebel power in a single organization is likely to be desirable, given that it is particularly difficult to bring civil wars with multiple, strong rebel groups to a long-lasting end.[16]

Window theory also suggests that counterinsurgents could try to cause inter-rebel war in the first place by engineering windows of opportunity and windows of vulnerability. In practice, however, the incumbent's leeway in inducing infighting is likely to be limited. Counterinsurgents could attempt to create windows of opportunity by providing weapons or money to some groups and reducing military pressure on them, thus generating circumstances conducive to a hegemonic bid; but rebel groups may reject this aid for fear of being branded as collaborators. Furthermore, whether the beneficiaries of government support would take the bait and exploit the incumbent-engineered window of opportunity remains an open question, as they may fear an opportunistic government attack when the insurgent movement is in the throes of infighting. As a matter of fact, the limited government threat associated with hegemonic bids in the cases analyzed in this book tended to be a function of hard-to-fake constraints to military resources and power projection rather than clever maneuvers by the government. Efforts to create windows of vulnerability for some rebel groups by providing support to other groups risk running into similar problems of limited rebel willingness to be seen as colluding with the enemy.

Third-party interveners may be in a better position to create windows by selectively supporting specific rebel groups, as there would typically be less of a stigma associated with external aid. Third-party states, however, would normally have less influence on the degree of threat posed by the government to the insurgents. Window theory also suggests that there may be substantial constraints to external interveners' ability to foster the growth of favorite rebel groups and weaken unpalatable ones. Besides operational difficulties involved in preventing spillover of aid to other organizations, selectively providing support to a subset of rebel groups (i.e., "picking winners") risks creating windows of vulnerability for other groups, prompting them to attack the beneficiaries of outside aid. Similarly, other groups may perceive the prospect of direct external military intervention (whether with airpower or by ground forces) in support of a rebel group as a window of vulnerability, triggering an attack to weaken the local allies of the intervener. This dynamic was likely at play in the late 2014 and early 2015 attacks by al-Qaeda affiliate al-Nusra on the main recipients of U.S. military aid among Syrian insurgents—the Hazzm Movement and the Syrian Revolutionaries Front—as well as on Division 30, the ill-fated rebel unit created by the Pentagon's train-and-equip program to fight ISIS.[17] Although picking winners is not doomed to failure, would-be interveners should incorporate in their plans measures to counter the unintended effects suggested by window theory. In particular, they should provide reliable protection for fledgling local allies.

This book offers two main lessons for rebel groups. First, power can be too much of a good thing if acquired very quickly. In an anarchic environment, needless to say, being strong is desirable. Yet a rebel group's rapid growth risks triggering gambles for resurrection by other groups experiencing a steep relative decline. Thus if extra power cannot be acquired instantaneously (which would remove incentives for preventive attacks by rivals), pacing one's growth may represent a prudent course of action to avoid inviting other groups' aggression without significant sacrifices of power over longer periods of time. Managing this balancing act is likely to be more easily said than done, but awareness of the tension between these competing concerns might help rebel leaders navigate the trade-off and be prepared for resurrection gambles by rivals.

Second, rebel groups bent on operating in areas inhabited by non-coethnic populations should opt for an indirect approach over trying to directly administer territory and control local civilians. Thus while ISIS and the Taliban (primarily Sunni Arab- and Pashtun-dominated organizations) have experienced particular difficulties operating in non-Sunni and non-Pashtun areas of Iraq and Afghanistan, respectively, the TPLF managed to move much beyond Tigray by propping up and allying with the Amhara Ethiopian People's Democratic Movement and the Oromo People's Democratic Movement.[18] Similarly, the Kurdish PYD in Syria has formed an alliance with various Sunni Arab armed organizations—the Syrian Defense Forces (SDF)—to fight against ISIS with the support of a broad U.S.-led international coalition. Through its significantly weaker, and thus subordinate, Sunni partners, the PYD has extended its writ to large, ethnically mixed or even primarily Arab swaths of northern Syria.[19]

Yet this indirect approach to extending a group's reach beyond its ethnic constituency is likely to encounter difficulties and succeed only under specific circumstances. Even in the case of the PYD, significant tensions came to the surface, with accusations that the organization resorted to ethnic cleansing against Arabs and Turkmens in some areas to increase Kurdish demographic dominance and acted as a foreign occupier.[20] Moreover, success in such ventures is likely to require capable ethnic-other allies with at least partially aligned preferences. As the failed U.S. attempt to cobble together anti-ISIS Sunni militias in Syria attests, assembling from scratch an armed organization is a far more daunting endeavor than propping up one that has already proven its viability and has an effective command-and-control system allowing it to put to good use the injection of financial and military support.

Acronyms

ACD2EPR	Armed Conflict Database-2-Ethnic Power Relations
AQI	al-Qaeda in Iraq
EDU	Ethiopian Democratic Union
ELF	Eritrean Liberation Front
ELF-PLF	Eritrean Liberation Front-People's Liberation Forces
ELM	Eritrean Liberation Movement
EPDM	Ethiopian People's Democratic Movement
EPLF	Eritrean People's Liberation Front
EPRLF	Eelam People's Revolutionary Liberation Front
EPRP	Ethiopian People's Revolutionary Party
EROS	Eelam Revolutionary Organization of Students
ERP	Ejército Revolucionario del Pueblo
FLN	National Liberation Front
FMLN	Farabundo Martí National Liberation Front
FNLA	National Front for the Liberation of Angola
FSA	Free Syrian Army
HuM	Hezb-ul-Mujahideen

IMK	Islamist Movement of Kurdistan
ISI	Islamic State of Iraq
ISIS	Islamic State of Iraq and Syria
JKLF	Jammu and Kashmir Liberation Front
KDP	Kurdistan Democratic Party
KDPI	Iranian Kurdistan Democratic Party
KRG	Kurdish Regional Government
LRA	Lord's Resistance Army
LTTE	Liberation Tigers of Tamil Eelam
MNA	Algerian National Movement
MNF	multinational force
MPLA	Popular Movement for the Liberation of Angola
MWC	minimum winning coalition
OPDM	Oromo People's Democratic Movement
PLO	Palestine Liberation Organization
PLOT	People's Liberation Organization of Tamil Eelam
PSP	Progressive Socialist Party
PUK	Patriotic Union of Kurdistan
PYD	Democratic Union Party
SCIRI	Supreme Council for Islamic Revolution in Iraq
TELO	Tamil Eelam Liberation Organization
TLF	Tigray Liberation Front
TPLF	Tigray People's Liberation Front
UCDP	Uppsala Conflict Data Program
UIFSA	United Islamic Front for the Salvation of Afghanistan
UPA	Uganda People's Army

Notes

1. Wars Within Wars

1. Reported in Robert S. Ross, "International Bargaining and Domestic Politics: U.S.-China Relations Since 1972," *World Politics* 38, no. 2 (January 1986): 255–87, quote on 263.
2. Bill Roggio and Lisa Lundquist, "Analysis: Shifting Dynamics of Rebel Infighting in Syria," *Long War Journal*, January 17, 2014.
3. Liz Sly, "On Third Anniversary of Syrian Rebellion, Assad Is Steadily Winning the War," *Washington Post*, March 14, 2014.
4. See, for example, Sam Dagher, "Fighting Among Rebels Boosts Syrian Regime," *Wall Street Journal*, January 13, 2014.
5. Stephen Biddle, Jeffrey A. Friedman, and Jacob N. Shapiro, "Testing the Surge: Why did Violence Decline in Iraq in 2007?" *International Security* 37, no. 1 (Summer 2012): 1–34; Jon R. Lindsay and Austin G. Long, "Correspondence: Assessing the Synergy Thesis in Iraq," *International Security* 37, no. 4 (Spring 2013): 173–98.
6. Inter-rebel war occurred in civil wars in the Middle East and North Africa, South Asia, Latin America, Sub-Saharan Africa, and Europe. For details, see online appendix at https://costantinopischedda.com/data-replication-materials-and-additional -materials/.
7. On relations between the rebel groups constituting the Farabundo Martí National Liberation Front (FMLN) in El Salvador, see Michael E. Allison and Alberto Martín Alvarez, "Unity and Disunity in the FMLN," *Latin American Politics and Society* 54, no. 4 (Winter 2012): 89–118; Hugh Byrne, *El Salvador's Civil War: A Study of Revolution* (Boulder, Colo.: Lynne Rienner, 1996); Cynthia McClintock, *Revolutionary Movements in Latin America: El Salvador's FMLN and Peru's Shining Path* (Washington, D.C.: United States Institute of Peace Press, 1998). On cooperation between the

Argentinian rebel groups Ejército Revolucionario del Pueblo (ERP) and the Montone-ros, see Richard Gillespie, "Political Violence in Argentina: Guerrillas, Terrorists, and Carapintadas," in *Terrorism in Context*, ed. Martha Crenshaw (University Park: Penn-sylvania State University Press, 1995), 230; Paul H. Lewis, *Guerrillas and Generals: The Dirty War in Argentina* (Westport, Conn.: Praeger, 2002), 111–13, 120–22, 126.

8. Kenneth Waltz, *Theory of International Politics* (Reading, Mass.: Addison-Wesley, 1979). "Balance of threat" theory suggests the same conclusion: the fact that the rebels and government are fighting implies the insurgents perceive a high degree of hostility in the incumbent's intentions, which, coupled with its typical military superiority, should make the government the most serious threat. See Stephen Walt, *Origins of Alliances* (Ithaca, N.Y.: Cornell University Press, 1987).

9. A key insight from the sociology of conflict is that conflict with "out-groups" tend to increase "in-group" cohesion. Georg Simmel, *Conflict: The Web of Group Affiliations* (Glencoe, Ill.: Free Press, 1955); Lewis A. Coser, *The Functions of Social Conflict* (New York: Free Press, 1956); Arthur Stein, "Conflict and Cohesion: A Review of the Litera-ture," *Journal of Conflict Resolution* 20, no. 1 (March 1976): 143–72; Gary Bornstein, "Intergroup Conflict: Individual, Group, and Collective Interests," *Personality and Social Psychology Review* 7, no. 2 (May 2003): 129–45.

10. The classic reference is Chaim D. Kaufmann, "Possible and Impossible Solutions to Ethnic Civil Wars," *International Security* 20, no. 4 (Spring 1996): 136–75. For micro-level evidence, see, for example, Omar Shahbudin McDoom, "The Psychology of Threat in Intergroup Conflict: Emotions, Rationality, and Opportunity in the Rwan-dan Genocide," *International Security* 37, no. 2 (Fall 2012): 119–55.

11. Relevant works, besides those discussed in this section, include Adria Lawrence, "Triggering Nationalist Violence: Competition and Conflict in Uprisings Against Colonial Rule," *International Security* 35, no. 2 (2010): 88–122; Navin A. Bapat and Kanisha D. Bond, "Alliances Between Militant Groups," *British Journal of Political Science* 42, no. 4 (2012): 793–824; Jesse Driscoll, "Commitment Problems or Bidding Wars? Rebel Fragmentation as Peace Building," *Journal of Conflict Resolution* 56, no. 1 (2012): 118–49; Theodore McLauchlin and Wendy Pearlman, "Out-Group Conflict, In-Group Unity? Exploring the Effect of Repression on Intramovement Cooperation," *Journal of Conflict Resolution* 56, no. 1 (2012): 41–66; Lee Seymour, "Alignment in Civil Wars: Rivalry, Patronage and Side Switching in Sudan," *International Security* 39, no. 2 (Fall 2014): 92–131; Emily Kalah Gade, Mohammed M. Hafez, and Michael Gab-bay "Networks of Cooperation: Rebel Alliances in Fragmented Civil Wars," *Journal of Conflict Resolution* 63, no. 9 (2019): 2071–97.

12. Hanne Fjelde and Desirée Nilsson, "Rebels Against Rebels: Explaining Violence Between Rebel Groups," *Journal of Conflict Resolution* 56, no. 4 (August 2012): 604–28. Lilja and Hultman argue that infighting among Tamil rebels in Sri Lanka resulted from competition for dominance in the insurgent movement, in particular in ethni-cally homogenous areas. Hafez and Mendelsohn separately put forth arguments about rebel infighting emphasizing, among other factors, the role of ideology, and tested them with case studies of Algeria's civil war in the 1990s. Gade and her coauthors find

that in the Syrian civil war ideological distance and power asymmetry increase the risk of infighting. Nygard and Weintraub present a formal bargaining model of inter-rebel fighting but no empirical test. Jannie Lilja and Lisa Hultman, "Intraethnic Dominance and Control: Violence Against Co-Ethnics in the Early Sri Lankan Civil War," *Security Studies*, 20, no. 2 (2011): 171–97; Mohammed M. Hafez, "Fratricidal Rebels: Ideological Extremity and Warring Factionalism in Civil Wars," *Terrorism and Political Violence* 32, no. 3 (2020): 604–29; Barak Mendelsohn, "The Battle for Algeria: Explaining Fratricide Among Armed Nonstate Actors," *Studies in Conflict & Terrorism* (forthcoming); Emily Kalah Gade, Mohammed M. Hafez, and Michael Gabbay, "Fratricide in Rebel Movements: A Network Analysis of Syrian Militant Infighting," *Journal of Peace Research* 56, no. 3 (2019): 321–35; Havard M. Nygard and Michael Weintraub, "Bargaining Between Rebel Groups and the Outside Option of Violence," *Terrorism and Political Violence* 27, no. 3 (2015): 557–80.

13. Fotini Christia, *Alliance Formation in Civil Wars* (New York: Cambridge University Press, 2012).

14. For more thorough critiques of Christia's argument and empirical findings, see the reviews of her book (including my own) in *H-Diplo/ISSF Roundtable Reviews* 6, no. 2 (2013).

15. Alistair Horne, *A Savage War of Peace: Algeria 1954–1962* (London: Macmillan, 1977), 136, 222; Rasmus Alenius Boserup, "Collective Violence and Counter-state Building," in *Crisis of the State: War and Social Upheaval*, ed. Bruce Kapferer and Bjorn Enge Bertelsen (New York: Berghahn Books, 2009), 249–50.

16. John H. Marcum, *The Angolan Revolution: Exile Politics and Guerrilla Warfare (1962–1976)* (Cambridge, Mass.: MIT Press, 1978), 9–61.

17. Paul Staniland, "Between a Rock and a Hard Place: Insurgent Fratricide, Ethnic Defection, and the Rise of ProState Paramilitaries," *Journal of Conflict Resolution* 56, no. 1 (February 2012): 16–40.

18. Peter Krause, *Rebel Power: Why National Movements Compete, Fight, and Win* (Ithaca, N.Y.: Cornell University Press, 2017).

19. Krause builds on the work of Bakke, Cunningham, and Seymour, which shows that the level of competition within self-determination movements—measured as the number of existing factions—affects the risk of infighting. My theory, like Krause's, emphasizes the balance of power between organizations, rather than their numbers in and of themselves, as a key factor shaping their relations with one another. Kristin M. Bakke, Kathleen Gallagher Cunningham, and Lee J. M. Seymour, "Shirts Today, Skins Tomorrow: Dual Contests and the Effects of Fragmentation in Self-Determination Disputes," *Journal of Conflict Resolution* 56, no. 1 (February 2012): 67–93; Kathleen Gallagher Cunningham, *Inside the Politics of Self-Determination* (Oxford: Oxford University Press, 2014).

20. Ben Hubbard, "U.S. Goal Is to Make Syrian Rebels Viable," *New York Times*, September 18, 2014.

21. Steven L. Burg and Paul S. Shoup, *The War in Bosnia Herzegovina: Ethic Conflict and International Intervention* (New York: M. E. Sharpe, 1999), 292–98.

22. Staniland, "Between a Rock and a Hard Place."

23. Biddle, Friedman, and Shapiro, "Testing the Surge"; Lindsay and Long, "Correspondence."

24. Ahmed Hashim, *When Counterinsurgency Wins: Sri Lanka's Defeat of the Tamil Tiger* (Philadelphia: University of Pennsylvania Press, 2013).

25. M. R. Narayan Swamy, *Inside an Elusive Mind, Prabhakaran: The First Profile of the World's Most Ruthless Guerrilla Leader* (Delhi: Konark, 2003), 211, 234–35, 238–39, 250–51.

26. For an analogous conceptualization of "windows" as causes of interstate wars, see Stephen Van Evera, *Causes of War: Power and the Roots of Conflict* (Ithaca, N.Y.: Cornell University Press, 1999). See also Richard Ned Lebow, "Windows of Opportunity: Do States Jump Through Them?," *International Security* 9, no. 1 (Summer 1984): 147–86.

27. Gambling for resurrection is "an attempt to maintain power by inducing massive change in the environment which has only a small chance of succeeding." Rui de Figueiredo and Barry R. Weingast, "The Rationality of Fear: Political Opportunism and Ethnic Conflict," in *Civil Wars, Insecurity, and Intervention*, ed. Barbara F. Walter and Jack L. Snyder (New York: Columbia University Press, 1999), 263. The term has been popularized in political science by George W. Downs and David M. Rocke, *Optimal Imperfection? Domestic Uncertainty and Institutions in International Relations* (Princeton, N.J.: Princeton University Press, 1995).

28. As many scholars of ethnic politics will no doubt receive this contention as controversial, it is important to note here that it is compatible with prevailing constructivist approaches. Though human beings' ethnic parochialism has deep evolutionary foundations, the specific identities available to and adopted by individuals result from processes of social construction.

29. Joseph Henrich, *The Secret of Our Success: How Culture Is Driving Human Evolution, Domesticating Our Species and Making Us Smarter* (Princeton, N.J.: Princeton University Press, 2016), 204.

30. See, among many others, Jack Levy, "Declining Power and the Preventive Motivation for War," *World Politics* 40, no. 1 (October 1987): 82–107; James D. Fearon, "Rationalist Explanations for War," *International Organization* 49, no. 3 (Summer 1995): 379–414; Robert Powell, "War as a Commitment Problem," *International Organization* 60, no. 1 (January 2006): 169–203; Randall L. Schweller, "Domestic Structure and Preventive War: Are Democracies More Pacific?," *World Politics* 44, no. 2 (January 1992): 235–69.

31. David Galula, *Counter-insurgency Warfare: Theory and Practice* (New York: Praeger, 1964), 8.

32. For a critique of Stephen Van Evera's *Causes of War* along these lines, see Richard K. Betts, "Must War Find a Way: A Review Essay," *International Security* 24, no. 2 (Fall 1999): 166–98, esp. 174–75.

33. Barry R. Posen, "The Security Dilemma and Ethnic Conflict," *Survival* 35, no. 1 (Spring 1993): 27–47; Kaufmann, "Possible and Impossible Solutions to Ethnic Civil Wars."

34. Kalyvas influentially argued that ideologies and ethnic identities are much less important predictors of civil war behavior than coercion and local-level relationships and disputes. Stathis N. Kalyvas, *The Logic of Violence in Civil War* (New York: Cambridge University Press, 2006).

35. Krause, *Rebel Power.*

36. I use the expressions "rebel groups," "rebel organizations," "insurgent groups," and "insurgent organizations" interchangeably. Following Kalyvas, I adopt a broad conceptualization of civil war, including anticolonial and antioccupation wars, in which the incumbent is a colonial power or a foreign occupier. Kalyvas, *The Logic of Violence in Civil War.*

37. Max Weber, *Economy and Society* (1922; Berkeley: University of California Press, 1978). Other works adopting Weber's conceptualization include Donald Horowitz, *Ethnic Groups in Conflict* (Berkeley: University of California Press, 1985); Andreas Wimmer, "The Making and Unmaking of Ethnic Boundaries: A Multilevel Process Theory," *American Journal of Sociology* 113, no. 4 (January 2008): 970–1022; Lars-Erik Cederman, Andreas Wimmer, and Brian Min "Why Do Ethnic Groups Rebel? New Data and Analysis," *World Politics* 62, no. 1 (January 2010): 87–119; Stuart J. Kaufman, *Nationalist Passions* (Ithaca, N.Y.: Cornell University Press, 2015). Note that this conceptualization is compatible with two pillars of the constructivist research agenda on ethnic politics—constrained malleability and multidimensional nature of identities. Kanchan Chandra, ed., *Constructivist Theories of Ethnic Politics* (New York: Oxford University Press, 2012), chap. 1.

38. For a similar approach to the association between rebel organizations and ethnic groups, see Julian Wucherpfennig et al., "Ethnicity, the State, and the Duration of Civil War," *World Politics* 64, no. 1 (January 2012): 79–115.

39. John J. Mearsheimer, *The Tragedy of Great Power Politics*, rev. ed. (New York: Norton, 2014), 370.

40. Staniland uses a similar definition for rebel groups that defect to the government side, in "Between a Rock and a Hard Place," 18–19.

41. Corinna Jentzsch, Stathis N. Kalyvas, and Livia Isabella Schubiger, "Militias in Civil War," *Journal of Conflict Resolution* 59, no. 5 (2015): 755–69; Sabine C. Carey and Neil J. Mitchell, "Progovernment Militias," *Annual Review of Political Science* 20 (2017): 127–47.

42. On the deviant case selection criterion, see Jason Seawright and John Gerring, "Case Selection Techniques in Case Study Research: A Menu of Qualitative and Quantitative Options," *Political Research Quarterly* 61, no. 2 (June 2008): 294–308, esp. 302–3.

43. See the discussion of the diverse case selection criterion in Seawright and Gerring, "Case Selection Techniques in Case Study Research," 300–301.

44. On the importance of testing theories on cases other than those used for developing them, see, among others, Alexander L. George and Andrew Bennett, *Case Studies and Theory Development in the Social Sciences* (Cambridge, Mass.: MIT Press, 2005), 75–76.

2. Windows of Opportunity, Windows of Vulnerability, and Inter-rebel War

1. Niccolò Machiavelli, *The Prince*, trans. and ed. Peter Bondanella (New York: Oxford University Press, 2005), 10.

2.   Quoted in Kenneth N. Waltz, *Man, the State, and War: A Theoretical Analysis* (New York: Columbia University Press, 1954), 187–88.

3.   Barbara F. Walter, "The Critical Barrier to Civil War Settlement," *International Organization* 51, no. 3 (Summer 1997): 338–40.

4.   Kenneth N. Waltz, *Theory of International Politics* (Reading, Mass.: Addison-Wesley, 1979), 118.

5.   Tanisha Fazal identifies nine instances of state death in the years 1946–1992, only two of which occurred through interstate war and conquest. Tanisha Fazal, "State Death in the International System," *International Organization* 58, no. 2 (Spring 2004): 311–44. Conversely, rebel groups' violent demise is frequent. See, for example, Timothy Wickham-Crowley, *Guerillas and Revolution in Latin America: A Comparative Study of Insurgents and Regimes Since 1956* (Princeton, N.J.: Princeton University Press, 1993), 16; Daniel Byman, *Understanding Proto-Insurgency* (Santa Monica, Calif.: RAND Corporation, 2007), 1.

6.   Peter Krause, "The Political Effectiveness of Non-State Violence: A Two-Level Framework to Transform a Deceptive Debate," *Security Studies* 22, no. 2 (2013): 259–94. See also Kristin M. Bakke, Kathleen Gallagher Cunningham, and Lee J. M. Seymour, "Shirts Today, Skins Tomorrow: Dual Contests and the Effects of Fragmentation in Self-Determination Disputes," *Journal of Conflict Resolution* 56, no. 1 (February 2012): 67–93.

7.   Window theory assumes that rebel groups primarily care about their survival as independent actors and success in the fight against the government. Even though naturally they prefer controlling a larger, rather than smaller, share of the ethnic community, rebel groups should be unwilling to take initiatives to expand that would put at risk those primary values, such as initiating aggression against another group in the absence of windows or trying to radically alter the inter-rebel balance of power through sustained coercive diplomacy, which could prompt other groups to gamble for resurrection. It seems highly plausible that in the real world groups with preference structures different from those I assume for theory building exist; if such groups are very prevalent (an open, factual question), empirical analysis should reveal limited explanatory power for my argument, as inter-rebel war would often occur when windows are not present.

8.   How quickly and cheaply is enough depends on the power of the government, in addition to the extent of its power projection constraints. In the typical scenario of limited government threat—when the incumbent is militarily superior overall but faces contingent constraints to power project—an inter-rebel war lasting more than a few months would probably be considered too risky. By contrast, in situations in which the government is weaker than the strongest rebel group, the latter would face a very broad window of opportunity and thus could afford a longer inter-rebel fight while also engaging in relatively intense combat against the government.

9.   Daniel Kahneman and Amos Tversky, "Prospect Theory: An Analysis of Decision Under Risk," *Econometrica* 47, no. 2 (1979): 263–91. For an application to preventive war, see Jack Levy, "Declining Power and the Preventive Motivation for War," *World*

Politics 40, no. 1 (October 1987): 82–107. For a discussion of the applicability of prospect theory to group-decision settings, see William A. Boettcher III, "The Prospects for Prospect Theory: An Empirical Evaluation of International Relations Applications of Framing and Loss Aversion," Political Psychology 25, no. 3 (June 2004): 331–62.

10. Dan Altman, "By Fait Accompli, Not Coercion: How States Wrest Territory from Their Adversaries," International Studies Quarterly 61, no. 4 (December 2017): 881–91.

11. Levy, "Declining Power."

12. When a dominant rebel group faces the prospect of rapid relative decline, the pressing need to forestall this development would add to the allure of using force to get rid of coethnic rivals on the cheap.

13. Groups facing a window of vulnerability also have the option of reaching out to the government in the hope of respite from counterinsurgency pressure or even help and protection in the inter-rebel struggle. However, I expect rebel groups to be even wearier of this option than gambling for resurrection. In fact, a rebel group in dire straits typically would be unable to extract significant concessions from the government, rendering whatever arrangement is reached vulnerable to other rebels' accusations of selling out, which would risk accelerating, rather than reversing, the group's decline. Thus we should tend to see rebel groups reaching cooperative arrangements with the government (if at all) only after the use of force against a rising rival has proven ineffective.

14. Not all hegemonic bids, of course, will be successful, as not all safe bets pan out. Leaders may miscalculate, misperceive, or make mistakes in the execution of sensible plans, and information about important factors may simply be unavailable (for example, intangible elements in the balance of power like the adversary's actual force employment or the cohesion of untested units). Moreover, as Carl von Clausewitz famously observed about war in general, there may well be a pervasive element of inherent unpredictability in inter-rebel war outcomes. Carl von Clausewitz, On War, ed. and trans. Michael Howard and Peter Paret (Princeton, N.J.: Princeton University Press, 1976).

15. Peter Krause, Rebel Power: Why National Movements Compete, Fight, and Win (Ithaca, N.Y.: Cornell University Press, 2017).

16. On resource cumulativity and interstate war, see Stephen Van Evera, Causes of War: Power and the Roots of Conflict (Ithaca, N.Y.: Cornell University Press, 1999).

17. As Stephen Van Evera points out, "Often resources empower their current owners but not a conqueror, or they empower the conqueror at a discount." Van Evera, Causes of War, 107. The most thorough discussion of cumulativity in the context of foreign occupations (in particular of industrial countries in the twentieth century) is Peter Liberman, Does Conquest Pay? The Exploitation of Occupied Industrial Societies (Princeton, N.J.: Princeton University Press, 1996).

18. Stathis N. Kalyvas, for example, reports various instances of progovernment militias recruited from rebellious ethnic groups. Kalyvas, "Ethnic Defection in Civil Wars," Comparative Political Studies 41, no. 3 (August 2008): 1043–68.

19. My argument is consistent with the long-standing view among scholars and practitioners of insurgency that to be viable, rebel organizations cannot rely exclusively on

coercion but also need some degree of consent from the civilian population under their influence, to be elicited through a mix of indoctrination and public goods provision. I contend that being able to present itself as a defender of the ethnic community against the ethnic-other forces of the government enormously facilitates the rebel group's task of gaining civilian consent to its rule. See, among many others, Mao Zedong, *On Guerrilla Warfare*, trans. Samuel B. Griffith (New York: Praeger, 1961); Zachariah C. Mampilly, *Rebel Rulers: Insurgent Governance and Civilian Life During War* (Ithaca, N.Y.: Cornell University Press, 2011); Anna Arjona, "Civilian Resistance to Rebel Governance," in *Rebel Governance in Civil War*, ed. Ana Arjona, Nelson Kasfir, and Zachariah Mampilly (New York: Cambridge University Press, 2015).

20. In practice, the existence of ethnically mixed areas reduces the sharpness of the distinction between pairs of coethnic rebel groups (relatively prone to inter-rebel war) and non-coethnic groups (less prone to inter-rebel war). Non-coethnic rebel groups may violently vie for control of an area where their respective potential supporters live intermingled. Unchallenged control of this area would offer the benefit of mobilizing and extracting resources from coethnics but may also entail the significant costs of policing a potentially hostile ethnic-other population or forcing it to leave (with the associated political and image negative consequences). Therefore inter-rebel war should be less likely between non-coethnic rebel groups whose distinct popular bases of support are partially intermingled than between coethnic rebel groups; and inter-rebel war should be more likely between non-coethnic rebel groups whose potential supporters live in ethnically mixed areas than between non-coethnic rebel groups whose supporters inhabit distinct areas.

21. Adnan R. Khan, "Life Under ISIS: Four Stories of Terror Endured," *Maclean's*, December 14, 2016.

22. Aymenn al-Tamimi, "The Islamic State and the Kurds: The Documentary Evidence," *CTC Sentinel* 10, no. 8 (September 2017): 33–38.

23. Nicholas Sambanis, Jonah Schulhofer-Wohl, and Moses Shayo, "Parochialism as a Central Challenge in Counterinsurgency," *Science* (May 2012): 805–8.

24. Robert H. Bates, "Ethnic Competition and Modernization in Contemporary Africa," *Comparative Political Studies* 6, no. 4 (January 1974): 457–84; Nicolas van de Walle, "Presidentialism and Clientelism in Africa's Emerging Party Systems," *Journal of Modern African Studies* 41, no. 2 (June 2003): 297–321; Kanchan Chandra, *Why Ethnic Parties Succeed: Patronage and Ethnic Head Counts in India* (New York: Cambridge University Press, 2004); Karen E. Ferree, "Explaining South Africa's Racial Census," *Journal of Politics* 68, no. 4 (November 2006): 803–15.

25. Raphaël Franck and Ilia Rainer, "Does the Leader's Ethnicity Matter? Ethnic Favoritism, Education, and Health in Sub-Saharan Africa," *American Political Science Review* 106, no. 2 (May 2012): 294–325; Daniel Corstange, *The Price of a Vote in the Middle East: Clientelism and Communal Politics in Lebanon and Yemen* (New York: Cambridge University Press, 2016).

26. James T. Quinlivan, "Coup-Proofing: Its Practice and Consequences in the Middle East," *International Security* 24, no. 2 (Fall 1999): 131–65; Theodore McLauchlin,

"Loyalty Strategies and Military Defection in Rebellion," *Comparative Politics* 42, no. 3 (2010): 333–50; Philip Roessler, "The Enemy Within: Personal Rule, Coups, and Civil War in Africa," *World Politics* 63, no. 2 (April 2011): 300–346; Julien Morency-Laflamme and Theodore McLauchlin, "The Efficacy of Ethnic Stacking: Military Defection During Uprisings in Africa," *Journal of Global Security Studies* (forthcoming).

27. James D. Fearon and David D. Laitin, "Explaining Interethnic Cooperation," *American Political Science Review* 90, no. 4 (December 1996): 715–35; James Habyariamana et al., *Coethnicity: Diversity and the Dilemmas of Collective Action* (New York: Russel Sage Foundation, 2009). Contrary to the prevailing view, in a field experiment in two Ugandan villages, Jennifer M. Larson and Janet I. Lewis find that ethnically homogenous networks are less dense than diverse ones. The study confirms that information does spread more widely through ethnically homogenous networks, but that is due to the higher willingness of individuals to share information with coethnics. Jennifer M. Larson and Janet I. Lewis, "Ethnic Networks," *American Journal of Political Science* 61, no. 2 (April 2017): 350–64.

28. Chandra, *Why Ethnic Parties Succeed*; Henry E. Hale, "Explaining Ethnicity," *Comparative Political Studies* 37, no. 4 (May 2004): 458–85; Daniel N. Posner, *Institutions and Ethnic Politics in Africa* (New York: Cambridge University Press, 2005); Corstange, *The Price of a Vote in the Middle East.*

29. On social identity theory, see Henri Tajfel, *Human Groups and Social Categories: Studies in Social Psychology* (New York: Cambridge University Press, 1981). On political socialization theory, see, for example, Keith Darden, "Resisting Occupation: Mass Schooling and the Creation of Durable National Loyalties," unpublished manuscript.

30. Donald L. Horowitz, *The Deadly Ethnic Riot* (Berkeley: University of California Press, 2001), 553–54; Roger D. Petersen, *Understanding Ethnic Violence, Fear, Hatred, and Resentment in Twentieth-Century Eastern Europe* (New York: Cambridge University Press, 2002); Ashutosh Varshney, "Nationalism, Ethnic Conflict, and Rationality," *Perspectives on Politics* 1, no. 1 (March 2003): 85–99.

31. As Robert Jervis notes in the different context of the divergence of policy views between U.S. presidents and their advisors, "role rather than individual difference can explain the discrepancies." Jervis, "Do Leaders Matter and How Would We Know?" *Security Studies* 22, no. 2 (2013): 159. There may also be a selection dynamic at play. People with a psychological predisposition for "Realpolitik" thinking (or "Machiavellism") may be particularly likely to rise through the ranks of rebel organizations by sidelining their internal rivals. On Realpolitik psychological orientation, see Brian Rathbun, "The Rarity of Realpolitik: What Bismarck's Rationality Reveals About International Politics," *International Security* 43, no. 1 (Summer 2018): 7–55.

32. Geoffrey Blainey makes this point in the context of interstate war with the parable of fighting waterbirds and the opportunistic fisherman. Richard Rosecrance labels the loss of relative power to a third party sitting on the sidelines as the "dilemma of the victor's inheritance." Geoffrey Blainey, *Causes of War* (New York: Free Press, 1973), 57–62; Richard Rosencrance, *Rise of the Trading State* (New York: Basic Books, 1986), 34.

33. I do not consider situations characterized by ongoing negotiations with the government as entailing significant opportunity costs for a rebel group in a position to launch a hegemonic bid. This is because the existence of coethnic competitors can trigger spoiling behavior, as weaker groups try to derail a peace process that risks marginalizing them. Moreover, the stronger rebel group should be able to extract more concessions from the government once in a hegemonic position. See Wendy Pearlman, "Spoiling Inside and Out: Internal Political Contestation and the Middle East Peace Process," *International Security* 33, no. 3 (Winter 2008–09): 79–109; Krause, *Rebel Power*.

34. Hegemonic bids therefore have something in common with Machiavelli's "well used cruelties," which "are carried out in a single stroke, done out of necessity to protect oneself and then are not continued, but are instead converted into the greatest possible benefits for the subjects.... Those who follow the first method [well-used cruelties] can remedy their standing both with God and with men." Machiavelli, *The Prince*, 33–34.

35. Paul Staniland, "States, Insurgents, and Wartime Political Orders," *Perspectives on Politics* 10, no. 2 (June 2012): 253.

36. Following analogous reasoning, Dale Copeland argues that in multipolar international systems a great power would launch a hegemonic bid only when markedly superior to all the other states, lest sideliners take advantage of the inevitable weakening of the aspiring hegemon in the lengthy and costly bilateral wars that it would have to wage sequentially against comparably powerful states. See Dale C. Copeland, *The Origins of Major War* (Ithaca, N.Y.: Cornell University Press, 2000), 15–20.

37. This is the motivating puzzle of the rational choice study of war: given that fighting is costly (and assuming risk neutrality or aversion), rational actors should agree on a peaceful division of the prize that leaves all better off than if they had settled the dispute with force. See James D. Fearon, "Rationalist Explanations for War," *International Organization* 49, no. 3 (Summer 1995): 379–414.

38. The fact that, as suggested by prospect theory, individuals become risk-acceptant when operating in the realm of losses may further reduce the bargaining range and thus the probability of finding a war-avoiding agreement. See Robert Jervis, *How Statesmen Think: The Psychology of International Politics* (Princeton, N.J.: Princeton University Press, 2017), 91.

39. Decline eventually could bring the group below what I dubbed the threshold of extreme weakness, where the huge imbalance of power would make resistance to any demand by a strong group pointless.

40. This is a specific variant of the commitment problem arising when actors negotiate over objects that are themselves a crucial source of bargaining power. Fearon, "Rationalist Explanations for War," 408–9; Robert Powell, "War as a Commitment Problem," *International Organization* 60, no. 1 (January 2006): 185–88.

41. Copeland makes the same point about the initiation of major war when there are more than two great powers in the international system. Copeland, *The Origins of Major War*, 23–24.

42. While, to my knowledge, there are no studies on these topics in the context of civil wars, the literature on buck passing and the collective action problem in international alliances is vast; see, in particular, Waltz, *Theory of International Politics*, 164–65; Barry R. Posen, *Sources of Military Doctrine* (Ithaca, N.Y.: Cornell University Press, 1984), 63–64; Stephen Walt, *Origins of Alliances* (Ithaca, N.Y.: Cornell University Press, 1987); Thomas J. Christensen and Jack L. Snyder, "Chain Gangs and Passed Bucks: Predicting Alliance Patterns in Multipolarity," *International Organization* 44, no. 2 (Spring 1990): 137–68; Glenn H. Snyder, *Alliance Politics* (Ithaca, N.Y.: Cornell University Press, 1997). On coalitional warfare in international politics, see Patricia A. Weitsman, "Alliance Cohesion and Coalition Warfare: The Central Powers and Triple Entente," *Security Studies* 12, no. 3 (2003): 79–113.

43. See notes 23–25 above.

44. On kin selection, see William D. Hamilton, "The Genetical Evolution of Social Behaviour," *Journal of Theoretical Biology* 7, no. 1 (1964): 1–16; Richard Dawkins, *The Selfish Gene* (New York: Oxford University Press, 1976); Steven Pinker, *How the Mind Works* (New York: Norton, 1997).

45. Gary R. Johnson, Susan H. Ratwik, and Timothy J. Sawyer, "The Evocative Significance of Kin Terms in Patriotic Speech," and Wolfgang Tönnesmann, "Group Identification and Political Socialisation," both in *The Sociobiology of Ethnocentrism: Evolutionary Dimensions of Xenophobia, Discrimination, Racism and Nationalism*, ed. Vernon Reynolds, Vincent Falger, and Ian Vine (Athens: University of Georgia Press, 1987); Azar Gat, *Nations: The Long History and Deep Roots of Political Ethnicity and Nationalism* (New York: Cambridge University Press, 2013). See also Bradley A. Thayer, *Darwin and International Relations: On the Evolutionary Origins of War and Ethnic Conflict* (Lexington: University Press of Kentucky, 2004), chap. 5.

46. Gat, *Nations*, 29.

47. Gat, *Nations*, 31–33; Colin J. Irwin, "A Study in the Evolution of Ethnocentrism," in *The Sociobiology of Ethnocentrism: Evolutionary Dimensions of Xenophobia, Discrimination, Racism and Nationalism*, ed. Vernon Reynolds, Vincent Falger, and Ian Vine (Athens: University of Georgia Press, 1987).

48. Joseph Henrich, *The Secret of Our Success: How Culture Is Driving Human Evolution, Domesticating Our Species and Making Us Smarter* (Princeton, N.J.: Princeton University Press, 2016).

49. Henrich, *The Secret of Our Success*, 57.

50. Lawrence H. Keeley, *War Before Civilization: The Myth of the Peaceful Savage* (New York: Oxford University Press, 1997); Azar Gat, *War in Human Civilization* (New York: Oxford University Press, 2006); Samuel Bowles and Herbert Gintis, *A Cooperative Species: Human Reciprocity and Its Evolution* (Princeton, N.J.: Princeton University Press, 2011).

51. Henrich, *The Secret of Our Success*, chap. 10.

52. Bowles and Gintis, *A Cooperative Species*, chap. 8.

53. After all, the minimal group school shows that it is possible to induce in-group bias by dividing subjects in laboratory-created groups based on trivial criteria such as the

tendency to underestimate or overestimate the number of dots on a screen. See Tajfel, *Human Groups and Social Categories*. In some civil wars (in particular those in Russia and Spain in the first half of the twentieth century), ideological identities have proven both relatively easy to observe and hard to change, thus resembling ethnic identities. See Kalyvas, "Ethnic Defection in Civil Wars"; Laia Balcells, *Rivalry and Revenge: The Politics of Violence During Civil War* (New York: Cambridge University Press, 2017).

54. On the tendency of violence to enhance the salience of ethnic categories and reinforce ethnic boundaries, see, among many others, James D. Fearon and David D. Laitin, "Violence and the Social Construction of Ethnic Identity," *International Organization* 54, no. 4 (Autumn 2000): 845–77; Steven I. Wilkinson, *Votes and Violence: Electoral Competition and Ethnic Riots in India* (New York: Cambridge University Press, 2004); Moses Shayo and Asaf Zussman, "Judicial Ingroup Bias in the Shadow of Terrorism," *Quarterly Journal of Economics* 126 (2011): 1447–84.

55. For similar reasoning about testing theories on the international balance of power, see William C. Wohlforth, *The Elusive Balance* (Ithaca, N.Y.: Cornell University Press, 1993); Copeland, *The Origins of Major War*.

56. On the method of interviewing elites in general and the importance of triangulating evidence in particular, see Layna Mosley, ed., *Interview Research in Political Science* (Ithaca, N.Y.: Cornell University Press, 2013); H. J. Davies, "Spies as Informants: Tri- angulation and Interpretation of Elite Interview Data in the Study of Intelligence and Security Services," *Politics* 21, no. 1 (2001): 73–80. In research on specific policy deci- sions there is typically a narrow population of relevant interviewees, and thus random sampling is not advisable. See Oisin Tansey, "Process Tracing and Elite Interviewing: A Case for Non-Probability Sampling," *PS: Political Science and Politics* 40, no. 4 (October 2007): 765–72; Julia F. Lynch "Aligning Sampling Strategies with Analytic Goals," in Mosley, *Interview Research in Political Science*. See the online appendix at https://constantinopischedda.com/data-replication-materials-and-additional-materials / for details on my "snowball" approach to finding appropriate interviewees and a com- plete list of my interview subjects.

57. On biases, see Robert Jervis "Understanding Beliefs," *Political Psychology* 27, no. 5 (2006): 641–63; Hartmut Blank, Jochen Musch, and Rüdiger F. Pohl, "Hindsight Bias: On Being Wise After the Event," *Social Cognition* 25, no. 1, (2007): 1–9. Perhaps the most radical objection to using decision makers' accounts as evidence comes from the experimental finding that much individual behavior is driven by unconscious feel- ings, preferences, and processes, and that actors' causal accounts of such behavior are no more accurate than those provided by outside observers. See Timothy D. Wilson, *Strangers to Ourselves: Discovering the Adaptive Unconscious* (Cambridge, Mass.: Har- vard University Press, 2004). This finding, however, has not gone unchallenged on theoretical and empirical grounds. See K. Anders Ericsson and Herbert A. Simon, "Verbal Reports as Data," *Psychological Review* 87, no. 3 (May 1980): 215–51; Igor Gavanski and Curt Hoffman, "Awareness of Influences on One's Own Judgments: The Roles of Covariation Detection and Attention to the Judgment Process," *Journal of Personality and Social Psychology* 52, no. 3 (1987): 453–63. Wilson himself

acknowledges that "often the conscious system gets it right" and "that people correctly recognize that their behavior was caused by situational demands" when "situational constraints or incentives are obvious." Wilson, *Strangers to Ourselves*, 128, 207.

58. In the jargon of political science, my case study inferential strategy combines process tracing and within-case congruence procedure. Process tracing involves reconstructing the chain of events and decisions leading to the outcomes of interest to see if it is consistent with the theory's observable implications. Congruence procedure consists in examining whether the independent variable (windows of opportunity and vulnerability) and dependent variable (inter-rebel war) covary as the theory suggests, holding constant background features of the case. See Alexander L. George and Andrew Bennett, *Case Studies and Theory Development in the Social Sciences* (Cambridge, Mass.: MIT Press, 2005), 181–204; Andrew Bennett and Jeffrey T. Checkel, eds., *Process Tracing: From Metaphor to Analytic Tool* (New York: Cambridge University Press, 2014).

59. On organizational cohesion as an aspect of insurgent military effectiveness, see Paul D. Kenny, "Structural Integrity and Cohesion in Insurgent Organizations: Evidence from Protracted Conflicts in Ireland and Burma," *International Studies Review* 12, no. 4 (2010): 533–55; Paul Staniland, *Networks of Rebellion: Explaining Insurgent Cohesion and Collapse* (Ithaca, N.Y.: Cornell University Press, 2014), 2–3. On tactical-operational skills as drivers of battlefield outcomes (in both interstate wars and fights involving nonstate actors), see Stephen Biddle, *Military Power: Explaining Victory and Defeat in Modern Battle* (Princeton, N.J.: Princeton University Press, 2004).

60. For example, if information is available on two dimensions of relative power, I code a group as stronger if it is clearly superior in at least one dimension and at least roughly equal in the other dimension.

61. On the trade-off between measurement validity and reliability, see David Collier, Henry E. Brady, and Jason Seawright, "Critiques, Responses, and Trade-Offs: Drawing Together the Debate," in *Rethinking Social Inquiry: Diverse Tools, Shared Standards*, ed. Henry E. Brady and David Collier, 2d ed. (Lanham, Md.: Rowman and Littlefield, 2010); John Gerring, *Social Science Methodology: A Unified Approach*, 2d ed. (New York: Cambridge University Press, 2012), chap. 7.

62. Besides the data reported in this book, the online appendix presents additional information and extensive quotations from primary and secondary sources used to code the presence of windows.

63. Krause, *Rebel Power*, 18, 206. Analogously, Daniel Corstange operationalizes "ethnic monopsony" as a situation in which a political constituency defined along ethnic lines is dominated by one vote-buying party rather than complete absence of any other party tapping into that pool of ethnic votes. Corstange, *The Price of a Vote*.

64. David E. Cunningham, "Veto Players and Civil War Duration," *American Journal of Political Science* 50, no. 4 (October 2006): 875–92; Hanne Fjelde and Desirée Nilsson, "The Rise of Rebel Contenders: Barriers to Entry and Fragmentation in Civil Wars," *Journal of Peace Research* 55, no. 5 (2018): 551–65; Barbara Walter, "Explaining the Number of Rebel Groups in Civil Wars," *International Interactions* 45, no. 1 (2019): 127.

192 2. Windows of Opportunity and Vulnerability

65. B. C. Upreti, "The Maoist Insurgency in Nepal: Nature, Growth and Impact," *South Asian Survey* 13, no. 1 (2006): 35–50; Janet I. Lewis, "How Does Ethnic Rebellion Start?" *Comparative Political Studies* 50, no. 10 (2017): 1420–50; Jennifer Larson and Janet I. Lewis, "Rumors, Kinship Networks, and Rebel Group Formation," *International Organization* 72, no. 4 (Fall 2018): 871–903.

66. Staniland, *Networks of Rebellion*. On the determinants of fragmentation in self-determination movements, see Lee Seymour, Kristin Bakke, and Kathleen Cunningham, "E Pluribus Unum, Ex Uno Plures: Competition, Violence, and Fragmentation in Ethnopolitical Movements," *Journal of Peace Research* 53, no. 1 (2016): 3–18.

67. Kenny, "Structural Integrity and Cohesion in Insurgent Organizations"; Victor Asal, Mitchell Brown, and Angela Dalton, "Why Split? Organizational Splits Among Ethnopolitical Organizations in the Middle East," *Journal of Conflict Resolution* 56, no. 1 (2012): 94–117; Fotini Christia, *Alliance Formation in Civil Wars* (New York: Cambridge University Press, 2012); Staniland, *Networks of Rebellion*; Henning Tamm, "Rebel Leaders, Internal Rivals, and External Resources: How State Sponsors Affect Insurgent Cohesion," *International Studies Quarterly* 60, no. 4 (2016): 599–610; Michael Woldemariam, *Insurgent Fragmentation in the Horn of Africa: Rebellion and its Discontents* (New York: Cambridge University Press, 2018); Eric S. Mosinger, "Balance of Loyalties: Explaining Rebel Factional Struggles in the Nicaraguan Revolution," *Security Studies* 28, no. 5 (2019): 935–75; Evan Perkoski, "Internal Politics and the Fragmentation of Armed Groups," *International Studies Quarterly*, 63, no. 4 (December 2019): 876–89.

68. Christopher H. Achen, *The Statistical Analysis of Quasi-Experiments* (Berkeley: University of California Press, 1986), 73–81.

69. Author's calculations based on data on self-determination movements worldwide from Seymour, Bakke, and Cunningham, "E Pluribus Unum."

70. Christia, *Alliance Formation in Civil Wars*.

71. Krause, *Rebel Power*.

72. This line of thinking can be inferred from the ethnic security dilemma literature. Barry R. Posen, "The Security Dilemma and Ethnic Conflict," *Survival* 35, no. 1 (Spring 1993): 27–47; Chaim D. Kaufmann, "Possible and Impossible Solutions to Ethnic Conflict," *International Security* 20, no. 4 (Spring 1996): 136–75.

73. For a review of arguments about the effects of leader-level attributes in international politics, see Jervis, "Do Leaders Matter?"

74. Matthew Kocher and coauthors argue that ideological differences along the left-right spectrum determined in which of two opposing camps self-proclaimed nationalists in occupied France ended up—those cooperating with the Nazis or those violently resisting them. Matthew A. Kocher, Adria K. Lawrence, and Nuno P. Monteiro, "Nationalism, Collaboration, and Resistance: France Under Nazi Occupation," *International Security* 43, no. 2 (Fall 2018): 117–50.

75. Window theory emphasizes the cumulativity of social resources over which coethnic rebel groups compete, but natural resources may offer an alternative explanation for inter-rebel war. Regardless of their ethnic or ideological backgrounds, rebel

groups may clash for control of assets such as oil and diamond fields, drug cultivation, and contraband routes, as these resources, besides potentially enriching their leadership, may significantly affect the outcome of the antigovernment struggle by enabling the purchase of more and better weapons as well as recruitment and retainment of fighters. I address this alternative explanation in the statistical analysis in chapter 6.

76. This distinction can be conceptualized in terms of the nature and scope of groups' policy goals (e.g., autonomy rather than independence) or of their willingness to pay costs and run risks to achieve their full objectives rather than accepting less extensive concessions from the government. See Stephen Stedman, "Spoiler Problems in Peace Processes," *International Security* 22, no. 2 (Fall 1997): 5–53; Andrew Kydd and Barbara Walter, "Sabotaging the Peace: The Politics of Extremist Violence," *International Organization* 56 no. 2 (Spring 2002): 263–96; Ethan Bueno de Mesquita, "Conciliation, Counterterrorism, and Patterns of Terrorist Violence," *International Organization* 59, no. 1 (January 2005): 145–76.

77. For an argument about how third-party states can affect inter-rebel relations by attenuating commitment problems among rebels, see Navin A. Bapat and Kanisha D. Bond, "Alliances Between Militant Groups," *British Journal of Political Science* 42, no. 4 (October 2012): 793–824. Tamm shows that carefully targeted external support can affect the balance of power among factions *within* rebel organizations. The same dynamic should apply to the balance of power between rebel organizations. This form of external influence could affect the prospects of inter-rebel war by creating windows of opportunity and windows of vulnerability, but it does not amount to a distinct alternative explanation, as infighting would occur through the mechanisms envisioned by window theory. Tamm, "Rebel Leaders, Internal Rivals."

78. For an argument about how government strategies may create fissures within rebel movements, see Patrick Johnston, "Negotiated Settlements and Government Strategy in Civil War: Evidence from Darfur," *Civil Wars* 9, no. 4 (2007): 359–77. On "wedge strategies" in international politics, see Timothy W. Crawford, "Preventing Enemy Coalitions: How Wedge Strategies Shape Power Politics," *International Security* 35, no. 4 (Spring 2011): 155–89.

79. Bakke, Cunningham, and Seymour, "Shirts Today, Skins Tomorrow"; Kathleen Gallagher Cunningham, *Inside the Politics of Self-Determination* (Oxford: Oxford University Press, 2014), 130–31. These studies suggest that this dynamic should be more likely the higher the number of coethnic organizations, so in the statistical analysis presented in chapter 6 I control for the number of coethnic rivals.

3. Inter-rebel War in the Shadow of Genocide

1. Author interview, Erbil, Iraq, November 2012.
2. Quoted in Chris Kutschera, *Le Défi Kurde ou le Rêve Fou de l'Indépendance* (Paris: Bayard Editions, 1997), 123 (interview by Kutschera, 1992).

3. Dietrich Rueschemeyer, "Can One or a Few Cases Yield Theoretical Gains?," in *Comparative Historical Analysis in the Social Sciences*, ed. James Mahoney and Dietrich Rueschemeyer (New York: Cambridge University Press, 2003), 316. As Donald Campbell observes, "Even in a single qualitative case study the conscientious social scientist often finds no explanation that seems satisfactory." Donald T. Campbell, "'Degrees of Freedom' and the Case Study," *Comparative Political Studies* 8, no. 2 (July 1975): 182.

4. Marc Trachtenberg, *The Craft of International History: A Guide to Method* (Princeton, N.J.: Princeton University Press, 2006).

5. Trachtenberg, *The Craft of International History*, 29.

6. While references to internecine Kurdish conflict are ubiquitous in the literature, systematic analyses are scarce. To my knowledge, the only publications specifically on the topic are Michael M. Gunter, "The KDP-PUK Conflict in Northern Iraq," *Middle East Journal* 50, no. 2 (Spring 1996): 224–41; Hanna Yousif Freij, "Tribal Identity and Alliance Behaviour Among Factions of the Kurdish National Movement in Iraq," *Nationalism and Ethnic Politics* 3, no. 3 (Fall 1997): 86–110.

7. See, for example, International Crisis Group, "Arming Iraq's Kurds: Fighting IS, Inviting Conflict," *Middle East Report* 158 (2015); Dexter Filkins, "Kurdish Dreams of Independence Delayed Again," *New Yorker*, October 16, 2017.

8. For an overview of earlier Kurdish history, see David McDowall, *A Modern History of the Kurds* (London: I. B. Tauris, 2007).

9. Edmund Ghareeb, *The Kurdish Question in Iraq* (Syracuse, N.Y.: Syracuse University Press, 1981), 35–40; Sa'ad Jawad, *Iraq and the Kurdish Question, 1958–1970* (London: Ithaca Press, 1981), 37–67; Nader Entessar, *Kurdish Politics in the Middle East* (Lanham, Md.: Lexington Books, 2010), 81.

10. Barzani received the honorary title of president of the KDP when in exile in the Soviet Union and maintained the position after his return to Iraq in 1958. Most politburo members were loyalists of Ahmed and Talabani. See McDowall, *A Modern History of the Kurds*, 302–6.

11. David Adamson, *The Kurdish War* (London: Allen & Unwin, 1964), 98; Ismet Chériff Vanly, *Kurdistan Irakien Entité Nationale: Étude de la Révolution de 1961* (Neuchâtel: Éditions de la Baconnière, 1970), 99–100; Edgar O'Ballance, *The Kurdish Revolt: 1961–1970* (Hamden, Conn.: Archon Books, 1973), 78–81; Jawad, *Iraq and the Kurdish Question*, 80–85; McDowall, *A Modern History of the Kurds*, 310–11.

12. Primary and secondary sources consistently describe the two groups as having distinct forces under separate chains of command and operating in distinct parts of Iraqi Kurdistan. For example, Dr. Mahmoud Osman, Barzani's close collaborator, describes the two entities in the following terms: "They operated in separate areas, they had separate forces under their command: essentially two separate regions and two separate revolutions with only weak connections between the two." Author interview, December 2012, Erbil, Iraq. See also O'Ballance, *The Kurdish Revolt*, 87–88; Jawad, *Iraq and the Kurdish Question*, 80–85; Nawshirwan Mustafa Amin, *From the Danube Shores to the Nawzang Valley: Political Events in Iraqi Kurdistan from 1975 to 1978* (Sulaimania, Iraqi Kurdistan, 1997), 65–66; Gareth R. V. Stansfield, *Iraqi*

Kurdistan: Political Development and Emergent Democracy (London: RoutledgeCur-
zon, 2003), 70.

13. Martin Van Bruinessen, "The Kurds Between Iran and Iraq," *MERIP Middle East
Report* 141 (1986): 14–27. Badinan largely corresponds to today's Duhok governorate
and part of the Erbil governorate north of the Great Zab River.

14. Vanly, *Kurdistan Irakien Entité Nationale*, 107, 145–77; O'Ballance, *The Kurdish Revolt*,
78–121; Ghareeb, *The Kurdish Question in Iraq*, 66–67; Jawad, *Iraq and the Kurdish
Question*, 142–73.

15. Author interview with Mahmoud Osman; Vanly, *Kurdistan Irakien Entité Nationale*,
224–25, 259–63; O'Ballance, *The Kurdish Revolt*, 125–27, 133–35; Jawad, *Iraq and the
Kurdish Question*, 173–80, 218n52; Van Bruinessen, "The Kurds Between Iran and
Iraq," 22.

16. Vanly, *Kurdistan Irakien Entité Nationale*, 274–75; O'Ballance, *The Kurdish Revolt*, 137,
151–52; Jawad, *Iraq and the Kurdish Question*, 205–14, 241–51; Van Bruinessen, "The
Kurds Between Iran and Iraq," 22; Michael M. Gunter, *The Kurdish Predicament in
Iraq: A Political Analysis* (New York: St. Martin's Press, 1999), 26.

17. Ghareeb, *The Kurdish Question in Iraq*, 136–37; Jawad, *Iraq and the Kurdish Question*,
250–52; McDowall, *A Modern History of the Kurds*, 326–27.

18. O'Ballance, *The Kurdish Revolt*, 159–63; Ghareb, *The Kurdish Question in Iraq*, 86, 100.
According to Adel Murad, the six thousand fighters under Talabani were integrated
on an individual basis in separate regional branches of the KDP forces. The late Adel
Murad was Barzani's affiliate at the time of the events and later one of the PUK's
founders; he was a high-ranking PUK member at the time of the interviews with the
author in November 2012 in Sulaimania, Iraq. Talabani was readmitted in the KDP
but was sent to Beirut (and later Damascus) as its representative in a soft form of exile,
while Ahmed did not return to Kurdistan. See Kamran Karadaghi, "The Two Gulf
Wars: The Kurds on the World Stage, 1979–1992," in *People Without a Country: The
Kurds and Kurdistan*, ed. Gérard Chaliand (London: Zed Press, 1993), 219; Gunter, *The
Kurdish Predicament in Iraq*, 26; McDowall, *A Modern History of the Kurds*, 343.

19. Ghareeb, *The Kurdish Question in Iraq*, 147–74; McDowall, *A Modern History of the
Kurds*, 327–35.

20. Asadollah Alam, *The Shah and I: The Confidential Diary of Iran's Royal Court, 1969–
1977* (New York: I. B. Tauris, 1991), 417–18; McDowall, *A Modern History of the Kurds*,
337–39; Ofra Bengio, *The Kurds of Iraq: Building a State Within a State* (Boulder, Colo.:
Lynne Rienner, 2012), 132–42; *Foreign Relations of the United States, 1969–1976*, vol. 27:
Iran; Iraq, 1973–1976, documents 275–76 and 279 (2012), available at https://history
.state.gov/historicaldocuments/frus1969-76v27; Arash Reisinezhad, *The Shah of Iran,
the Iraqi Kurds, and the Lebanese Shia* (Cham, Switzerland: Palgrave Macmillan,
2019), 147–49, 162–73, 212–28.

21. Ghareeb, *The Kurdish Question in Iraq*, 156–74; Bengio, *The Kurds of Iraq*, 142–48.

22. Van Bruinessen, "The Kurds Between Iran and Iraq," 22–26; Mustafa, *Danube Shores
to the Nawzang Valley*, 43–65; Kutschera, *Le Défi Kurde*, 31–46; McDowall, *A Modern
History of the Kurds*, 343–47. The Socialist Party came into existence in August 1979 as

one of the constitutive PUK's factions—the Social Democratic Movement—splintered off and merged with a small group led by Mahmoud Osman. The Communist Party found refuge in the Kurdish mountains in the fall of 1979, after its expulsion from the ruling National Front.

23. Van Bruinessen, "The Kurds Between Iran and Iraq," 24.

24. Author interviews in December 2012 in Sulaimania, Iraq, with Shoresh Hadji, PUK military commander during the Iran-Iraq War and member of the Kurdish Regional Government (KRG) Parliament with the opposition party Gorran at the time of the interview; Mohammad "Hama" Tofiq, high-ranking member of the PUK at the time of the events and senior Gorran member at the time of the interview; Farid Asasard, senior PUK member since 1978; and Mala Baxtiar, PUK military commander at the time of the events and PUK politburo member at the time of the interview.

25. Van Bruinessen, "The Kurds Between Iran and Iraq," 19, 25–26.

26. Nawshirwan Mustafa Amin, *Going Around in Circles: The Inside Story of Events in Iraqi Kurdistan, 1984–1988* (Sulaimania, Iraqi Kurdistan, 1999), 72–85; Kutschera, *Le Défi Kurde*, 70–75; McDowall, *A Modern History of the Kurds*, 348–51.

27. Anthony H. Cordesman and Abraham R. Wagner, *The Lessons of Modern War*, vol. 2: *The Iran-Iraq War* (Boulder, Colo.: Westview Press, 1990), 178–216; McDowall, *A Modern History of the Kurds*, 351–52; Joost R. Hiltermann, *A Poisonous Affair: America, Iraq, and the Gassing of Halabja* (New York: Cambridge University Press, 2007), 90–92; Steven R. Ward, *Immortal: A Military History of Iran and Its Armed Forces* (Washington, D.C.: Georgetown University Press, 2009), 265–66.

28. Cordesman and Wagner, *The Lessons of Modern War*, 353–403; McDowall, *A Modern History of the Kurds*, 352–60; Hiltermann, *A Poisonous Affair*.

29. Sheri Laizer, *Martyrs, Traitors and Patriots: Kurdistan After the Cold War* (London: Zed Books, 1996), 2–52; Gordon W. Rudd, *Humanitarian Intervention: Assisting the Iraqi Kurds in Operation PROVIDE COMFORT, 1991* (Washington, D.C.: Department of the Army, 2004).

30. O'Ballance, *A Modern History of the Kurds*, 387–91.

31. Adamson, *The Kurdish War*, 91; Vanly, *Kurdistan Irakien Entité Nationale*, 99–100; O'Ballance, *The Kurdish Revolt*, 84–85; Jawad, *Iraq and the Kurdish Question*, 80–85. Jawad explicitly speaks of the Ahmed-Talabani group's "inferior fighting capacity" (84).

32. Author interview, November 2012, Erbil, Iraq. Khursheed Shera was KDP member of the KRG Parliament at the time of the interview. In an interview with the author, Mahmoud Osman also noted the military superiority of the Barzani faction.

33. The only exception is O'Ballance, who claims that the Ahmed-Talabani fighters "were better disciplined, organized and controlled" but also reports a much larger numerical imbalance between the two factions than other sources (about 15,000 vs. 650 fighters), leaving in any case little doubt about the overall superiority of Barzani's forces. O'Ballance, *The Kurdish Revolt*, 104.

34. O'Ballance, *The Kurdish Revolt*, 88–89. Barzani's forces managed to disrupt the preparations for a large-scale government offensive due to start in mid-May 1962. See Dana Adams Schmidt, *Journey Among Brave Men* (Boston: Little, Brown, 1964), 82–84.

35. For a discussion of the ideological position of the Arab nationalist forces (and the Baath Party in particular) opposed to Qassem, see, for example, Vanly, *Kurdistan Irakien Entité Nationale*, 159–60. Vanly also reports that in December 1962 (two months before the coup), the KDP politburo issued a resolution concluding that Iraq's nationalist parties (including the Baath) had a "chauvinist attitude, against the Kurdish people, against its national demands, against our revolution."

36. Chris Kutschera, *Le Mouvement National Kurde* (Paris: Frammarion, 1979), 226; O'Ballance, *The Kurdish Revolt*, 97–98; Kenneth M. Pollack, *Arabs at War: Military Effectiveness, 1948–1991* (Lincoln: University of Nebraska Press, 2002), 158–59; McDowall, *A Modern History of the Kurds*, 313. In November 1962 a Lebanese newspaper revealed that a group of officers of the Iraqi general staff had presented a memorandum to Qassem criticizing his management of the war along the lines mentioned. See Vanly, *Kurdistan Irakien Entité Nationale*, 158–59.

37. Eric Rouleau, "Bagdad Accorde l'Autonomie au Kurdistan Irakien," *Le Monde*, March 12, 1963.

38. Pollack, *Arabs at War*, 158.

39. Jawad reports that in "March and April both sides [the rebels and the government] began to reinforce their positions." Jawad, *Iraq and the Kurdish Question*, 146.

40. O'Ballance, *The Kurdish Revolt*, 107–15. The fellow Baathist Syrian government had contributed a five-thousand-strong brigade (and airpower support) to the Iraqi government's offensive against the Kurds in the summer of 1963.

41. Jawad, *Iraq and the Kurdish Question*, 158–59, 165; McDowall, *A Modern History of the Kurds*, 316; author interview with Mahmoud Osman.

42. Several observers report that Barzani was deeply concerned about the exhaustion of the Kurdish population. See, for example, Kutschera, *Le Mouvement National Kurde*, 245–46; Nawshirwan Mustafa Amin, *Fingers That Break Each Other: Political Events in Kurdistan from 1979 to 1983* (Sulaimania, Iraqi Kurdistan, 1998), 74.

43. Author interview, November 2012, Erbil, Iraq. Later on Sa'id Kaka became a military leader in the PUK (1975–1979) and the Socialist Party (from 1979); at the time of the interview, he was a KDP member of the KRG Parliament. In another interview, Khursheed Shera, a peshmerga on Barzani's side from 1961 and later KDP commander, corroborates this account, noting that "the Iraqi army was tired and needed a break, as it was busy killing Baathists. They needed a break to reorganize. They did not consider it [the February 1964 ceasefire] a final agreement. . . . Barzani understood Baghdad's position on this." Importantly, the Ahmed-Talabani group shared this assessment of the government's political and military weakness. See Kutschera, *Le Mouvement National Kurde*, 246–47; O'Ballance, *The Kurdish Revolt*, 114, 119.

44. Jonathan Randal, *Kurdistan: After Such Knowledge, What Forgiveness?* (London: Bloomsbury, 1998), 177.

45. Tensions between the two groups had existed since before the onset of the war against Baghdad. See Jawad, *Iraq and the Kurdish Question*, 160–63. Several observers report that since 1962 Barzani expressed to visitors his contempt and distrust toward the Ahmed-Talabani faction; on his part, Ahmed labeled Barzani as repressive, tribal, and

"a Kurdish de Gaulle." See Adamson, *The Kurdish War*, passim; Vanly, *Kurdistan Irakien Entité Nationale*, 221; Jawad, *Iraq and the Kurdish Question*, 184. Reportedly, in 1963 Barzani accused the Ahmed-Talabani faction of collusion with the government for not doing anything to ease the pressure on his forces during an earlier offensive by Qassem. See Jawad, *Iraq and the Kurdish Question*, 163. According to Vanly, in 1963 Barzani gave an ominous hint of what was to follow, saying that he "might have to bring to reason the faction of the politburo [the Ahmed-Talabani group]." Vanly, *Kurdistan Irakien Entité Nationale*, 221.

46.   Author interview. Osman was a member of the KDP leadership since 1964 and is often referred to in the literature as Barzani's right hand and de facto foreign minister. After 1975 Osman vehemently criticized Barzani for his mismanagement of the struggle in its last phases. This does not necessarily undermine, however, the credibility of his account of the 1964 events. Osman would not have an interest in portraying Barzani in a negative light in this episode because he himself was indirectly implicated as a new member of the leadership of Barzani's group. Moreover, he has long been an independent figure in Iraqi Kurdistan's political landscape and is widely respected as a nonpartisan, balanced observer. Several authors offer a consistent reading of the events of 1964. See, e.g., Jawad, *Iraq and the Kurdish Question*, 153–76; John Bulloch and Harvey Morris, *No Friends but the Mountains: The Tragic History of the Kurds* (London: Viking, 1992), 127.

47.   O'Ballance reports that after defeating the Ahmed-Talabani group, Barzani "was able to strengthen his grass roots support and his hold on the Kurdish political machine which was fast developing in Kurdish territory." O'Ballance, *The Kurdish Revolt*, 121. See also Kutschera, *Le Mouvement National Kurde*, 250–53. For a detailed description of the complex institutional apparatus through which Barzani's KDP controlled the Kurdish movement and the liberated areas after the episode of inter-rebel war, see Vanly, *Kurdistan Irakien Entité Nationale*, 238–52. After its flip to Baghdad's side in 1966, the Ahmed-Talabani group had a presence in Kurdistan only in Sulaimania, Kirkuk, and Erbil, which remained under government control as other major urban centers. See Vanly, *Kurdistan Irakien Entité Nationale*, 275.

48.   Kutschera, *Le Mouvement National Kurde*, 252–53.

49.   Mustafa, *Danube Shores to the Nawzang Valley*, 71, 93–96.

50.   The PUK was born from the merger of three smaller groups: Komala (a Marxist-Leninist, Kurdish nationalist organization that had operated clandestinely in Sorani areas since 1970), the Social Democratic Movement (led by former prominent KDP members, in particular Ali Askari), and the General Line (a group of influential Kurdish personalities who returned from abroad and did not have a large organization on the ground in Kurdistan). Positions in PUK leadership organs and local branches were allocated so as to ensure the representation of each of its components. It is nonetheless appropriate to speak of the PUK as a single rebel organization because it had a unified chain of command under Talabani's leadership; none of the three components had authority over military issues, finances, and political relations with other groups and the government, nor did they have their own distinct peshmerga forces. See

Christiane More, *Les Kurdes Auhjourd'hui: Mouvement National and Partis Politiques* (Paris: L'Harmattan, 1984), 120–22; Mustafa, *Danube Shores to the Nawzang Valley*, 171–75, 336; Stansfield, *Iraqi Kurdistan*, 79–84.

51. PUK Declaration of Formation, June 1, 1975, Damascus, Syria (provided to the author by Faridoun Abd-Al Qader, PUK founding member). See also McDowall, *A Modern History of the Kurds*, 343.

52. At least according to PUK sources. See Mustafa, *Danube Shores to the Nawzang Valley*, 95.

53. Karadaghi, "The Two Gulf Wars," 219–20; Kutschera, *Le Défi Kurde*, 40. Buoyed by rapidly expanding oil revenues, Baghdad conducted a major buildup of its armed forces in the aftermath of the Algiers Agreement of 1975. See Bengio, *The Kurds of Iraq*, 153–55.

54. Mustafa, *Danube Shores to the Nawzang Valley*, 130, 144–47, 157. In the summer of 1977 Nawshirwan Mustafa, PUK's unofficial deputy commander, briefed Talabani on the dire conditions of the organization's forces in the field, describing the intense pressure brought on them by the government offensive, which had caused a large number of defections from the insurgent ranks. Mustafa, *Danube Shores to the Nawzang Valley*, 166. See also Kutschera, *Le Défi Kurde*, 40, for a description of the massive forces deployed by Baghdad in Kurdistan in the summer of 1977. The government kept up the pressure in 1978. See Mustafa, *Danube Shores to the Nawzang Valley*, 211–16.

55. Libya was also supporting the PUK, but for geographical reasons its aid needed to go through Syria to reach Iraqi Kurdistan. The shortage of weapons in Kurdistan was especially acute because the Iraqi government had launched a successful weapons buyback program after defeating the Kurds in 1975, offering financial rewards for turning in guns and threatening capital punishment for illegal possession; the government collected over 150,000 small arms. See Mustafa, *Danube Shores to the Nawzang Valley*, 96.

56. Mustafa, *Danube Shores to the Nawzang Valley*, 95–96; Kutschera, *Le Défi Kurde*, 42; Farid Asasard, *Political Atlas of Kurdistan Region, 1914–2005* (Sulaimania, Iraqi Kurdistan, 2010), 125–26. As Nawshirwan Mustafa put it in his memoirs, "Badinan . . . was the only way to get to the outside world, the only gateway for weapons and ammunition and so we could not give up on it" (125).

57. McDowall, *A Modern History of the Kurds*, 344; Van Bruinessen, "The Kurds Between Iran and Iraq," 23.

58. Thomas Schelling, *Arms and Influence* (New Haven, Conn.: Yale University Press, 1966), 66–69.

59. Mustafa, *Danube Shores to the Nawzang Valley*, 121–23, 178–79.

60. For example, in an interview with the author, PUK founding member Adel Murad expressed his strong suspicion that the attacks were part of an overarching KDP plan to nip in the bud the PUK, but he acknowledged not to have seen direct evidence of such a plan. Moreover, until 1979 the KDP political leadership (mostly based outside of Iraq) was not fully in control of the military commanders on the ground; it is thus possible that the two small-scale attacks occurred without the leadership's orders or

authorization. See Kutchera, *Le Défi Kurde*, 39. Nawshirwan Mustafa reports that there were also skirmishes between PUK and the KDP forces in Sorani areas; the PUK either disarmed the local KDP forces, absorbed them in the organization, or pushed them out of the region. Mustafa, *Danube Shores to the Nawzang Valley*, 195–96, 218–19.

61. Talabani sent several letters to this effect to KDP leaders. See Mustafa, *Danube Shores to the Nawzang Valley*, 96.

62. Mustafa, *Danube Shores to the Nawzang Valley*, 121–23, 129.

63. Mustafa, *Danube Shores to the Nawzang Valley*, 130–31, 135.

64. Mustafa, *Danube Shores to the Nawzang Valley*, 158–59, 161–62, 178; author interviews with Omar Said Ali, high-ranking PUK member at the time of the events (in the leadership of Gorran Party at the time of the interview), December 2012, Sulaimania, Iraq; and Adel Murad.

65. For example, in an interview with the author, Khursheed Shera argued that by creating the PUK, "Talabani wanted somehow to get back at Barzani," and that the primary conclusion of one of the PUK's first meetings was that the KDP should be considered an enemy. Muhsin Dizai (close advisor to Mullah Mustafa Barzani and senior KDP member at the time of the interview) claimed that the tensions between the two organizations were due to the fact that the PUK wanted to control Badinan. Author interview, November 2012, Erbil, Iraq. Even if Talabani repeatedly tried to cooperate with the KDP, the PUK's Declaration of Formation and subsequent communiques did lend themselves to an aggressive interpretation: the PUK accused the KDP leadership of having colluded with imperialist forces hostile to the Kurdish people and having shamefully abandoned the battlefield in 1975; the PUK also proclaimed its duty to be the leader of the new revolution.

66. In an interview with the author, Omar Said Ali (high-ranking PUK member at the time) hinted that a change in the group's intentions over time was not a far-fetched possibility, as he noted that within the PUK in those early years two views confronted each other—one was in favor of cooperation with the KDP against the common enemy (Baghdad), while the other advocated fighting against Kurdish conservative forces (the KDP).

67. Mustafa, *Danube Shores to the Nawzang Valley*, 168–70, 179.

68. Mustafa, *Danube Shores to the Nawzang Valley*, 256, 264–65.

69. Mustafa, *Danube Shores to the Nawzang Valley*, 266–69; Farid Asasard, *Political Atlas of Kurdistan Region*, 131–32.

70. Mustafa, *Danube Shores to the Nawzang Valley*, 270–71. See also More, *Les Kurdes Auhjourd'hui*, 124.

71. McDowall, *A Modern History of the Kurds*, 344–45; Mustafa, *Danube Shores to the Nawzang Valley*, 273–77, 278–89.

72. Mustafa, *Danube Shores to the Nawzang Valley*, 321; author interview with Omar Said Ali.

73. Author interviews with Mulazin Omar (PUK military commander from the group's early days; no longer politically active at the time of the interview), November 2012,

Sulaimania, Iraq; Salar Aziz (member of the Ahmed-Talabani faction and then high-ranking PUK member since the organization's early days; senior figure of the Gorran Party at the time of the interview), December 2012, Sulaimania, Iraq; Fouad Yassin (KDP peshmerga until 1975 and then PUK foot soldier in the years 1976–1978; not politically active at the time of the interview), November 2012, Sulaimania, Iraq; Shoresh Hadji; Mohammad Tofiq; Omar Said Ali; Farid Asasard; and Mala Baxtiar. Importantly, these PUK-related subjects do not necessarily have similar incentive structures: as several of them left the PUK and publicly or privately criticized it, their consistent accounts of the group's preference for avoiding military confrontation gain credibility.

74. Author interviews with Shoresh Hadji and Omar Said Ali. According to the KDP's narrative of the event, the PUK had planned to destroy the KDP headquarters on its way to Syria. See Van Bruinessen, "The Kurds Between Iran and Iraq," 24; author interview with Mala Mohamed (high-ranking KDP member at the time of the events and of the interview), December 2012, Salahadin, Iraq. Some renowned scholars implicitly endorse the KDP's interpretation of the event, but they do not provide specific supporting evidence. See Stansfield, *Iraqi Kurdistan*, 87–89; McDowall, *A Modern History of the Kurds*, 344–45.

75. The estimates of the PUK's manpower losses range quite widely, from around 25 percent (according to Van Bruinessen and Kutschera) to almost 60 percent (according to Stansfield and my interviewee Salar Aziz); the percentages are calculated based on a total figure of twelve hundred peshmerga put forth by my interviewee Farid Asasard. Van Bruinessen, "The Kurds Between Iran and Iraq," 24; Kutschera, *Le Défi Kurde*, 42; Stansfield, *Iraqi Kurdistan*, 88. Nawshirwan Mustafa reports that "the PUK lost most of its forces," in *Danube Shores to the Nawzang Valley*, 289.

76. Kutschera, *Le Défi Kurde*, 42–43; Van Bruinessen, "The Kurds Between Iran and Iraq," 23–26. The PUK's breakaway faction merged with Mahmoud Osman's tiny group to form the Socialist Party. After the KDP's debacle in 1975, Osman had openly criticized Barzani and created an organization, the KDP-Preparatory Committee, later renamed the United Socialist Party of Kurdistan. Several observers link the PUK's defeat in 1978 to its subsequent fragmentation. See, in particular, Mustafa, *Danube Shores to the Nawzang Valley*, 336; Van Bruinessen, "The Kurds Between Iran and Iraq," 25.

77. More, *Les Kurdes Auhjourd'hui*, 142; Kutschera, *Le Défi Kurde*, 45–47.

78. Van Bruinessen, "The Kurds Between Iran and Iraq," 26–27; Mehrdad R. Izady, *The Kurds: A Concise Handbook* (Washington, D.C.: Taylor & Francis, 1992), 215; Tareq Y. Ismael, *The Rise and Fall of the Communist Party of Iraq* (New York: Cambridge University Press, 2008), 192, 289–91.

79. Both Nawshirwan Mustafa and Shoresh Hadji stress the reduced threat posed by Baghdad as the war with Iran started. Mustafa, *Fingers That Break Each Other*, 182; author interview with Shoresh Hadji.

80. Van Bruinessen, "The Kurds Between Iran and Iraq," 27.

81. Author interview with Farid Asasard.

82. Author interviews with Khursheed Shera, Mulazin Omar, and Mahmoud Osman.

83. Van Bruinessen, "The Kurds Between Iran and Iraq," 26–27.

84. Adnan Mufti (high-ranking Socialist Party member at that time of the events and member of the PUK politburo at the time of the interview) observed that the fact that the Socialist and Communist Parties operated in Sorani areas and thus were inevitably involved with the PUK in a power struggle for control of those areas influenced their decision to ally with the KPD rather than the PUK. Moreover, he suggested that the Socialist Party's desire to establish warmer relations with Iran, which was allied with the KDP, played a role in the Socialists' decision to ally with the KDP. Author interview, December 2012, Erbil, Iraq. The group Pasok was also a member of the alliance. I do not include the organization in the analysis because of the dearth of information about it. The fact that several important sources do not even mention Pasok (for example, Van Bruinessen's "The Kurds Between Iran and Iraq"), and those that do mention it hint at its small size, suggests that it was below the threshold of extreme weakness, even though precise figures for group members are hard to come by. More, *Les Kurdes Auhjourd'hui*, 136, reports that the other Kurdish rebel groups estimated the membership of Pasok at less than a hundred in 1983. See also Kutschera, *Le Défi Kurde*, 318n27; Mustafa, *Danube Shores to the Nawzang Valley*, 221–22. When the PUK attacked the bases of the National Democratic Front in 1983, Pasok forces too were expelled from Soran.

85. In 1981 the Front members combined had twice as many fighters as the PUK. See Van Bruinessen, "The Kurds Between Iran and Iraq," 27.

86. Kutschera, *Le Défi Kurde*, 56. As Adnan Mufti noted in an interview with the author when discussing the skirmishes between the PUK and the other parties operating in Sorani areas, "Often the fighting was not preplanned; there were disputes in villages, sometimes about a girl, sometimes a local commander would try to show he was especially tough." Consistently, Nawshirwan Mustafa describes a pattern of clashes sparked by local and personal disputes, rather than an all-out fight directed by the organizations' leaderships. Mustafa, *Fingers That Break Each Other*, 188–92, 207–20.

87. Mustafa, *Fingers That Break Each Other*, 222; author interviews with Shoresh Hadji, Omar Said Ali, and Mala Baxtiar. Secondary sources make similar observations. See, e.g., Van Bruinessen, "The Kurds Between Iran and Iraq," 25–26.

88. Mustafa, *Fingers That Break Each Other*, 252–56.

89. Kutschera, *Le Défi Kurde*, 56–58; Mustafa, *Fingers That Break Each Other*, 279; McDowall, *A Modern History of the Kurds*, 347.

90. Author interviews with Faridoun Abd-Al Qader, senior PUK member involved in diplomatic contacts with both the Iranian and Iraqi governments (November 2012, Sulaimania, Iraq), and Farid Asasard.

91. Author interview with Faridoun Abd-Al Qader. In an interview with the author, Shoresh Hadji also stressed how the PUK saw Iran's religious leaders as inevitably ill-disposed toward the group for ideological, ethnic, and religious reasons. In the face of a low chance of Iranian support, the PUK's ideological and emotional reluctance to abandon the KDPI prevailed. See interviews with Faridoun Abd-Al Qader, Mulazin Omar, and Shoresh Hadji, as well as Mustafa, *Fingers That Break Each Other*, 267.

3. Inter-rebel War in the Shadow of Genocide   203

92. Mustafa, *Fingers That Break Each Other*, 204–5.

93. Cordesman and Wagner, *The Lessons of Modern War*, 153–65.

94. Kutschera, *Le Défi Kurde ou le Rêve Fou de l'Indépendance*, 60; Mustafa, *Fingers that Break Each Other*, 264.

95. Cordesman and Wagner, *The Lessons of Modern War*, 166.

96. Van Bruinessen, "The Kurds Between Iran and Iraq," 26; Ismael, *The Rise and Fall of the Communist Party of Iraq*, 201–2.

97. Mustafa, *Fingers That Break Each Other*, 280, 289–90.

98. As Nawshirwan Mustafa implies in his memoir, the PUK leadership was aware that supporting the KDPI in its fight against Iran would do little to endear itself to Tehran: "The PUK's stance was more an emotional reaction than a strategic calculation. KDPI was defeated and pushed out of Iran. . . . The PUK's help could not have sufficed to defend the KDPI but it would anger Iran." Mustafa, *Fingers That Break Each Other*, 267. We should be careful not to rely unduly on hindsight in making sense of the PUK's calculus: the two Iranian offensives in areas of PUK operations in 1983 (aimed at both weakening Iraqi forces and finishing off the KDPI) occurred in the summer and fall, that is, just *after* this episode of inter-rebel war. See Cordesman and Wagner, *The Lessons of Modern War*, 166–67, 175–78; Bulloch and Morris, *No Friends but the Mountains*, 152; Hiltermann, *A Poisonous Affair*, 29–32; Ibrahim Al-Marashi and Sammy Salama, *Iraq's Armed Forces: An Analytical History* (New York: Routledge, 2008), 142. The PUK, however, likely saw with concern the presence of Iranian forces across the border, in a context in which Iran was openly hostile toward the group and had launched several cross-border offensives further south against Iraqi forces.

99. Mustafa, *Fingers That Break Each Other*, 296.

100. The military arm of the Supreme Council for Islamic Revolution in Iraq (SCIRI, a Shia antigovernment group supported by Iran) participated in the offensives and established a foothold in Iraqi Kurdistan. The KDP-SCIRI is a pair of non-coethnic rebel groups that could have fought each other but did not, as window theory predicts. However, given the paucity of the evidence at my disposal and the fact that Iranian sponsorship of both groups is also a plausible explanation for the absence of inter-rebel war, I do not include SCIRI in the analysis. See Hanna Batatu, "Shi'i Organizations in Iraq: Ad-Da'wah al-Islamiyah and al-Mujahidin," in *Shi'ism and Social Protest*, ed. Juan R. I. Cole and Nikki R. Keddie (New Haven, Conn.: Yale University Press, 1986), 197; Dilip Hiro, *The Longest War: The Iran-Iraq Military Conflict* (New York: Routledge, 1991), 96–97, 150; Hiltermann, *A Poisonous Affair*, 29.

101. PUK leaders Mulazin Omar, Faridoun Abd-Al Qader (in interviews with the author), and Nawshirwan Mustafa (in *Fingers That Break Each Other*, 331–32) explicitly said that the decision to negotiate with Baghdad was dictated by the difficult military position of the group, in addition to the hope that Saddam Hussein might be willing to make real concessions given Iranian successes on the battlefield. These accounts are made more credible by the fact that Adel Murad, who opposed the decision to negotiate with Baghdad in 1983, responded as follows to my direct question about whether there were realistic alternatives for the organization to negotiating with Baghdad:

"Not really. That was a really dark moment; Iran had a very bad attitude towards PUK and had a good relationship with KDP. . . . The [PUK] peshmerga needed a break, they had been fighting since 1976; plus there was a sense that Saddam was weak (Iran had made some advances in the South), so he would make concessions." Several analysts concur in interpreting the PUK's decision as driven by its unsustainable military position. See, in particular, Kutschera, *Le Défi Kurde*, 60–61; McDowall, *A Modern History of the Kurds*, 348–49; Hiltermann, *A Poisonous Affair*, 31–32.

102. Turkey's veto of the agreement is emphasized in my interviews with Adel Murad and Faridoun Abd-Al Qader and in Nawshirwan Mustafa's memoir, as well as in the secondary literature. See Mustafa, *Going Around in Circles*, 81; Kutschera, *Le Défi Kurde*, 63–65; Quil Lawrence, *Invisible Nation: How The Kurds' Quest for Statehood Is Shaping Iraq and the Middle East* (New York: Walker, 2008), 32. Likely a significant improvement in Iraq's position in its war against Iran in 1984 and early 1985 (Iraq had managed to blunt the Iranian offensive in spring 1984 and started receiving more support from the United States) contributed to Baghdad's decision to turn its back to the PUK. See Bulloch and Morris, *No Friends but the Mountains*, 156–57; Kutschera, *Le Défi Kurde*, 64; Efraim Karsh, *The Iran-Iraq War, 1980–1988* (Oxford: Osprey, 2002), 47; Hiltermann, *A Poisonous Affair*, 40–56.

103. Mustafa, *Going Around in Circles*, 83; author interview with Faridoun Abd-Al Qader; Stephen C. Pelletiere, *The Kurds: An Unstable Element in the Gulf* (Boulder, Colo.: Westview Press, 1984), 186–87; McDowall, *A Modern History of the Kurds*, 351.

104. Author interviews with Faridoun Abd-Al Qader and Adel Murad.

105. Van Bruinessen, "The Kurds Between Iran and Iraq," 27; author interviews with Mulazin Omar and Shoresh Hadji.

106. Van Bruinessen, "The Kurds Between Iran and Iraq," 27.

107. Author interview with Adel Murad; Mustafa, *Going Around in Circles*, 115.

108. As PUK leading figure Nawshirwan Mustafa put it, "We had come to the conclusion that in order to reach intra-Kurdish peace we needed to make peace with Iran." Mustafa, *Going Around in Circles*, 102.

109. Author interview with Faridoun Abd-Al Qader. Tehran's fears that the PUK may still have been engaged in negotiations with Baghdad apparently subsided when a delegation of Iranian intelligence officers visiting Talabani witnessed Iraqi airplanes bombing the group's headquarters. See interview with Sherdel Abdullah Howeizi, PUK liaison with the Iranian intelligence at the time of the events, reported in Hiltermann, *A Poisonous Affair*, 90.

110. According to my PUK interviewee Faridoun Abd-Al Qader, "Iran . . . was in a difficult military position and needed PUK's help. . . . Iran was now much more forthcoming because of its need." Several other PUK-affiliated subjects made similar observations in interviews or, in the case of Nawshirwan Mustafa, their memoirs. See author interviews with Adel Murad, Mulazin Omar, Mala Baxtiar, and Mam Rostam (PUK military commander at the time of the events and member of Gorran Party at the time of the interview), November 2012, Sulaimania, Iraq; Mustafa, *Going Around in Circles*, 103–6. For a description of the more difficult situation Iran faced from the spring of

1984, see Cordesman and Wagner, *The Lessons of Modern War*, 178–213; Karsh, *The Iran-Iraq War*, 47, 74–75. PUK-related subjects also argue that Iran's new disposition was influenced by its perception that the PUK was indeed a powerful organization because, when Baghdad and the group reached a ceasefire in 1983, Iraq was able to move a large number of forces to the southern front; moreover, after the end of negotiations with Baghdad, Iranian intelligence officers visiting PUK areas of operation could see that its peshmerga near Iraqi towns were able to put serious pressure on the regime. See author interview with Faridoun Abd-Al Qader; interviews with Faridoun Abd-Al Qader and Sherdel Abdullah Howeizi reported in Hiltermann, *A Poisonous Affair*, 90–91.

111. Mustafa, *Going Around in Circles*, 106; author interviews with Mulazin Omar and Mohammad Tofiq.

112. Human Rights Watch, *Genocide in Iraq: The Anfal Campaign Against the Kurds* (New Haven, Conn.: Yale University Press, 1993); Human Rights Watch, *Claims in Conflict: Reversing Ethnic Cleansing in Northern Iraq* (New York: Human Rights Watch, 2004); Hiltermann, *A Poisonous Affair*, 134–35. In the course of the 1974–1975 offensive against Barzani's forces and in its aftermath, the scale of civilian killing and displacement perpetrated by the Iraqi government, while appalling, was significantly smaller. Another well-known instance of Iraqi mass violence against the Kurdish people is the killing of up to eight thousand male members (including children) of the Barzani tribe in 1983 in retaliation for the KDP's cooperation with Tehran during the Iran-Iraq War.

113. Laizer, *Martyrs, Traitors and Patriots*, 113.

114. For example, O'Ballance reports that in April 1994, shortly before the outbreak of KDP-PUK infighting, Kurdish "authorities apprehensively claimed that Saddam Hussein already had 200,000 troops in readiness to cross the 36th parallel as soon as 'Operation Poised Hammer' was wound up." O'Ballance, *The Kurdish Struggle*, 230. After the withdrawal of allied ground forces from Kurdistan in the summer of 1991, the international community relied on allied warplanes based in southern Turkey to deter Saddam's aggression against the Kurdish region, subject to Turkish approval for renewal every six months.

115. McDowall, *A Modern History of the Kurds*, 384, 394n40.

116. Stansfield, *Iraqi Kurdistan*, 98–99; McDowall, *A Modern History of the Kurds*, 388. Based on the definition provided in the first chapter of this book, the KDP should therefore be considered a counterinsurgent militia for at least part of 1996, when it fought the PUK in close cooperation with government forces.

117. McDowall, *A Modern History of the Kurds*, 368.

118. McDowall, *A Modern History of the Kurds*, 369–73.

119. The KDP and PUK agreed to split executive power equally after the first round of presidential elections, where Massoud Barzani (KDP) and Jalal Talabani (PUK) received 47.5 percent and 45 percent of the votes, respectively. The KDP and the PUK obtained, respectively, 50.22 and 49.78 percent of the parliamentary votes (excluding the votes for all other parties). Michael M. Gunter, "A De Facto Kurdish State in

Northern Iraq," *Third World Quarterly* 14, no. 2 (1993): 295–319; Stansfield, *Iraqi Kurdistan*, 129–31; McDowall, *A Modern History of the Kurds*, 380–81.

120.   Kutschera, *Le Défi Kurde*, 133.

121.   As Gareth Stansfield notes, "KDP and PUK handed over control of revenue sources to the KRG in name only, and the KRG exerted little control over the main crossing points." Stansfield, *Iraqi Kurdistan*, 152. See also O'Ballance, *The Kurdish Struggle*, 201; David Romano, *The Kurdish Nationalist Movement: Opportunity, Mobilization and Identity* (New York: Cambridge University Press, 2006), 209; Sarah Graham-Brown, *Sanctioning Saddam: The Politics of Intervention in Iraq* (New York: I. B. Tauris, 1999), 222.

122.   *Military Balance* (London: International Institute for Strategic Studies, 1992–1994).

123.   The key border crossing point is Habur, also known as Ibrahim Khalil, near the city of Zakho.

124.   Robert Baer, *See No Evil: The True Story of a Ground Soldier in the CIA's War on Terrorism* (New York: Random House, 2002), 192–93. The PUK controlled much of the significantly less profitable border with Iran. See Graham-Brown, *Sanctioning Saddam*, 224; Freij, "Tribal Identity and Alliance Behaviour Among Factions of the Kurdish National Movement in Iraq," 101; Andrew Cockburn and Patrick Cockburn, *Out of the Ashes: The Resurrection of Saddam Hussein* (New York: Harper Collins, 1999), 178–79.

125.   McDowall, *A Modern History of the Kurds*, 390.

126.   Stansfield, *Iraqi Kurdistan*, 149, 232n12.

127.   Stansfield, *Iraqi Kurdistan*, 151–52.

128.   Gunter, *The Kurdish Predicament in Iraq*, 67–109.

129.   Romano, *The Kurdish Nationalist Movement*, 210.

130.   See, for example, Kutschera, *Le Défi Kurde*, 133; Graham-Brown, *Sanctioning Saddam*, 225.

131.   Gunter, "The KDP-PUK Conflict in Northern Iraq," 235–37; Kutschera, *Le Défi Kurde*, 133.

132.   Baer, *See No Evil*, 196.

133.   Robert H. Pelletreau, "Negotiating with the Kurds," *Mideast Mirror*, August 3, 1998. The PUK's offensive aimed at taking over a major border crossing with Iran (Hajj Omran) under KDP control, which would have partially offset the PUK's financial decline. Kutschera, *Le Défi Kurde*, 137–38.

134.   Stansfield, *Iraqi Kurdistan*, 99.

135.   Romano, *The Kurdish Nationalist Movement*, 210.

136.   Kutschera, *Le Défi Kurde*, 122; Anthony H. Cordesman, *Iran and Iraq: The Threat from the Northern Gulf* (Boulder, Colo.: Westview Press, 1994), 229–30.

137.   Kutschera, *Le Défi Kurde*, 140.

138.   The implementation of oil-for-food—a UN sanction-relief program allowing Iraq to sell some of its oil to buy food and various humanitarian items, with 13 percent of the revenues allocated to the Kurdish region—may have contributed to improving the PUK's financial position. Though the KDP continued to benefit from controlling

the border with Turkey, the PUK gained a substantial source of income, which hitherto it had sorely lacked. The United Nations and the Iraqi government reached the oil-for-food agreement in 1996, but the program started having effects on the ground in spring 1997. See Graham-Brown, *Sanctioning Saddam*, 284; Tim Niblock, *Pariah States and Sanctions in the Middle East* (Boulder, Colo.: Lynne Rienner, 2001), 117–28; Gareth Stansfield, "Governing Kurdistan: The Strengths of Division," in *The Future of Kurdistan in Iraq*, ed. Brendan O'Leary, John McGarry, and Khaled Salih (Philadelphia: University of Pennsylvania Press, 2005), 204–9; Alan Makovsky, "Kurdish Agreement Signals New U.S. Commitment," *PolicyWatch* 341 (Washington Institute for Near East Policy, 1998).

139. Stansfield, *Iraqi Kurdistan*, 100–102; Owen Bowcott "New Dawn for Iraqi Kurds as Warring Factions Bury Hatchet, *Guardian*, February 10, 1999; "Iraq: PUK Says Rival KDP Responsible for Failure of Inter-Kurdish Peace Talks," *BBC Monitoring Middle East*, September 15, 2000.

140. Stansfield observes that after the last PUK's attempt at breaking the deadlock in the fall of 1997, both parties recognized that "they did not possess the strength to usurp the other." Stansfield, *Iraqi Kurdistan*, 1. Likewise, according to a Saudi newspaper, the end of the Kurdish infighting was due at least in part to "a feeling by both parties that neither is capable of eliminating the other by military means." Reported in "Turkey in the Arab (and Kurdish) Dock," *Mideast Mirror*, September 10, 1998.

141. U.S. pressure on the KDP and the PUK may have also been important to produce the agreement and keep the peace. The United States had mediated between the warring parties before, but Washington became determined to stop the Kurdish infighting only in 1998, once it concluded that a stable Kurdistan was needed to confront Saddam Hussein. See Cockburn and Cockburn, *Out of the Ashes*, 290; Mahmoud Osman, "The Kurdish Internal Conflict, Peace Process and Its Prospects," *Kurdistan Observer*, March 14, 2001. (Osman was involved in earlier mediation efforts as an independent Kurdish figure.)

142. As many as five hundred people (counting both combatants and civilians) may have died in the fighting. Amnesty International, "Human Rights Abuses in Iraqi Kurdistan Since 1991," February 1995, 95.

143. David Romano, *An Outline of Kurdish Islamist Groups in Iraq*, Occasional Paper (Jamestown Foundation, 2007), 9; Cordesman, *Iran and Iraq*, 229–30. Moreover, the IMK presidential candidate in 1992, ranking third after Massoud Barzani and Jalal Talabani, received only 4 percent of the votes.

144. McDowall, *A Modern History of the Kurds*, 386–87; Laizer, *Martyrs, Traitors and Patriots*, 117, 131–32.

145. Stansfield suggests as much, based on the highly ambiguous statement by an IMK military leader that "Kurdish parties [presumably the KDP] forced the IMK to fight." Stansfield, *Iraqi Kurdistan*, 97, 225n12.

146. Fotini Christia, *Alliance Formation in Civil Wars* (New York: Cambridge University Press, 2012).

147.   In the spring of 1963, at the apex of their territorial control before 1991, the combined areas under the full control of the Barzani and the Ahmed-Talabani groups amounted to 33 percent of Iraqi Kurdistan. See figure A.1 in the online appendix at https://costantinopischedda.com/data-replication-materials-and-additional-materials/.

148.   Christia's argument could be interpreted as suggesting that the relevant territory is not the Kurdish region but Iraq as a whole, as it contained population and resources that the government could mobilize in the course of the civil war. If we were to consider the entire country, the balance of power, of course, would be even more favorable to the government.

149.   Schmidt, *Journey Among Brave Men*, 70; Vanly, *Kurdistan Irakien Entité Nationale*, 147; Pollack, *Arabs at War*, 158–61, 165.

150.   Van Bruinessen reports that in the post-1975 round of rebellion, the Kurdish insurgents did not have "liberated areas," as the government was able to move troops wherever it wished in Kurdistan. The insurgents were especially weak in the first years after the 1975 defeat. Van Bruinessen, "The Kurds Between Iran and Iraq," 27n5. See also Mustafa, *Danube Shores to the Nawzang Valley*, 173, 212–14.

151.   Nawshirwan Mustafa reports at 200,000 the size of Iraqi armed forces in this period. According to the International Institute for Strategic Studies, the Iraqi armed forces grew from 158,000 to 222,000 in the years 1976–1980. Mustafa, *Danube Shores to the Nawzang Valley*, 278; *Military Balance* (1976–1980). There are no precise figures on the size of insurgent groups in 1978, but they were certainly in the low thousands. In an interview with the author, Farid Asasard estimated the number of PUK fighters in 1978 at 1,200; Van Bruinessen reports an estimate of 9,000 fighters in 1981 for all the main groups operating in Kurdistan combined (PUK, KDP, Socialist Party, and Communist Party). Van Bruinessen, "The Kurds Between Iran and Iraq," 27. The figure would be significantly lower for the KDP and the PUK in 1976–1978 (the two groups active at the time), as they grew rapidly only after the beginning of the Iran-Iraq War. See my interview with Shoresh Hadji.

152.   Van Bruinessen, "The Kurds Between Iran and Iraq," 27; author interviews with Shoresh Hadji and Adnan Mufti.

153.   The troop figure does not include the paramilitary forces of the Popular Army, which grew from about 250,000 at the beginning of the Iran-Iraq War to around 500,000 in the following years. See *Military Balance* (1980–1983); Pollack, *Arabs at War*, 182; Al-Marashi and Salama, *Iraq's Armed Forces*, 154. For figures on the rapid growth of the Iraqi ground forces over the period 1980–1987, see Shahram Chubin and Charles Tripp, *Iran and Iraq at War* (Boulder, Colo.: Westview, 1988), 294.

154.   There are no precise figures on the number of Iraqi troops actually deployed in Kurdistan and rebel fighters in this period, but there is no doubt that there were many more government troops in the region than all rebels combined. Van Bruinessen estimates at about nine thousand and thirteen thousand the overall size of the rebel forces in Kurdistan in 1981 and 1985, respectively; thirteen thousand can thus be taken as the highest plausible estimate of rebel numerical strength in the years 1979–1983 (a period of steady growth of the rebel ranks). Consistently, Nawshirwan Mustafa reports that

the PUK had forty-five hundred fighters in late 1983. According to McDowall, after the PUK and Baghdad reached a ceasefire agreement in late 1983, Iraq could move four to six divisions that had been battling the PUK to the southern front, while Farid Asasard claimed that the PUK was able to pin down one fourth of the Iraqi ground forces. All this implies that at the very least forty thousand Iraqi troops (conservatively assuming four divisions of ten thousand troops each) were deployed in areas where the PUK operated. Moreover, the government presence in Kurdistan included regular units deployed against the KDP and the other rebel groups (for which I do not have specific figures) and thousands of counterinsurgent militias. Van Bruinessen, "The Kurds Between Iran and Iraq," 27; Mustafa, *Fingers That Break Each Other*, 332; McDowall, *A Modern History of the Kurds*, 351; author interview with Farid Asasard.

155. By contrast, Baghdad maintained a stark advantage in terms of troop numbers and weaponry over the Kurdish organizations in this period too.

156. The significance of the ideological differences between the KDP and the PUK appears to have waned over time. Several of my non-PUK interviewees attribute what they saw as PUK's aggressive behavior in the 1970s and 1980s to the group's Marxist fanaticism. By the 1990s, however, the two parties had become hardly distinguishable in terms of ideology. See Romano, *The Kurdish Nationalist Movement*, 197; Bengio, *The Kurds of Iraq*, 161.

157. Jawad, *Iraq and the Kurdish Question*, 176–78.

158. Jawad, *Iraq and the Kurdish Question*, 205–14.

159. All the main Kurdish rebel groups joined an alliance in 1988—the Iraqi Kurdistan Front—with the common objectives of Saddam's overthrow, the creation of a democratic system, and the recognition of Kurdish national rights.

160. McDowall, *A Modern History of the Kurds*, 380.

161. For one example about the KDP and one about the PUK, see, respectively, Kutschera, *Le Défi Kurde*, 39; and Mustafa, *Going Around in Circles*, 31.

162. Mustafa, *Fingers That Break Each Other*, 332.

163. See, for example, Gunter, "The KDP-PUK Conflict in Northern Iraq," 228.

164. On necessary conditions counterfactuals, see Jack Levy and Gary Goertz, eds., *Explaining War and Peace: Case Studies and Necessary Condition Counterfactuals* (New York: Routledge, 2007).

165. See note 45 above.

166. In fact, the immediate impetus for Barzani's hegemonic bid is unlikely to have been fear of defection as the Ahmed-Talabani faction opposed the ceasefire agreement of 1964, claiming the government was weak and thus insurgents should not relent in their operations.

167. By contrast, there is no indication that Baghdad provoked the episode of inter-rebel war in 1978. The PUK had meetings with representatives of the Iraqi government in 1977 and then in the aftermath of the clash. On both occasions the contacts did not make headway as the Iraqi government was unwilling to make concessions (besides co-optation offers for the PUK leadership) given the position of weakness of the rebels; so the group continued its guerrilla activities. In 1979 Baghdad had similarly

inconclusive contacts with the Socialist Party. See Kutschera, *Le Défi Kurde*, 42; author interview with Adel Murad; Mustafa, *Danube Shores to the Nawzang Valley*, 181–85, 337–38.

168.   The latter is one of the mechanisms driving infighting in self-determination movements suggested by Kristin M. Bakke, Kathleen Gallagher Cunningham, and Lee J. M. Seymour, "Shirts Today, Skins Tomorrow: Dual Contests and the Effects of Fragmentation in Self-Determination Disputes," *Journal of Conflict Resolution* 56, no. 1 (February 2012): 67–93; and Kathleen Gallagher Cunningham, *Inside the Politics of Self-Determination* (Oxford: Oxford University Press, 2014). According to Mahmoud Osman, in 1982 the Iraqi government asked him to prove that the Socialist Party controlled the area it claimed, which he interpreted as an exhortation to attack other groups; he also interpreted the 1983 attack by the PUK as motivated by a similar request. Reported in Van Bruinessen, "The Kurds Between Iran and Iraq," 27.

169.   Mustafa, *Fingers That Break Each Other*, 332. This battle is also reported in More, *Les Kurdes Auhjourd'hui*, 125; Kutschera, *Le Défi Kurde*, 64.

170.   Freij, "Tribal Identity and Alliance Behaviour"; Gunter, "The KDP-PUK Conflict in Northern Iraq"; Martin Van Bruinessen, "Nationalisme Kurde et Ethnicités intra-Kurdes," *Peuples Méditerranéens*, no. 68–69 (1994): 11–37.

171.   Theodore McLauchlin and Wendy Pearlman, "Out-Group Conflict, In-Group Unity? Exploring the Effect of Repression on Intramovement Cooperation," *Journal of Conflict Resolution* 56, no. 1 (February 2012): 41–66.

172.   To be clear, the point is that window theory can explain more of the variation in Kurdish inter-rebel fighting, not that McLauchlin and Pearlman's argument is inconsistent with the evidence. McLauchlin and Pearlman aim, more narrowly, to explain variation in conflict within ethno-national movements in the aftermath of government repression (in the Kurdish case, following two government military victories against the rebels) as a function of the constituent organizations' degree of satisfaction with existing institutional arrangements in the movement.

173.   Timothy W. Crawford, "Preventing Enemy Coalitions: How Wedge Strategies Shape Power Politics," *International Security* 35, no. 4 (Spring 2011): 155–89. There is, indeed, some evidence of thinking along these lines in the Iraqi government apparatus. For example, in a document dated April 3, 1988, addressed to the General Military Intelligence Directorate, an Iraqi intelligence officer recommended sustaining, rather than reducing, military pressure on the rebels so as to create "division among the insurgency movements in order to reach a state of confusion and disharmony among them." See Conflict Records Research Center, Saddam Hussein Collection-GMID-D-000-859, 11.

174.   I do not have direct evidence on government decision making in this episode, but various observers buttress my interpretation of Baghdad's actions as driven by an urgent need for a break from the fight. See Vanly, *Kurdistan Irakien Entité Nationale*, 216–17; O'Ballance, *The Kurdish Revolt*, 120; Jawad, *Iraq and the Kurdish Question*, 154; author interviews with two Barzani affiliates, Sa'id Kaka and Khursheed Shera.

175.   Graham-Brown, *Sanctioning Saddam*, 68–69; Baer, *See No Evil*, 288.

4. Parallel Paths to Ethnic Hegemony

1. Reported in Dan Connell, *Against All Odds: A Chronicle of the Eritrean Revolution* (Trenton, N.J.: Red Sea Press, 1993), 85.

2. David Pool, *From Guerrillas to Government: The Eritrean People's Liberation Front* (Oxford: James Currey, 2001), 36–53. Eritrea had enjoyed significant autonomy as a federal unit from the time of its reunification with Ethiopia, following Italian colonial rule and British transitional administration. In 1962 Addis Ababa downgraded Eritrea to the status of Ethiopian province.

3. John Markakis, *National and Class Conflict in the Horn of Africa* (New York: Cambridge University Press, 1987), 104–9; Gaim Kibreab, *Critical Reflections on the Eritrean War of Independence: Social Capital, Associational Life, Religion, Ethnicity, and Sowing Seeds of Dictatorship* (Trenton, N.J.: Red Sea Press, 2008), 149–52.

4. Michael Woldemariam, *Insurgent Fragmentation in the Horn of Africa: Rebellion and its Discontents* (New York: Cambridge University Press, 2018), 137–50; Pool, *From Guerrillas to Government*, 63–70; Kibreab, *Critical Reflections*, 164–74.

5. Pool, *From Guerrillas to Government*, 71; Kibreab, *Critical Reflections*, 179. The group's name was Eritrean People's Liberation Forces (rather than Front) until its first congress in 1977.

6. On the Ethiopian revolution, see Christopher S. Clapham, *Transformation and Continuity in Revolutionary Ethiopia* (New York: Cambridge University Press, 1990); Edmond J. Keller, *Revolutionary Ethiopia: From Empire to People's Republic* (Bloomington: Indiana University Press, 1991).

7. Haggai Erlich, *The Struggle Over Eritrea, 1962–1978* (Stanford, Calif.: Hoover Press Publication, 1983), 43–54; John Markakis, *National and Class Conflict in the Horn of Africa* (New York: Cambridge University Press, 1987), 136–44; Pool, *From Guerrillas to Government*, 136–40.

8. Richard Sherman, *Eritrea: The Unfinished Revolution* (New York: Praeger, 1980), 62–66; Markakis, *National and Class Conflict*, 138–42; Pool, *From Guerrillas to Government*, 140–42.

9. Pool, *From Guerrillas to Government*, 143–47.

10. Aregawi Berhe, *A Political History of the Tigray People's Liberation Front (1975–1991): Revolt, Ideology, and Mobilization in Ethiopia* (Los Angeles: Tsehai, 2009), 74; Gebru Tareke, *The Ethiopian Revolution: War in the Horn of Africa* (New Haven, Conn.: Yale University Press, 2009), 86–87.

11. René Le Fort, *Ethiopia: An Heretical Revolution?* (London: Zed Press, 1983), 187; Clapham, *Transformation and Continuity*, 185; Berhe, *Tigray People's Liberation Front*, 79–84, 103–12, 117–24; Andargachew Tiruneh, *The Ethiopian Revolution, 1974–1987: A Transformation from an Aristocratic to a Totalitarian Autocracy* (New York: Cambridge University Press, 1993), 124–31, 205–8; John Young, *Peasant Revolution in Ethiopia: The Tigray People's Liberation Front, 1975–1991* (New York: Cambridge University Press, 1997), 100–13; Kiflu Tadesse, *The Generation, Part 1: The History of the Ethiopian*

People's Revolutionary Party (Lanham, Md.: University Press of America, 1998), 434–37.

12. For detailed accounts of the key battles, see Tareke, *The Ethiopian Revolution*; Fantahun Ayele, *The Ethiopian Army: From Victory to Collapse, 1977–1991* (Evanston, Ill.: Northwestern University Press, 2014).

13. The Eritrean and Tigrayan identities emerged and then solidified as a result of complex historical processes, involving Italy's colonization of Eritrea, large-scale intrastate violence, political exclusion along ethnic lines, and ethnonational mythmaking. See Ruth Iyob, *The Eritrean Struggle for Independence: Domination, Resistance, Nationalism, 1941–1993* (New York: Cambridge University Press, 1995); John Young, "Ethnicity and Power in Ethiopia," *Review of African Political Economy* 23, no. 70 (December 1996): 531–42; Alemseged Abbay, *Identity Jilted or Re-imagining Identity? The Divergent Paths of the Eritrean and Tigrayan Nationalist Struggles* (Lawrenceville, N.J.: Red Sea Press, 1998); Roy Pateman, *Eritrea: Even the Stones Are Burning* (Lawrenceville, N.J.: Red Sea Press, 1998).

14. Eritrea has a Muslim minority of over one-third of the population, nine languages, and eleven named ethnic groups. See Kibreab, *Critical Reflections*, 388n3.

15. Although the ELM leaders were Eritrean Muslims living in Sudan, the organization had a secular outlook and attracted both Christians and Muslims in the Sahel and in Keren, Massawa, and Asmara. The ELF initially drew most of its members from the province's Muslim-dominated lowlands. The organization, however, always had a substantial Christian component. Moreover, during the 1972–1974 armed conflict between the ELF and the EPLF, Eritrean civilians consistently appealed to both groups to set aside their differences and fight together for their common cause of Eritrean independence. Often individuals would join one organization rather than the other for contingent reasons, such as the fact that they had a friend in one of the groups or that they happened to cross into a group's area of operations when fleeing their home. By 1975 the bulk of the rank and file of the ELF, as the EPLF, were Christian highlanders. See Kibreab, *Critical Reflections*, 337, 415n1; Pool, *From Guerrillas to Government*, 141–42; Dawit Wolde Giorgis, *Red Tears: War, Famine and Revolution in Ethiopia* (Trenton, N.J.: Red Sea Press, 1989), 88; Woldemariam, *Insurgent Fragmentation*, 104–5; Connell, *Against All Odds*, 84.

16. The ELM had existed since 1958 but initially opted for a coup strategy, rather than guerrilla warfare, to achieve national liberation, by infiltrating the government security apparatus in the province. Only after the ELF took up arms and the government started rounding up the ELM underground cells did the organization embrace armed struggle. Ethiopian security forces had thwarted several previous attempts in 1962–1965 by the ELM to start military operations. The ELM's attempt to initiate a guerrilla campaign in Eritrea in 1965 was apparently prompted by the group's acquisition of arms in the black market that emerged owing to the insurgency in South Sudan. See Markakis, *National and Class Conflict*, 104–9; Iyob, *The Eritrean Struggle for Independence*, 99–107.

17.   Markakis, *National and Class Conflict*, 109, 113. The document "From the Experiences of the Eritrean Liberation Army" (part 1) (2005) reports that the ELF had about eight hundred fighters by the end of 1964. See http://www.nharnet.com/Editorials/TodayinEr-iHistory/NharnetTeam_Jan13.htm. The document is drawn from an Arabic-language book published by ELF's leaders Abdullah Idris and Mohammed Hasab, *Experiences of the ELA: 1961–1981* (not dated). In my interviews, ELF-related subjects readily pointed out the group's military superiority vis-à-vis the ELM's force. See, for example, author interview with Ahmed Nasser (ELF member from 1963 and in leadership positions from 1971), Stockholm, August 2013.

18.   Kibreab, *Critical Reflections*, 150–51.

19.   Markakis, *National and Class Conflict*, 121. See also Erlich, *The Struggle Over Eritrea*, 35–36.

20.   An Israeli-trained counterinsurgency force known as the "commandos" or "101," which would prove highly effective in denying rebel access to the Christian-populated Eritrean highlands, was created only in late 1965. See Tareke, *The Ethiopian Revolution*, 62; Woldemariam, *Insurgent Fragmentation*, 94.

21.   Erlich, *The Struggle Over Eritrea*, 37–38; Markakis, *National and Class Conflict*, 121–22.

22.   "From the Experiences of the Eritrean Liberation Army" (parts 2 and 5).

23.   Interview reported in Redie Bereketeab, *Eritrea: Making of a Nation* (Trenton, N.J.: Red Sea Press, 2007), 177.

24.   Mohammed Ibrahim Bahdurai (ELF member from 1961) offers a consistent account: "The ELF's success against the armed bands of the ELM was welcomed by all national-ists because everyone knew that the presence of more than one organization in the country would invite divisions based not on political lines but on the backward regional and confessional sentiments." See "Interview with Mohammed Ibrahim Bah-durai," *Eritrean Newsletter* 44, September 1, 1981, http://www.nharnet.com/Archives /Arch_2004/Oct_2004/NharnetTeam_Oct01.htm.

25.   *Eritrean Newsletter* 44, September 1, 1981, 3; Markakis, *National and Class Conflict*, 109; Iyob, *The Eritrean Struggle for Independence*, 104–5; interview with ELM cofounder Saleh Ahmed Eyay, conducted by Günter Schröder in 2004.

26.   Pool, *From Guerrillas to Government*, 64–68; Kibreab, *Critical Reflections*, 220n54; Woldemariam, *Insurgent Fragmentation*, 149.

27.   Author interviews with Mesfin Hagos, July and August 2013, Frankfurt, Germany. This imbalance of power clearly emerges from several other EPLF and ELF subjects' accounts and the secondary literature. For example, according to Markakis, *National and Class Conflict*, 133, in early 1972 the ELF could marshal about two thousand fight-ers, while the splinter groups combined had less than five hundred.

28.   Woldemariam, *Insurgent Fragmentation*, 150–51. Osman Saleh Sabbe's connections quickly bore fruit, as by 1973 the EPLF had gained access to more modern small arms than those at the ELF's disposal. See author interview with Ahmed Nasser; Markakis, *National and Class Conflict*, 135; and Tewdros Gebrezghier's memoir in "The Near

Liquidation of the (E)PLF," a collection of memoirs of EPLF fighters and other documents covering the years 1972 and 1973, compiled in 1993 by Aida Kidane, http://www
.eritrios.net/1970s.htm.

29. Richard Sherman, *Eritrea: The Unfinished Revolution* (New York: Praeger, 1980), 80–
82; Pateman, *Eritrea*, 132–33; Bowyer Bell, "Endemic Insurgency and International
Order: The Eritrean Experience," *Orbis* 18, no. 2 (Summer 1974): 427–50.

30. Author interview with Gime Ahmed, July 2013, Addis Ababa.

31. Woldemariam, *Insurgent Fragmentation*, 101–2. Woldemariam reports that contemporary U.S. intelligence and British diplomatic assessments of the government-rebels
military balance consistently described a stalemated battlefield in the years 1971–1973.

32. Author interview with Ahmed Nasser, an ELF leader at the time of the events. The text
of the resolution is reported in Kibreab, *Critical Reflections*, 173–74. The secondary
literature offers a consistent account. See, for example, Pool, *From Guerrillas to Government*, 71.

33. Markakis, *National and Class Conflict*, 134–35; Pool, *From Guerrillas to Government*,
133–36; Bereket Habte Selassie, *The Crown and the Pen: The Memoirs of a Lawyer
Turned Rebel* (Trenton, N.J.: Red Sea Press, 2007), 306–9; interview with Ahmed
Karar, Sudan's chief of security at the time, conducted by Günter Schröder, 1981,
Khartoum.

34. Author interview with Nasser. See also interview with Tesfay Degiga (ELF member
from 1973) and *Eritrean Newsletter*, September 1, 1981, 11–13.

35. Interview with *Ma'ariv*, October 21, 1974, reported in Erlich, *The Struggle Over Eritrea*,
52. Osman Saleh Sabbe was an ELF founding member and influential EPLF figure
until 1976. Haile Menkerios (EPLF member from 1973) also pointed to the widespread
perception that government weakness provided a clear chance for achieving independence. Author interview with Menkerios, July 2013, Addis Ababa.

36. Erlich, *The Struggle Over Eritrea*, 71–78; Markakis, *National and Class Conflict*, 136–
44; Woldemariam, *Insurgent Fragmentation*, 105.

37. Markakis, *National and Class Conflict*, 134. Wolde-Yesus Ammar (ELF member from
1965 and subsequently head of the group's Foreign Office) noted that the realization
that defeating the EPLF would be very difficult convinced the ELF to stop the infighting. Author interview with Wolde-Yesus Ammar, August 2013, Frankfurt, Germany.
The ELF probably witnessed with much apprehension the growth of its rival's strength
during the two years of infighting. We should not, however, expect the ELF to respond
to the unfavorable power trend with a gamble for resurrection, precisely because the
group's leadership by 1974 had had ample opportunity to realize the ineffectiveness of
the military approach in tackling the challenge posed by the EPLF; expansion in the
face of the collapse of government authority, instead, represented an untested potential avenue to reverse the group's relative decline.

38. By 1979 the Ethiopian army had grown to include more than 200,000 soldiers, compared to fewer than 50,000 when the Derg took power; 120,000 heavily armed troops
participated in the first offensive. See Connell, *Against All Odds*, 157–94; Awet T. Weldemichael, "The Eritrean Long March: The Strategic Withdrawal of the Eritrean

People's Liberation Front (EPLF), 1978–1979," *Journal of Military History* 73, no. 4 (October 2009): 1231–71.

39. Weldemichael, "The Eritrean Long March," 1232.

40. Awet Tewelde Weldemichael, *Third World Colonialism and Strategies of Liberation: Eritrea and East Timor Compared* (New York: Cambridge University Press, 2013), 154.

41. For example, in an interview with the author, the ELF's Gime Ahmed described "anarchic divisions" in the group. This is a recurring theme in the secondary literature, too. See Iyob, *The Eritrean Struggle for Independence*, 120–21; Pool, *From Guerrillas to Government*, 147.

42. Author interviews with Mesfin Hagos. Another military commander, Adhanom Gebremariam, provided a similar assessment in my interview with him, April 2014, New York.

43. The much touted sixth offensive (Operation Red Star) would be launched in February 1982, after two years of planning. An important reason for the delay was the training of four mountain infantry divisions (recommended by Soviet advisors as the only way to overrun the last Eritrean rebel stronghold in the Sahel mountains), which experienced recruitment and troop accommodation constraints. Moreover, with only two out of four of the new divisions ready, the Ethiopian army launched a large-scale offensive (Operation Lash) in the Southeast of Ethiopia against Somali forces in late August 1980, which had been under well-publicized preparation for months. The ELF-EPLF war started on the same day. See Tareke, *The Ethiopian Revolution*, 225–46; Ayele, *The Ethiopian Army*, 31–33.

44. See also the interview with Isaias Afewerki, currently president of Eritrea and top EPLF leader at that time, in *Adulis* 1, nos. 4–5 (1984), 9–15; EPLF, "Ethiopia's Sixth Offensive and Developments in the Eritrean Struggle," August 25, 1982. The EPLF had detailed intelligence on Addis Ababa's intentions and military planning, thanks to "innumerable infiltrators and agents placed in the armed forces as well as in various government offices." Moreover, both the EPLF and the TPLF were "able not only to decipher all [government] coded messages but also to identify army commanders by their names." See Ayele, *The Ethiopian Army*, 96, 98.

45. Author interview with Adhanom Gebremariam. Mesfin Hagos made a similar statement in an interview with the author.

46. Author interview with Wolde-Yesus Ammar (in the ELF Foreign Office at that time); see also Markakis, *National and Class Conflict*, 140; Pool, *From Guerrillas to Government*, 141.

47. The ELF-PLF's figure is from Dan Connell, "Eritrean Liberation Struggle Escalates," *Guardian*, July 6, 1977. The ELF's estimate is from Woldemariam, *Insurgent Fragmentation*, 132, which reports a roughly stable group size from 1975 to 1982.

48. Author interview with Tesfay Degiga.

49. Author interviews with Ahmed Nasser; Wolde-Yesus Ammar; Menghesteab Asmeron (ELF senior cadre at the time of the events), July 2013, Frankfurt, Germany; and Tewolde Gebrselassie (ELF member from 1974), July 2013, Addis Ababa.

50. Author interview with Tewolde Gebrselassie.

51.   The ELF-PLF's figures are from Dan Connell, "Eritrean Forces Resume Guerrilla Attacks," *Guardian*, January 3, 1979; and from an interview with John Duggan, who visited ELF-PLF bases in the summer of 1978, conducted by the Eritrean Gruppen Stockholm, December 7, 1978, in Stockholm, provided to the author by Günter Schröder. In interviews with the author, Menghesteab Asmeron, Tesfay Degiga, and Tewolde Gebrselassie (ELF members at the time of the events) stressed the weakness and small size of the ELF-PLF compared to the ELF. The ELF had roughly eighteen thousand fighters, according to Woldemariam, *Insurgent Fragmentation*, 132.

52.   Author interview with Wolde-Yesus Ammar.

53.   Dan Connell, "Ethiopia Prepares Eritrea Offensive," *Guardian*, November 22, 1978; Weldemichael, "The Eritrean Long March." Nonetheless, according to ELF-related interviewees, the decision to attack the ELF-PLF was at least in part motivated by the ELF's fear that if the government, at some point down the road, had redirected its attention to the areas of northwestern Eritrea where the group operated, it might have had to fight a war on two fronts against the ELF-PLF and Addis Ababa's forces. Author interviews with Tesfay Degiga and Tewolde Gebrselassie.

54.   Berhe, *Tigray People's Liberation Front*, 278 (emphasis in original).

55.   Some TPLF sources posit a pre-existing plan to eliminate the TLF. See Kahsay Berhe, *Ethiopia: Democratization and Unity* (Münster, Germany: Monsenstein und Van-nerdat, 2005), 62; author interview with Gebru Asrat (TPLF member from 1975 and subsequently in leadership positions), July 2013, Addis Ababa. Others argue that the TPLF leaders were genuinely interested in a merger with the TLF, but the TPLF rank and file's opposition to the merger prevailed. Author interviews with Aregawi Berhe (chairman of the TPLF at the time), August 2013, The Hague, Netherlands; and Ghidey Zeratsion (TPLF founding member), August 2013, Oslo.

56.   Berhe, *Tigray People's Liberation Front*, 81–84.

57.   In separate interviews with the author, Aregawi Berhe, Gebru Asrat, and Tedros Hagos (TPLF member from 1976, interviewed in July 2013, Mekele, Ethiopia) did not provide precise size figures, simply describing the TLF as "smaller" than the TPLF and rife with internal tensions. By contrast, Mokonnen Mokonnen (TPLF member from 1975, inter-view with the author in September 2013, Silver Spring, Maryland) reports that the TPLF had about twice as many fighters as the TLF when they fought (45–50 to 25). In his book, *Tigray People's Liberation Front*, 81–82, Berhe reports a more than 3:1 size advantage for the TPLF, but he is considering only the main faction of the TLF, not the other two fac-tions whose whereabouts were unknown at the time of the TPLF-TLF fight.

58.   Berhe, *Tigray People's Liberation Front*, 93. The negligible Derg presence in Tigray's countryside until 1978 is reported in the secondary literature, too. See Young, *Peasant Revolution in Ethiopia*, 93, 97.

59.   Woldemariam estimates the size of the ELF and the EPLF in 1975 at eighteen thousand and ten thousand, respectively, in *Insurgent Fragmentation*, 132, 164.

60.   In October 1975 the TPLF had about a hundred fighters. Berhe, *Tigray People's Libera-tion Front*, 139.

61. Young, *Peasant Revolution in Ethiopia*, 100. The Amhara were Ethiopia's politically dominant group both before and after the Derg took power.

62. Young, *Peasant Revolution in Ethiopia*, 102–3; Berhe, *Tigray People's Liberation Front*, 105; author interviews with Gebru Asrat and Mokonnen Mokonnen.

63. Berhe, *Tigray People's Liberation Front*, 103–4; author interview with Ghidey Zeratsion; Young, *Peasant Revolution in Ethiopia*, 100–102.

64. Author interview with Ghidey Zeratsion.

65. Author interviews with Ghidey Zeratsion; Aregawi Berhe; Tesfay Atsbeha (TPLF senior military figure at the time), August 2013, Cologne, Germany; and Mulugeta Gebrehiwot (TPLF foot soldier at the time), July 2013, Addis Ababa. Berhe reports in *Tigray People's Liberation Front*, 170, that the size of the TPLF in July 1976 was about one thousand fighters. Historical accounts are replete with references to Teranafit's lack of a coherent organization and the prevalence among its rank and file of criminals who had opportunistically joined for looting and peasants lured with false economic promises and not deeply committed to the group.

66. Author interviews with Ghidey Zeratsion and Aregawi Berhe.

67. Author interview with Ghidey Zeratsion. Other interviewees, in particular Aregawi Berhe and Mulegeta Gebrehiwot, made similar observations. See also Berhe, *Tigray People's Liberation Front*, 105.

68. Berhe, *Tigray People's Liberation Front*, 127–28.

69. Berhe, *Tigray People's Liberation Front*, 56.

70. Author interview with Aregawi Berhe. Moreover, the TPLF's predicament was exacerbated by news of an EDU contingent inside Ethiopia after Sihul's death. See Berhe, *Tigray People's Liberation Front*, 106–7. Ghidey Zeratsion also reports, in an interview with the author, that the expectation of the EDU's imminent arrival undermined the TPLF's initial plan.

71. Author interview with Tedros Hagos; Berhe, *Tigray People's Liberation Front*, 107–8.

72. Author interview with Ghidey Zeratsion. Aregawi Berhe made a similar observation in an interview with the author.

73. Tadesse, *The Generation*, 390–91; Berhe, *Tigray People's Liberation Front*, 142–45. As EPRP leader Kiflu Tadesse notes in *The Generation*, 229, "Resolving the national question had remained one of the major issues for the organization." The TPLF-EPRP ideological disagreements were about whether the class or the national/ethnic issue should be considered priority number one. I do not have data on the ethnic background of EPRP fighters. EPRP and TPLF interview subjects as well as the secondary literature report that the EPRP leadership was dominated by Tigrayans. See Sarah Vaughan, "Ethnicity and Power in Ethiopia," Ph.D. dissertation, University of Edinburgh, 2003, 166; author interviews with Begasho Gurmo Ashenafi (EPRP foot soldier), August 2013, Frankfurt, Germany; and Tekleweini Assefa (early TPLF member), July 2013, Addis Ababa. That the two groups had overlapping bases is clearly illustrated by their competition for recruits and supporters, reported by TPLF and EPRP sources: both were able to recruit in eastern Tigray, and both tried to convince

supporters of their rivals to switch sides. See Tadesse, *The Generation*, 394; Kahsay Berhe, *Ethiopia*, 75.

74. The groups were unsuccessful in negotiating an agreement to cooperate against the government and end the skirmishes involving their respective fighters and supporters. See Tadesse, *The Generation*, 88, 390–99; Berhe, *Tigray People's Liberation Front*, 143–47; author interview with Ghidey Zeratsion, who was the TPLF representative at the negotiations.

75. The EDU apparently expected to march triumphantly to Mekele (Tigray's capital) and then Addis Ababa, rolling up on its way the much weaker TPLF. EDU leaders may have also thought they would be able to tap into the TPLF's social base of support, owing to the absence, in practice, of sharp distinction between EDU and the Tigrayan Teranafit: as noted, EDU's founder and prominent (but not sole) leader Ras Mengesha was a symbol of Tigrayan identity, and some Teranafit forces defeated by the TPLF joined the EDU, where they remained as a distinct unit. The TPLF eventually prevailed against the EDU after a government offensive significantly weakened the group. See the online appendix at https://costantinopischedda.com/data-replication -materials-and-additional-materials/ for more information on this episode of inter-rebel war.

76. Tadesse, *The Generation*, 434–37, 471; Berhe, *Tigray People's Liberation Front*, 149–51.

77. According to EPRP Kiflu Tadesse and Begasho Ashenafi, in early 1978 the EPRP had about a thousand fighters in eastern Tigray. Aregawi Berhe notes that in late spring 1978 the TPLF could marshal about a thousand soldiers. According to Tesfay Atsbeha (TPLF commander at that time), the two groups were equal in terms of numbers of soldiers and weapons, but the TPLF was stronger because its fighters were significantly more experienced. See Tadesse, *The Generation*, 404; author interviews with Begasho Ashenafi and Tesfay Atsbeha; Berhe, *Tigray People's Liberation Front*, 178.

78. Author interview with Aregawi Berhe. Consistently, in interviews with the author Ghidey Zeratsion and Mokonnen Mokonnen stressed that the TPLF emerged battle-hardened from its fight against the EDU, and Gebru Asrat reported that the TPLF leadership believed that the group could easily defeat the EPRP by the time the fight against the EDU was ending. See also Kahsay Berhe, *Ethiopia*, 58. The EPRP's problems of combat readiness and its limited military experience (often a source of discontent among the organization's rank and file) are a leitmotiv in Tadesse's *The Generation*, in particular 188, 370, 374, and 381. In interviews with the author, Begasho Ashenafi and an anonymous EPRP foot soldier (interviewed in August 2013, Addis Ababa) stressed the group's almost complete lack of battlefield experience at the beginning of the inter-rebel war, too.

79. Author interview with Aregawi Berhe; Tadesse, *The Generation*, 374–83. In 1977 the government eradicated the EPRP's urban infrastructure; hundreds of militants took refuge in the group's base area in Tigray, causing internal unrest. See Tadesse, *The Generation*, 269–301, 308–9.

80. In interviews with the author, Gebru Asrat and Tekleweini Assefa report similar assessments.

81. Berhe, *Tigray People's Liberation Front*, 225–53. See also Tadesse, *The Generation*, 407; Kahsay Berhe, *Ethiopia*, 75–76.

82. Kahsay Berhe, *Ethiopia*, 49–52; Aregawi Berhe, *Tigray People's Liberation Front*, 251–55; Awet T. Weldemichael, "Formative Alliances of Northeast African Insurgents: Eritrean Liberation Strategy and Ethiopian Armed Opposition," *Northeast African Studies* 14, no. 1 (March 2014): 83–122.

83. Weldemichael, "Formative Alliances."

84. Weldemichael, "Formative Alliances"; author interviews with EPLF Mesfin Hagos and with TPLF Ghidey Zeratsion and Aregawi Berhe.

85. Weldemichael "Formative Alliances," 103–8; Berhe, *Tigray People's Liberation Front*, 272–73, 315; author interviews with Aregawi Berhe, Mesfin Hagos, and Haile Menkerios.

86. Author interviews with Mesfin Hagos.

87. Tareke, *The Ethiopian Revolution*, 109.

88. In an interview with the author, Ahmed Nasser claimed that the battle was unplanned, which appears plausible given that only a relatively small ELF contingent was involved. See also Berhe, *Tigray People's Liberation Front*, 257.

89. Tadesse, *The Generation*, 436–37; Berhe, *Tigray People's Liberation Front*, 257–59.

90. Author interview with Gebru Asrat.

91. Quoted in Abbay, *Identity Jilted or Re-imagining Identity?*, 114.

92. As senior TPLF member Mokonnen Mokonnen noted in an interview with the author, "We wanted the EPLF to stay in power; otherwise, the Derg would focus all its forces on us."

93. As discussed earlier, there were about three thousand Ethiopian troops deployed in Eritrea (plus the local police) facing approximately a thousand insurgents. The force ratio obviously would be much more favorable to the government if one considered the entirety of Ethiopian armed forces (about forty thousand strong). While the insurgents were lightly armed, the Ethiopian forces benefited from heavier military equipment and training provided by the United States. See Woldemariam, *Insurgent Fragmentation*, 96; Jeffrey Alan Lefebvre, *Arms for the Horn: U.S. Security Policy in Ethiopia and Somalia, 1953–1991* (Pittsburgh: University of Pittsburgh Press, 1991), 109–10, 116; author interviews with Mesfin Hagos and Gime Ahmed.

94. Woldemariam, *Insurgent Fragmentation*, 101–6; Weldemichael, *Third World Colonialism*, 119–25; *Military Balance* (1971). In 1972 the ELF had grown to two thousand fighters but had a somewhat narrower operational reach than in 1965. While the Ethiopian armed forces had only marginally expanded by 1972, from 1967 on all three brigades of the Second Division had been deployed in Eritrea (in addition to the Israeli-trained "commandos"), so the force ratio in the province was more favorable to the government than in 1965.

95. Woldemariam, *Insurgent Fragmentation*, 101.

96. At some point between 1975 and 1977, the Eritrean rebels managed to wrest 90 percent of the province from government control. Based on Christia's favored measure of power, by 1977 the ELF constituted a minimum winning coalition on its own, as it

controlled more than 50 percent of Eritrean territory (assuming that the surface of the province, rather than the whole country, is the relevant denominator). Thus infighting between the two groups in this period would have been consistent with MWC theory, but the ELF and the EPLF continued to jointly fight the government, as predicted by window theory. See Woldemariam, *Insurgent Fragmentation*, 105–6.

97.   Berhe, *Tigray People's Liberation Front*, 95, 139; Young, *Peasant Revolution in Ethiopia*, 98.

98.   Peter Krause, *Rebel Power: Why National Movements Compete, Fight, and Win* (Ithaca, N.Y.: Cornell University Press, 2017). See in particular Krause's analysis of the Eritrean case, "Coercion by Movement: How Power Drove the Success of the Eritrean Insurgency, 1960–1993," in *Coercion: The Power to Hurt in International Politics*, ed. Kelly M. Greenhill and Peter Krause (New York: Oxford University Press, 2018).

99.   Krause's own assessment of the balance of power in the Eritrean movement supports my claim. The movement leader ELF attacked the challengers ELM and EPLF in 1965 and 1972, respectively, while the EPLF attacked the weaker ELF in 1980. Krause, "Coercion by Movement," 148, 150, 153–54.

100. For example, Krause reports in "Coercion by Movement," 153–54, that the EPLF overtook the ELF as movement leader by 1977, but infighting occurred only in 1980.

101. See, for example, Connell, *Against All Odds*, 180–81; Pool, *From Guerrillas to Government*, 76–87.

102. See, for example, Tareke, *The Ethiopian Revolution*, 101–2.

103. Interview with Osman Saleh Sabbe, conducted by Günter Schröder, December 1980, Khartoum. Similar initiatives by Sudan, Somalia, and various Arab countries are also reported by Ahmed Karar, Sudan's chief of security at the time (interviewed by Günter Schröder), and by Haile Menkerios, Tesfay Degiga, and Ahmed Nasser in interviews with the author.

104. I thank Will Reno for pointing this out.

105. See, for example, Connell, *Against All Odds*.

106. Awet T. Weldemichael, "African Diplomacy of Liberation: The Case of Eritrea's Search for an 'African India,'" *Cahiers d'Études Africaines* 212, no. 4 (2013): 867–94; Tareke, *The Ethiopian Revolution*, 74.

107. Weldemichael, "African Diplomacy of Liberation," 879. External support for the EPLF significantly declined after Osman Saleh Sabbe left the organization in 1977. See Pool, *From Guerrillas to Government*, 142.

108. Young, *Peasant Revolution in Ethiopia*, 102, 129–30; Berhe, *Tigray People's Liberation Front*, 107–8, 111–12.

109. Tadesse, *The Generation*, 130; author interviews with Tesfay Degiga and Ahmed Nasser.

110. Author interviews with Aregawi Berhe, Ghidey Zeratsion, and Gebru Asrat.

5. Inter-rebel War in Lebanon, Sri Lanka, and Syria

1.   Charles Winslow, *Lebanon: War and Politics in a Fragmented Society* (New York: Routledge, 1996), 220, 249, 269.

2. See, for example, Erik Melander, Thérése Pettersson, and Lotta Themnér, "Organized Violence, 1989–2015," *Journal of Peace Research* 53, no. 5 (2016): 727–42.

3. Theodor Hanf, *Coexistence in Wartime Lebanon: Decline of a State and Rise of a Nation* (London: Centre for Lebanese Studies, 1993), 75–97.

4. Walid Khalidi, *Conflict and Violence in Lebanon: A Confrontation in the Middle East* (Cambridge, Mass.: Center for International Affairs, Harvard University, 1979), 68–72; Lewis W. Snider, "The Lebanese Forces: Their Origins and Role in Lebanon's Politics," *Middle East Journal* 38, no. 1 (1984): 1–33.

5. Khalidi, *Conflict and Violence in Lebanon*, 72–82; Hanf, *Coexistence in Wartime Lebanon*, 181–94, 206–10; Winslow, *Lebanon*, 208–12; Tony Badran, "Lebanon's Militia Wars," in *Lebanon: Liberation, Conflict and Crisis*, ed. Barry Rubin (New York: Palgrave, 2009).

6. Hanf, *Coexistence in Wartime Lebanon*, 218.

7. Khalidi, *Conflict and Violence in Lebanon*, 56–65, 82–84; Lawrence L. Whetten, "The Military Dimension," in *Lebanon in Crisis: Participants and Issues*, ed. P. Edward Haley and Lewis W. Snider (Syracuse, N.Y.: Syracuse University Press, 1979); Hanf, *Coexistence in Wartime Lebanon*, 210–12, 215–26; Edgar O'Ballance, *Civil War in Lebanon, 1975–92* (New York: St. Martin's Press, 1998), 48; Jawaid Iqbal, *The Lebanese Civil War: Issues, Actors and Outcome* (Aligarh, India: Centre for West Asian Studies, 1998), 72–75, 79–80.

8. Even coethnic rebel groups should have been deterred by the likely high costs of infighting in 1976. At first, when the National Movement was winning on the battlefield, infighting would have entailed significant opportunity costs in terms of forgone military gains. Later, once Syria had turned against the rebels, infighting would have worsened the already difficult military situation that the National Movement was facing.

9. Khalidi, *Conflict and Violence in Lebanon*, 110–11; Wadi Haddad, *Lebanon: The Politics of Revolving Doors* (New York: Praeger, 1985), 57–58; Yair Evron, *War and Intervention in Lebanon: The Israeli-Syrian Deterrence Dialogue* (Baltimore: Johns Hopkins University Press, 1987), 66–67; Hanf, *Coexistence in Wartime Lebanon*, 231–32; O'Ballance, *Civil War in Lebanon*, 65–66.

10. Hanf, *Coexistence in Wartime Lebanon*, 237–40; Antoine J. Abraham, *The Lebanon War* (Westport, Conn.: Praeger, 1996), 113–14, 117–21.

11. Hanf, *Coexistence in Wartime Lebanon*, 239.

12. The Phalanges did clash against the Marada Brigade in the spring of 1978. The episode, however, does not amount to inter-rebel war as Marada was an ally of Syria, not a rebel group, as noted. See Hanf, *Coexistence in Wartime Lebanon*, 234–36.

13. Abraham, *The Lebanon War*, 121.

14. Hanf, *Coexistence in Wartime Lebanon*, 231–43.

15. In discussing Syria's gradual disengagement from Lebanese affairs in late 1978–1980, Itamar Rabinovich notes that "the other protagonists in the struggle over Lebanon's future were fully aware of the extent to which the [Syrian] regime's weakness and preoccupation with other matters limited its ability to pursue its objectives in Lebanon."

Rabinovich, *The War for Lebanon, 1970–1985* (Ithaca, N.Y.: Cornell University Press, 1985), 113. Similarly, after analyzing the challenges Syria was facing in 1978–1980, Robert G. Rabil observes that "neither Bashir [the Phalanges leader] nor the Israelis failed to notice Syria's weakness and preoccupation with domestic matters, which limited its ability to influence events in Lebanon." Rabil, *Embattled Neighbors: Syria, Israel and Lebanon* (Boulder, Colo.: Lynne Rienner, 2003), 62. See also Hanf, *Coexistence in Wartime Lebanon*, 246; O'Ballance, *Civil War in Lebanon*, 93.

16. Evron, *War and Intervention in Lebanon*, 90.

17. In 1978 Syria's Muslim Brotherhood intensified its militant activities, and in 1979 it massacred dozens of Alawite cadets in Aleppo; the following year Assad himself would narrowly escape an assassination attempt by the group.

18. Rabinovich, *The War for Lebanon*, 113, 114.

19. Hanf, *Coexistence in Wartime Lebanon*, 247–48. See also Rabinovich, *The War for Lebanon*, 114.

20. Rabil, *Embattled Neighbors*, 60.

21. Hanf, *Coexistence in Wartime Lebanon*, 247.

22. Badran, "Lebanon's Militia Wars," 164.

23. Badran, "Lebanon's Militia Wars," 163–65, 173–75.

24. Farid El-Khazen, *The Breakdown of the State in Lebanon, 1967–1976* (Cambridge, Mass.: Harvard University Press, 2000), 303–4.

25. Badran, "Lebanon's Militia Wars," 166. Hanf reports in *Coexistence in Wartime Lebanon*, 191, that Tanzim "was not so much a fighting force as an organization for training guerrillas," while the "Guardians of the Cedars were a marginal group." Jonathan C. Randal describes the Tanzim and the Guardians as "much smaller" than the Tigers and Phalanges. Randal, *Going All the Way: Christian Warlords, Israeli Adventurers, and the War in Lebanon* (New York: Viking, 1984), 117.

26. Hanf, *Coexistence in Wartime Lebanon*, 247.

27. Rabinovich, *The War for Lebanon*, 114. Similarly, just before discussing the destruction of the Tigers, Rabil implies that the Phalangist leader thought force could be used to get rid of threatening rivals and grow at their expense: "Bashir [Gemayel] had a clear-cut plan.... He perceived power as emanating from the barrel of a gun. He believed that political predominance in Lebanon had to be based on military power to be effective. For this reason, he strove to unify Christian military power under his command. Inveterate Maronite squabbling was a luxury he could not afford." Rabil, *Embattled Neighbors*, 59.

28. Rabinovich, *The War for Lebanon*, 115; Hanf, *Coexistence in Wartime Lebanon*, 333.

29. Randal, *Going All the Way*, 140. In *Embattled Neighbors*, 59, Rabil points out that "Bashir [Gemayel] was able to mobilize the Christian community and draw support from a large segment of the population who not too long before disapproved of and even despised the Phalangists."

30. Randal, *Going All the Way*, 224–26; Hanf, *Coexistence in Wartime Lebanon*, 248–52; Winslow, *Lebanon*, 240–41.

31. Randal, *Going All the Way*, 248–71; Evron, *War and Intervention in Lebanon*, 129–54; Hanf, *Coexistence in Wartime Lebanon*, 256–64; Elizabeth Picard, *Lebanon, a Shattered Country: Myths and Realities of the Wars in Lebanon* (New York: Holmes and Meier, 2002), 123–25.

32. Rabil reports that at a meeting of Lebanese Forces leaders in June 1982 (which he attended), Bashir Gemayel spoke of "Israel's invasion as the single most important event in Lebanon's civil war" and "explained that if the Christians played their cards right, they would emerge as the real victorious party in the war for Lebanon." Rabil, *Embattled Neighbors*, 68.

33. Hanf, *Coexistence in Wartime Lebanon*, 275–76. Controlling the Chouf would allow the Lebanese Forces to ensure the safety of the Christian population living there and establish a land link between the Christian stronghold in central Lebanon and Israel.

34. Rabil, *Embattled Neighbors*, 71.

35. The killing of a large number of civilians in the Palestinian camps of Sabra and Shatila in West Beirut was perpetrated by elements of the Lebanese Forces; the Israeli army, however, was accused of connivance as it controlled the areas surrounding the camps and thus presumably had knowledge of the events taking place inside them over the span of several days. See Evron, *War and Intervention in Lebanon*, 160–61; Rabil, *Embattled Neighbors*, 74.

36. Rabinovich, *The War for Lebanon*, 174–79; Hanf, *Coexistence in Wartime Lebanon*, 282–93; O'Ballance, *Civil War in Lebanon*, 137–38; Rabil, *Embattled Neighbors*, 73–75.

37. Limited clashes in February 1986 represented the main exception. See Hanf, *Coexistence in Wartime Lebanon*, 310.

38. Amal had long held the PLO responsible for the suffering of Lebanon's Shia population, caught in the crossfire between the Palestinian insurgents and Israel. The group did not participate in the Lebanese civil war until 1984 but had clashed with Palestinian forces in the South between 1979 and 1982.

39. Badran reports that the PSP joined the fight on Amal's side only when the latter experienced difficulties in defeating Mourabitoun. Badran, "Lebanon's Militia Wars," 43–44; see also Augustus Richard Norton, *Amal and the Shi'a: Struggle for the Soul of Lebanon* (Austin: University of Texas Press, 1987), 134. By contrast, Hanf mentions an earlier clash between the PSP and Mourabitoun in the summer of 1984, in *Coexistence in Wartime Lebanon*, 297.

40. Joe Stork, "The War of the Camps, the War of the Hostages," *MERIP Reports* 133 (1985); Rami Siklawi, "The Dynamics of the Amal Movement in Lebanon 1975–90," *Arab Studies Quarterly* 34, no. 1 (2012): 4–26.

41. Norton, *Amal and the Shi'a*, 134–36; Hanf, *Coexistence in Wartime Lebanon*, 302–5, 312–18; Winslow, *Lebanon*, 261–62; Picard *Lebanon, a Shattered Country*, 135; Badran, "Lebanon's Militia Wars," 46–47.

42. Hanf, *Coexistence in Wartime Lebanon*, 336–37. See also Badran, "Lebanon's Militia Wars," 36–37. West Beirut represents an exception to the rule. The PLO capitulated to the Israeli siege and bombardment, while the pro-Syrian groups did not challenge the

takeover of the city by superior Israeli forces and the subsequent transfer to the Lebanese army. The joint offensive by Amal, PSP, and Mourabitoun in 1984, however, retook West Beirut with relative ease, as its primarily Muslim inhabitants welcomed Syria's allies and Shia units in the army sided with Amal.

43.   Hanf, *Coexistence in Wartime Lebanon*, 296.

44.   To be sure, reintensification of the fighting is always possible; after all, even once belligerents sign a peace agreement and disarmament and demobilization are under way, there is a nonnegligible risk of civil war recrudescence. The point is that there may be circumstances, like those prevailing in Lebanon in 1985–1989, in which rebel groups are confident that in the absence of a major shock (in this case, Syria's departing from its well-established practice of preventing either side from achieving outright victory), infighting would carry such low costs as to make it an acceptable course of action even without the relatively high benefits associated with a shared ethnic identity among rebels. Compare the situation in 1985–1989 with that in 1983–1984: benefiting from significant Syrian support, the PSP and Amal were making major territorial gains in the Chouf and West Beirut in 1983 and 1984, which infighting might have jeopardized; in 1985–1989, instead, there was no significant fighting, let alone shifts in territorial control between the two civil war camps.

45.   Magnus Ranstorp, *Hizb'Allah in Lebanon: The Politics of the Western Hostage Crisis* (London: Palgrave, 1997), 101. While there had been sporadic clashes before, the "Shi'i civil war proper broke out April 1988." See Hanf, *Coexistence in Wartime Lebanon*, 317.

46.   Augustus Richard Norton reports that "although its leading members refer to 1982 as the year the group was founded, Hezbollah did not exist as a coherent organization until the mid-1980s. From 1982 through the mid-1980s it was less an organization than a cabal." Norton, *Hezbollah: A Short History* (Princeton, N.J.: Princeton University Press, 2007), 34. See also Hala Jaber, *Hezbollah: Born with a Vengeance* (New York: Columbia University Press, 1997), 53–54, 62.

47.   Eitan Azani, *The Story of the Party of God: From Revolution to Institutionalization* (New York: Palgrave, 2009), 63.

48.   A. Nisar Hamzeh, "Lebanon's Hizbullah: From Islamic Revolution to Parliamentary Accommodation," *Third World Quarterly* 14, no 2 (1993): 321–37, esp. 322; Azani, *Party of God*, 60–61. Norton reports that, following Israel's 1982 invasion, Syria allowed the establishment of a thousand-man contingent of Iranian Revolutionary Guards in the Bekaa both to fight Israel and to get Hezbollah off the ground; but as Damascus regained strength, it became more lukewarm toward the new organizations. See Norton, *Amal and the Shi'a*, 100–101. See also William Harris, "The View from Zahle: Security and Economic Conditions in the Central Bekaa 1980–1985," *Middle East Journal* 39, no. 3 (1985): 270–86, esp. 281; and Jaber, *Hezbollah*, 31.

49.   Azani, *Party of God*, 63–64. Timur Goksel, the spokesperson of the UN peacekeeping mission in southern Lebanon, offered a similar assessment of Amal's initial view of Hezbollah: "Since 1985, Hizballah started to share Amal's domination of the Shi'i community. Initially Amal did not care too much, as it was confident that it was untouchable. Amal did not pay a lot of attention to Hizballah as it did not think

Hizballah was going to be well organized, active and a serious challenger." Reported in Siklawi, "Dynamics of the Amal Movement," 20–21.

50. Stork, "The War of the Camps"; Siklawi, "Dynamics of the Amal Movement," 20; Hanf, *Coexistence in Wartime Lebanon*, 317; Picard, *Lebanon*, 136; Azani, *Party of God*, 73.

51. Norton notes that Hezbollah was "numerically inferior to Amal," which in particular had a 5:1 advantage in Beirut. He also estimates that at the end of the Lebanese civil war in 1990 Amal and Hezbollah had 6,500 and 3,500 fighters, respectively. Norton, *Amal and the Shi'a*, 101; and Norton, "Lebanon After Ta'if: Is the Civil War over?," *Middle East Journal* 45, no. 3 (1991): 468.

52. This suggests that Amal may have committed a crucial miscalculation in allowing Hezbollah's rise while fighting against the PSP and the PLO. I do not have enough information to assess the balance of power between Amal and Hezbollah during their fight in terms of other relevant measures of power, but it is plausible that Amal's loss of members created some problems of internal cohesion negatively affecting its military effectiveness.

53. Siklawi, "Dynamics of the Amal Movement," 21–22; Azani, *Party of God*, 76–82; Dominique Avon and Anaïs-Trissa Khatchadourian, *Hezbollah: A History of the "Party of God"* (Cambridge, Mass.: Harvard University Press, 2012), 36.

54. Ronald D. McLaurin, "From Professional to Political: The Redecline of the Lebanese Army," *Armed Forces and Society* 17, no. 4 (1991): 551; Hanf, *Coexistence in Wartime Lebanon*, 572–73; Winslow, *Lebanon*, 271–72.

55. Hanf, *Coexistence in Wartime Lebanon*, 599. The three Muslims whom Aoun nominated as members of his government, in keeping with Lebanon's power-sharing formula, did not accept the posts, so the cabinet consisted of only three Christian ministers. Aoun's pro-Christian position became more explicit later, when he publicly opposed the September 1989 agreement reducing Christian influence in the power-sharing system and legitimizing the continued involvement in Lebanon of Syria, that is, the ally of the Sunni political leaders, the Shia Amal, and the Druze PSP.

56. In fact, "the Syrian government had officially warned Aoun that he might do as he wished in 'his' part of the country, but they would not tolerate any action against militias in other parts of the country." Hanf, *Coexistence in Wartime Lebanon*, 573.

57. Hanf, *Coexistence in Wartime Lebanon*, 572–74. I do not have information on the other dimensions of the balance of power at this time, besides the fact that both sides were heavily armed.

58. Hanf, *Coexistence in Wartime Lebanon*, 572–73; Winslow, *Lebanon*, 271.

59. Hanf, *Coexistence in Wartime Lebanon*, 573–90; Winslow, *Lebanon*, 272–75.

60. Hanf, *Coexistence in Wartime Lebanon*, 598–621; Winslow, *Lebanon*, 276–82; Rabil, *Embattled Neighbors*, 78–80.

61. Amal was still engaged in its intra-Shia fight against Hezbollah until the fall of 1990 and did not play an important role in the final phase of the civil war. Besides the Syrian forces, the two key actors in the final attack on Aoun's stronghold in October 1990 were the Hrawi government and the Lebanese Forces. Window theory would correctly

predict the absence of infighting between them too as non-coethnic (Hrawi's soldiers were primarily Muslim).

62. Hanf, *Coexistence in Wartime Lebanon*, 596. McLaurin reports (without providing supporting evidence) that army officers believed that Aoun's forces would quickly defeat the Lebanese Forces. However, he then lists ten reasons why this "remarkable assessment" was wrong and the fight would be indecisive. McLaurin, "From Professional to Political," 556–58.

63. McLaurin, "From Professional to Political," 599; Winslow, *Lebanon*, 276–77.

64. Hanf, *Coexistence in Wartime Lebanon*, 598. See also McLaurin, "From Professional to Political," 555–56.

65. Fotini Christia, *Alliance Formation in Civil Wars* (New York: Cambridge University Press, 2012).

66. Khalidi, *Conflict and Violence in Lebanon*, 103; Robert Fisk, *Pity the Nation: The Abduction of Lebanon* (New York: Thunder's Mouth, 1990), 86–87; Hanf, *Coexistence in Wartime Lebanon*, 225–26, 236, 254; Badran, "Lebanon's Militia Wars," 38–46.

67. Peter Krause, *Rebel Power: Why National Movements Compete, Fight, and Win* (Ithaca, N.Y.: Cornell University Press, 2017).

68. Hanf, *Coexistence in Wartime Lebanon*, 248, 598; Winslow, *Lebanon*, 276–77; Sandra Mackey, *A Mirror of the Arab World: Lebanon in Conflict* (New York: Norton, 2008), 133–34.

69. Hanf, *Coexistence in Wartime Lebanon*, 303–5, 312–15. During the fight, Syria provided fifty tanks to Amal but none to the PSP.

70. Azani, *Party of God*, 79–81. Hezbollah's main foreign sponsor, Iran, also seems to have opposed the intra-Shia fighting, as it publicly condemned both Amal and Hezbollah for their fratricide. See Avon and Khatchadourian, *Hezbollah*, 36.

71. Paul Staniland, "Between a Rock and a Hard Place: Insurgent Fratricide, Ethnic Defection, and the Rise of Pro-State Paramilitaries," *Journal of Conflict Resolution* 56, no. 1 (February 2012): 16–40; Staniland, *Networks of Rebellion: Explaining Insurgent Cohesion and Collapse* (Ithaca, N.Y.: Cornell University Press, 2014), 149–54. The rebel groups had distinct but highly overlapping social bases among Sri Lanka's Tamil population; in fact, "up to this time [1985] the Tamil population had hardly differentiated between rival groups. They were all referred to as boys and even Tigers." University Teachers for Human Rights (Jaffna), *The Broken Palmyra* (Sri Lanka, 1990), chap. 5, http://www.uthr.org/BP/volume1/Chapter5.htm.

72. Brendan O'Duffy, "LTTE: Majoritarianism, Self-Determination, and Military-to-Political Transition in Sri Lanka," in *Terrorism, Insurgency, and the State: Ending Protracted Conflict*, ed. Marianne Heiberg, Brendan O'Leary, and John Tirman (Philadelphia: University of Pennsylvania Press, 2007), 257. See also Rohan Gunaratna, *Indian Intervention in Sri Lanka: The Role of India's Intelligence Agencies* (Colombo: South Asian Network on Conflict Research, 1993), 411; Stephen Hopgood, "Tamil Tigers, 1987–2002," in *Making Sense of Suicide Missions*, ed. Diego Gambetta (Oxford: Oxford University Press, 2005).

73. For analyses of the factors that may have contributed to the LTTE's defeat, see Niel A. Smith, "Understanding Sri Lanka's Defeat of the Tamil Tigers," *Joint Forces Quarterly*, 59, no. 4 (2010): 40–44; Ahmed Hashim, *When Counterinsurgency Wins: Sri Lanka's Defeat of the Tamil Tiger* (Philadelphia: University of Pennsylvania Press, 2013), 132–96.

74. Gunaratna, *Indian Intervention in Sri Lanka*, 411.

75. For an account of the sporadic attacks conducted by Tamil militants in the decade before 1983, see M. R. Narayan Swamy, *Tigers of Lanka: From Boys to Guerrillas* (Delhi: Konark, 1994), 23–91. For an analysis of the outbidding dynamics among Sinhala political parties over the issue of the country's official language that brought about the Sinhala-Tamil conflict after Sri Lanka's independence, see Stanley Tambiah, *Sri Lanka: Ethnic Fratricide and the Dismantling of Democracy* (Chicago: University of Chicago Press, 1986).

76. Swamy, *Tigers of Lanka*, 93–97; John Richardson, *Paradise Poisoned: Learning About Conflict, Terrorism and Development from Sri Lanka's Civil Wars* (Kandy, Sri Lanka: International Center for Ethnic Studies, 2005), 523–28. Swamy (104) points out that none of the Tamil armed groups had more than fifty members before the onset of the war in 1983. Likewise, O'Duffy, in "LTTE," 257, reports that before the fateful ambush the LTTE consisted of "30 poorly armed dissidents."

77. Richardson, *Paradise Poisoned*, 530.

78. Swamy, *Tigers of Lanka*, 109.

79. Richardson, *Paradise Poisoned*, 530, 545–46.

80. Swamy, *Tigers of Lanka*, 147.

81. M. R. Narayan Swamy, *Inside an Elusive Mind, Prabhakaran: The First Profile of the World's Most Ruthless Guerrilla Leader* (Delhi: Konark, 2003), 132. Similarly, Ketheshwaran Loganathan (former EPRLF spokesperson) observes that "amongst the non-LTTE organizations, it was TELO, with a record of sensational attacks against the security forces that came anywhere close to matching LTTE's prowess in the battlefield." Loganathan, *Sri Lanka: Lost Opportunities, Past Attempts at Resolving Ethnic Conflict* (Colombo: Centre for Policy Research and Analysis, 1996), 119.

82. Swamy, *Tigers of Lanka*, 143.

83. Swamy, *Tigers of Lanka*, 178.

84. Swamy, *Tigers of Lanka*, 179–83; Dagmar Hellmann-Rajanayagam, *The Tamil Tigers: Armed Struggle for Identity* (Stuttgart, Germany: Steiner, 1994), 42–43; Ambalavanar Sivarajah, *Politics of Tamil Nationalism in Sri Lanka* (New Delhi: South Asian, 1996), 134–35; Swamy, *Inside an Elusive Mind*, 132; Mark Whitaker, *Learning Politics from Sivaram: The Life and Death of a Revolutionary Tamil Journalist in Sri Lanka* (London: Pluto Press, 2007), 92–95. Thus the observations that "in early 1985, the P.L.O.T.E., L.T.T.E. and T.E.L.O. were considered fairly evenly balanced" appears inaccurate. In fact, the same source indirectly acknowledges PLOT's inferiority by pointing out that while "militarily the T.E.L.O. had come to rival the L.T.T.E.," PLOT lacked battlefield experience, and "by mid-1986 the organisation had suffered from neglect from the

leadership in India and was poorly armed." See University Teachers for Human Rights (Jaffna), *The Broken Palmyra*, chap. 5.

85. In the words of Swamy, EROS and EPRLF found themselves "plodding behind in the race for militant leadership" According to Swamy, EROS "was largely seen as a group of intellectuals based in London," and Hellmann-Rajanayagam observes that it "kept an extremely low profile," focusing on terrorist attacks in the South rather than engaging the government forces in battle in the North. The EPRLF too had largely been inactive on the battlefield until 1986 and was generally considered "militarily weak," as Swamy notes. Gunaratna reports that in early 1986 TELO had more fighters at its disposal than EROS and EPRLF combined. Swamy, *Tigers of Lanka*, 102, 104, 203, 209; Hellmann-Rajanayagam, *The Tamil Tigers*, 81; Gunaratna, *Indian Intervention in Sri Lanka*, 140, 148, 155.

86. University Teachers for Human Rights (Jaffna), *The Broken Palmyra*, chap. 5.

87. Swamy, *Inside an Elusive Mind*, 135.

88. Swamy, *The Tigers of Lanka*, 189–90.

89. University Teachers for Human Rights (Jaffna), *The Broken Palmyra*, chap. 5; Swamy, *Tigers of Lanka*, 191–96.

90. Swamy, *Inside an Elusive Mind*, 143.

91. Swamy, *Tigers of Lanka*, 207–9; Whitaker, *Learning Politics from Sivaram*, 94–95.

92. As Swamy puts it in *Tigers of Lanka*, 223, by the end of 1986, "PLOT had ceased to exist for all intents and purposes." See also Hellmann-Rajanayagam, *The Tamil Tigers*, 44; Staniland, *Networks of Rebellion*, 164.

93. Swamy, *Tigers of Lanka*, 203–9; Gunaratna, *Indian Intervention in Sri Lanka*, 147–49; University Teachers for Human Rights (Jaffna), *The Broken Palmyra*, chap. 5.

94. Swamy, *Tigers of Lanka*, 221–22.

95. Richardson, *Paradise Poisoned*, 531. The emergence of TELO's internal unrest marked the opening of a window of vulnerability for the EPRLF and the PLOT, in addition to a window of opportunity for the LTTE, as the other Tamil groups could have expected the LTTE to grow stronger by defeating TELO and absorbing its resources. According to window theory, however, a hegemonic bid by the Tigers was more likely than a gamble for resurrection by the EPRLF and the PLOT: weaker groups typically would be reluctant to act until less risky paths out of their predicament have been ruled out; moreover, EPRLF and PLOT would have also experienced collective action problems in mounting a joint attack. By contrast, the would-be hegemon would have an incentive to act swiftly.

96. Staniland, *Networks of Rebellion*, 165.

97. Both Swamy and the University Teachers for Human Rights (Jaffna) report that EROS was the smallest of the main Tamil armed organizations. Swamy, *The Tigers of Lanka*, 186; Teachers for Human Rights (Jaffna), *The Broken Palmyra*, chap. 5. There are no reports, unlike for the EPRLF, that EROS overcame its lack of battlefield experience in 1986.

98. Interview by Jon Lee Anderson with Anton Balasingham, 1987, in Jon Lee Anderson and Scott Anderson, *War Zones* (New York: Dodd Mead, 1988), 200.

99.   Swamy, *Tigers of Lanka*, 223.

100. Gunaratna, *Indian Intervention in Sri Lanka*, 361.

101. Swamy, *Tigers of Lanka*, 169–71. In fact, in the course of the year, Colombo's forces unsuccessfully tried several times to break the encirclement of their bases by the Tamil insurgents.

102. Richardson, *Paradise Poisoned*, 545–46. See also Swamy, *Tigers of Lanka*, 202–3. For a discussion of the problems at the root of the Sri Lankan army's indecisive approach to counterinsurgency up to 1987, see Hashim, *When Counterinsurgency Wins*, 90–93.

103. Swamy, *Tigers of Lanka*, 190–91.

104. Swamy, *Tigers of Lanka*, 212–13; Loganathan, *Sri Lanka*, 108–15.

105. University Teachers for Human Rights (Jaffna), *The Broken Palmyra*, chap. 5. See also Hellmann-Rajanayagam, *The Tamil Tigers*, 13–14; Gunaratna, *Indian Intervention in Sri Lanka*, 164–65.

106. Dayan Jayatilleka, *The Indian Intervention in Sri Lanka, 1987–1990: The North-east Provincial Council and Devolution of Power* (Kandy, Sri Lanka: International Centre for Ethnic Studies, 1999), 21.

107. University Teachers for Human Rights (Jaffna), *The Broken Palmyra*, chaps. 7–8; S. D. Muni, *Pangs of Proximity: India and Sri Lanka's Ethnic Crisis* (Oslo: PRIO, 1993); Swamy, *Tigers of Lanka*, 225–50.

108. Swamy, *Tigers of Lanka*, 255–68; Loganathan, *Sri Lanka*, 126–34; Gunaratna, *Indian Intervention in Sri Lanka*, 236–40.

109. Swamy, *Tigers of Lanka*, 270, 271–80.

110. Loganathan, *Sri Lanka*, 139; Swamy, *Tigers of Lanka*, 286. As Dagmar Hellmann-Rajanayagam observes, "The EPRLF could only survive with India's help." Hellmann-Rajanayagam, *The Tamil Tigers*, 121.

111. Gunaratna, *Indian Intervention in Sri Lanka*, 391.

112. William Clarance, *Ethnic Warfare in Sri Lanka and the UN Crisis* (London: Pluto Press, 2007), 54; Swamy, *Tigers of Lanka*, 300–319; Loganathan, *Sri Lanka*, 156–62; Gunaratna, *Indian Intervention in Sri Lanka*, 433–40.

113. Paul Staniland, "Explaining Cohesion, Fragmentation, and Control in Insurgent Groups," Ph.D. dissertation, Massachusetts Institute of Technology, 2010, 456. For similar observations, see, for example, Hellmann-Rajanayagam, *The Tamil Tigers*, 1; Swamy, *Inside an Elusive Mind*, 211. For a detailed description of the state-like system of governance established by the LTTE in areas under its control, see Zachariah C. Mampilly, *Rebel Rulers: Insurgent Governance and Civilian Life During War* (Ithaca, N.Y.: Cornell University Press, 2011), 108–13.

114. For example, Swamy reports that the LTTE hunted down many TELO members after the group's defeat, but others were allowed to join the Tigers' ranks. Moreover, Whitaker reports that the Tigers demanded that the PLOT, before leaving Jaffna, hand over to them five hundred trained cadres based in Tamil Nadu awaiting deployment in Sri Lanka. Swamy, *Tigers of Lanka*, 191–96; Whitaker, *Learning Politics from Sivaram*, 95. Other rebel groups appear to have realized the implications of a shared ethnic constituency, though they miscalculated their chances of success in the intraethnic

struggle. In particular, TELO's head is said to have claimed that "LTTE guerrillas would flock to the TELO if only the Tiger boss was done away with." See Swamy, *Inside an Elusive Mind*, 133.

115.   Swamy, *Tigers of Lanka*, 169. The rebel groups claimed (and the LTTE eventually controlled) as the Tamil homeland much larger swaths of Tamil-inhabited territory than the Jaffna peninsula.

116.   The LTTE's figure is from Swamy, *Tigers of Lanka*, 280. Sri Lanka's armed forces were forty-eight thousand strong (with forty thousand soldiers in the army, including active reservists). No information is available on the number of Sri Lanka's troops deployed in Tamil areas, but they are likely to have constituted a large share, given that its forces were not involved in other military operations until the Sinhalese rebellion in the South following the India-Sri Lanka Accord. See *Military Balance* (1986–1987).

117.   Krause, *Rebel Power*.

118.   Swamy, *Inside an Elusive Mind*, 200, 135. See also Gunaratna, *Indian Intervention in Sri Lanka*, 403–12.

119.   See, for example, Staniland, *Networks of Rebellion*, chap. 6. The relative degree of group cohesion is indeed an important part of the explanation of the Tigers' behavior—the LTTE attacked its rivals when they were immersed in internal strife—but this is fully consistent with window theory, which identifies organizational cohesion as one of the key dimensions of the inter-rebel balance of power.

120.   As Richardson notes in *Paradise Poisoned*, 528, "RAW's [Research and Analysis Wing, India's external intelligence agency] strategy was to maintain control by preventing any one group from becoming dominant." As part of this strategy, RAW arm-twisted the Tigers into joining the Eelam National Liberation Front (ENLF), an umbrella organization composed of TELO, EROS, and EPRLF. See Swamy, *Tigers of Lanka*, 143; Swamy, *Inside an Elusive Mind*, 119–20. Sri Lanka's intelligence operatives too "assessed that RAW was not behind LTTE plans to achieve total control of the political, economic and social life in the Jaffna peninsula. They also assessed that RAW had not encouraged LTTE to eliminate rival groups." See Gunaratna, *Indian Intervention in Sri Lanka*, 166.

121.   Stephen Hopgood, "Tamil Tigers."

122.   See in particular, Swamy, *Tigers of Lanka*, 330.

123.   Swamy, *Inside an Elusive Mind*, 2003, 91; Muni, *Pangs of Proximity*, 67.

124.   Muni's book is the only source reporting that in 1985 PLOT struck an agreement with Colombo to find a negotiated settlement and fight other Tamil organizations. Muni, *Pangs of Proximity*, 67. In any case, the fact that fears of rivals' defection to the government may affect rebels' threat perception and thus contribute to motivate inter-rebel war is not at odds with my argument. Window theory would be falsified only if fears of defection (whether arising spontaneously or through manipulation by the government) tended to be sufficient to cause inter-rebel war, regardless of the presence of windows of opportunity and windows of vulnerability.

125.   Hellman-Rajanayagam, *The Tamil Tigers*, 121; Staniland, "Between a Rock and a Hard Place," 32.

126. Hashim, *When Counterinsurgency Wins*, 90–92. See also Raj Vijayasiri, "A Critical Analysis of the Sri Lankan Government's Counterinsurgency Campaign," Master's thesis, Command and Staff College, Fort Leavenworth, Kansas, 1999.

127. "All this time [during the LTTE-TELO fight] the Sri Lankan army had remained quiet except for a bit of helicopter firing here and there." University Teachers for Human Rights (Jaffna), *The Broken Palmyra*, chap. 5.

128. See, for example, William McCants, *The ISIS Apocalypse* (New York: St. Martin's Press, 2015); Graeme Wood, "What ISIS Really Wants," *Atlantic* (March 2015). For a different view, positing that ISIS's extremism serves the vital functions of signaling the group's strong commitment to a political cause and thus attracting and retaining both recruits and civilian supporters, see Barbara F. Walter, "The Extremist's Advantage in Civil Wars," *International Security* 42, no. 2 (Fall 2017): 7–39.

129. Anonymous, "The Mystery of ISIS," *New York Review of Books*, August 13, 2015.

130. Mohammed M. Hafez, "Fratricidal Jihadists: Why Islamists Keep Losing Their Civil Wars," *Middle East Policy* 25, no. 2 (2018): 86–99, quote on 94.

131. ISIS fought in a multiparty civil war across the border too, coordinating its summer 2014 offensive against the Iraqi government with several other Sunni rebel groups. I focus on Syria's civil war because the information on the other rebel groups in Iraq and their relations with ISIS over time is relatively scant. See Charles Lister, *The Syrian Jihad: Al-Qaeda, the Islamic State and the Evolution of an Insurgency* (New York: Oxford University Press, 2015), 231–32.

132. Michael Weiss and Hassan Hassan, *ISIS: Inside the Army of Terror* (New York: Regan Arts, 2015), 132–42. While there certainly were non-Alawites in regime ranks, members of the Alawite minority dominated executive power in Syria. Alawites also dominated the military elite, whereas Sunni Arabs constituted the bulk of the rank and file (as well as the vast majority of the thousands of defecting soldiers). This is of course not to say that the regime had no support among Syria's Sunni Arab population. As Kevin Mazur shows, at least in the first year of the Syrian uprising, Sunni communities that were integrated in regime patronage networks were relatively quiescent. See Kevin Mazur, "State Networks and Intra-Ethnic Group Variation in the 2011 Syrian Uprising," *Comparative Political Studies* 52, no. 7 (June 2019): 995–1027. On Alawite dominance, see Christopher Phillips, "Sectarianism and Conflict in Syria," *Third World Quarterly* 36, no. 2 (2015): 357–76, esp. 366; Theodore McLauchlin, "The Loyalty Trap: Regime Ethnic Exclusion, Commitment Problems, and Civil War Duration in Syria and Beyond," *Security Studies* 27, no. 2 (2018): 296–317, esp. 305–6.

133. International Crisis Group, "Tentative Jihad: Syria's Fundamentalist Opposition," *Middle East Report* 131 (2012): 1–2; Elizabeth O'Bagy, "The Free Syrian Army," *Middle East Security Report* 9 (Institute for the Study of War, 2013); Valerie Szybala, "Al-Qaeda Shows Its True Colors in Syria," *Backgrounder* (Institute for the Study of War, 2013). In keeping with much literature on the Syrian civil war, by "Jihadist" I mean rebel organizations that see themselves as engaged in a global Jihad (struggle/war) on behalf of the umma (the worldwide Sunni community), such as al-Qaeda and ISIS. "Salafist" refers to rebel organizations (e.g., Ahrar al-Sham) that propound a literalist

interpretation of Islamic scriptures, a revival of the practices of Islam's forefathers (the "Salaf"), and the establishment of a religious state; they too consider themselves as engaged in Jihad, but its scope is limited to Syria rather than transnational. "Moderate Islamist" indicates rebel organizations with a broad range of political views inspired by Islam but generally less extreme than Salafists and Jihadists (for example, envisioning a separation of state and religion or at least strong legal protections for other religions); many groups affiliated with the FSA and Syria's Muslim Brotherhood fall into this category.

134. International Crisis Group, "Tentative Jihad," 21; Phillips, "Sectarianism and Conflict in Syria," 369. The most prominent exception is the Kurdish Islamic Front, a primarily Kurdish Islamist group, which Ahrar al-Sham helped create. See Aron Lund, "The Politics of the Islamic Front, Part 5: The Kurds," *Diwan* blog (Carnegie Endowment for International Peace), January 30, 2014, https://carnegie-mec.org/diwan/54367.

135. Ahmed S. Hashim, "The Islamic State: From al-Qaeda Affiliate to Caliphate," *Middle East Policy* 21, no. 4, (2014): 69–83; Andrew W. Terrill, "Confronting the 'Islamic State': Understanding the Strengths and Vulnerabilities of ISIS," *Parameters* 44, no. 3 (2014): 13–23; Aymenn Jawad al-Tamimi, "The Dawn of the Islamic State of Iraq and ash-Sham," *Current Trends in Islamist Ideology* 16 (Hudson Institute, 2014).

136. Al-Tamimi, "Dawn of the Islamic State," 6; International Crisis Group, "Rigged Cars and Barrel Bombs: Aleppo and the State of the Syrian War," *Middle East Report* 55 (2014): 5.

137. Aaron Y. Zelin, "The War Between ISIS and al-Qaeda for Supremacy of the Global Jihadist Movement," *Research Notes* (Washington Institute for Near East Policy, 2014); Lister, *The Syrian Jihad*, 139–49; McCants, *The ISIS Apocalypse*, 89–96.

138. Lister, *The Syrian Jihad*, 159–60; Isabel Nassief, "The Campaign for Homs and Aleppo," *Middle East Security Report* 17 (Institute for the Study of War, 2014), 27–35.

139. On Sunni rebels' clashes with the PYD and its armed wing, see, for example, Lister, *The Syrian Jihad*, 95–96, 153–54, 289–96.

140. International Crisis Group, "Flight of Icarus? The PYD's Precarious Rise in Syria," *Middle East Report* 151 (2014): i, 7.

141. Barak Barfi, "Ascent of the PYD and the SDF," Research Notes 32, Washington Institute for Near East Policy (April 2016), 6. See also Ozlem Kayhan Pusane, "How to Profile PYD/YPG as an Actor in the Syrian Civil War: Policy Implications for the Region and Beyond," in *Violent Non-state Actors and the Syrian Civil War: The ISIS and YPG Cases*, ed. Özden Zeynep Oktav, Emel Parlar Dal, and Ali Murat Kurşun (New York: Springer, 2018), 77–78.

142. Patrick Cockburn, "Syria Civil War: Kurdish Leader Says Collapse of Assad Regime 'Would Be a Disaster' Despite Its Treatment of His People," *Independent*, September 24, 2015.

143. International Crisis Group, "Rigged Cars and Barrel Bombs," 6; Lister, *The Syrian Jihad*, 157–58, 166.

144. Hassan Hassan, "Rebel vs. Rebel," *Foreign Policy*, September 18, 2013; "Syrian Rebel Factions Tell Al Qaeda Groups to Withdraw," *France24*, October 3, 2013, http://www

.france24.com/en/20131003-syrian-rebels-tell-qaeda-groups-withdraw-homs-isil-azaz); Lister, *The Syrian Jihad*, 162, 166–67, 175.

145. It is important to use information that was plausibly available to the rebels at the time rather than committing the fallacy of relying on the hindsight knowledge that, from the second half of 2014, ISIS grew exponentially and managed to take over large swaths of Iraqi and Syrian territory, prompting a U.S.-led intervention to contain its rampage.

146. Lister, *The Syrian Jihad*, 166. ISIS would be smaller (if marginally) than Ahrar al-Sham even if one included in the calculation the Islamic State's troops in Iraq. On the groups' size estimates, see "Syria's Islamist Fighters: Competition Among Islamists," *Economist*, July 20, 2013; James Traud, "Everyone Is Scared of ISIS," *Foreign Policy*, October 4, 2013, http://foreignpolicy.com/2013/10/04/everyone-is-scared-of-isis/; "Syria Crisis: Guide to Armed and Political Opposition," *BBC News*, December, 13, 2013, http://www.bbc.co.uk/news/worldmiddle-east-24403003; "What ISIS, an al-Qaeda Affiliate in Syria, Really Wants," *The Economist Explains* (blog), January 20, 2014, http://www.economist.com/blogs/economist-explains/2014/01/economist-explains-12; Mapping Militant Organizations database, https://cisac.fsi.stanford.edu/mappingmilitants/profiles/ (entries for the three groups).

147. For descriptions of al-Nusra's and Ahrar al-Sham's disciplined and tightly organized nature as well as their battlefield prowess and significant firepower, see, for example, Szybala, "Al-Qaeda Shows Its True Colors in Syria," 6n28; "Syria Crisis"; "Syria's Islamist Fighters: Competition Among Islamists," *Economist*; Jennifer Cafarella, "Jabat al-Nusra in Syria: An Islamic Emirate for al-Qaeda," Middle East Security Report 25 (Institute for the Study of War, 2014); Lister, *The Syrian Jihad*, 146.

148. International Crisis Group, "Rigged Cars and Barrel Bombs," 10–12; Charles C. Caris and Samuel Reynolds, "ISIS Governance in Syria," *Middle East Security Report* 22 (Institute for the Study of War, 2014), 12–13; Lister, *The Syrian Jihad*, 187–91; Weiss and Hassan, *ISIS*, 194–95.

149. Lister, *The Syrian Jihad*, 190.

150. International Crisis Group, "Rigged Cars and Barrel Bombs," 11. The fact that Ahrar al-Sham's fighters in eastern Syria offered safe passage to ISIS's contingents in two circumstances, even though the organization as a whole had been an active participant in the fight against the Islamic State around Aleppo, may have been of crucial help to ISIS. Moreover, ISIS's recovery was probably facilitated by the fact the Syrian government focused its attention mostly on the rest of the opposition forces, rarely targeting ISIS. Analysts have suggested that the government's restraint toward ISIS in this period was due to the fact that the areas in the East controlled by the group were of lesser strategic importance than those contested by the rest of the opposition (e.g., Aleppo). Moreover, Assad supposedly reasoned that countries of the West would have no choice but to support him against ISIS once less extreme insurgents had been disposed of. See, for example, International Crisis Group, "Rigged Cars and Barrel Bombs," 12; Terrill, "Confronting the 'Islamic State,'" 18.

151.   Anne Barnard, "Dual Threat Has Mainstream Syrian Rebels Fearing Demise: Facing Both ISIS Militants and Bashar al-Assad's Forces in Syria," *New York Times*, August 15, 2014; Jeffrey White, "ISIS, Iraq, and the War in Syria: Military Outlook," *Policywatch* 2273 (Washington Institute, 2014); Fabrice Balanche, "L'Inflexible Progression del'Etat Islamique," *Libération*, October 3, 2014; Terrill, "Confronting the 'Islamic State,'" 18.

152.   Before the fall of Mosul, ISIS's size was typically estimated at around ten thousand fighters, roughly equally distributed between Iraq and Syria. See, for instance, "The Islamic State of Iraq and Greater Syria: Two Arab Countries Fall Apart," *Economist*, June 14, 2014; Ehab Zahriyeh, "How ISIL Became a Major Force with Only a Few Thousand Fighters," *Al Jazeera*, June 19, 2014, http://america.aljazeera.com/articles/2014/6/19/isil-thousands-fighters.html. Subsequently, U.S. intelligence agencies' estimates went up to twenty to thirty thousand, owing to massive inflows of new members. See Ceylan Yeginsu, "ISIS Draws a Steady Stream of Recruits from Turkey," *New York Times*, September 15, 2014; Robert Windrem, "ISIS by the Numbers: Foreign Fighter Total Keeps Growing," *NBC News*, February 28, 2015, http://www.nbcnews.com/storyline/isis-terror/isis-numbers-foreign-fighter-total-keeps-growing-n314731. Analyst Daveed Gartenstein-Ross puts forth a more plausible estimate of around 100,000 fighters. Gartenstein-Ross, "How Many Fighters Does the Islamic State Really Have?" *War on the Rock*, February 9, 2015, http://warontherocks.com/2015/02/how-many-fighters-does-the-islamic-state-really-have/. On the expansion of ISIS's finances, see Patrick B. Johnston, "Countering ISIL's Financing," testimony presented before the House Financial Services Committee, November 13, 2014.

153.   Lister, *The Syrian Jihad*, 186.

154.   Weiss and Hassan, *ISIS*, 224–29.

155.   International Crisis Group, *Rigged Cars and Barrel Bombs*, 5.

156.   Brian Michael Jenkins, "Brothers Killing Brothers: The Current Infighting Will Test al Qaeda's Brand," *Perspective* (RAND Corporation, 2014), 3. Consistent with my interpretation, Jenkins suggests that the threat posed by a rising ISIS was a key factor driving the anti-ISIS offensive in 2014.

157.   International Crisis Group, *Rigged Cars and Barrel Bombs*, 6–7, 10 (based on interviews with officials from al-Tawhid Brigade, Ahrar al-Sham, Suqur al-Sham Brigades, and Jaysh al-Islam, conducted in Gaziantep, Istanbul, and Reyhanli, Turkey, in March–June 2014).

158.   International Crisis Group, *Rigged Cars and Barrel Bombs*, 7, 10 (interview conducted in Kilis, Turkey). Ahrar al-Sham, the strongest member of the Islamic Front, was reportedly the most reluctant to use force in debates that took place within the alliance in the weeks leading up to the attack against ISIS.

159.   Lister, *The Syrian Jihad*, 171. The formation of the Islamic Front alliance in late November (including five of the six groups in question) may have represented a balancing effort against ISIS, aiming at deterring further piecemeal aggression and, if that failed, facilitating coordination in an all-out fight against ISIS. The Syrian Revolutionaries Front alliance, formed in early December 2013, plausibly may have served a similar

balancing function. By contrast, the Jaysh al-Mujahidin, announced only days before the anti-ISIS attack, probably had a more straightforward war-fighting raison d'être.

160. Interestingly, ISIS spokesman, Abu Mohammed al-Adnani, provided an interpretation of the attack consistent with window-of-vulnerability logic, as in an audio clip posted online he said that his group's rivals tried to defeat it "when they saw it was getting more powerful." See "ISIL Says It Faces War with Nusra in Syria," *Al Jazeera*, March 8, 2014, https://www.aljazeera.com/news/middleeast/2014/03/isil-says-it-faces -war-with-nusra-syria-20143719484991740.html.

161. International Crisis Group, *Rigged Cars and Barrel Bombs*, 7–9; Nassief, "The Campaign for Homs and Aleppo," 31–36.

162. International Crisis Group, *Rigged Cars and Barrel Bombs*, 12–13. According to al-Tawhid Brigade's official, the insurgents had to use against ISIS ammunition that they had been saving for an operation to take over the Aleppo airport (interview conducted in Gaziantep, Turkey, in March 2014). Moreover, ISIS followed through on a threat to end its contribution to the fight against government forces in and around Aleppo unless the insurgents stopped attacking it.

163. Gade, Hafez, and Gabbay find that in Syria's civil war, ideologically distant rebel groups are more likely to clash and more extreme ones (and ISIS in particular) are distinctively prone to engage in infighting. Gade, Hafez, and Gabbay, "Fratricide in Rebel Movements." There is, of course, also the possibility that a shared ideology works like shared ethnicity as propellant, rather than suppressant, of inter-rebel war.

164. See, for instance, Lister, *The Syrian Jihad*, 181. For arguments positing Jihadist organizations' inherent tendency to attack other rebels, see Hafez, "Fratricidal Jihadists."

165. Analogous reasoning points to the limited explanatory power of arguments emphasizing individual leaders' characteristics and rebel organizations' internal cohesion. The fact that a broad array of rebel groups (presumably with a range of different personalities at their helm) decided to attack ISIS in early 2014 points to situational factors as more important forces behind their actions. Similarly, both relatively undisciplined FSA-affiliated groups and the "extremely tightly controlled" al-Nusra participated in the fight against ISIS. See Lister, *The Syrian Jihad*, 103. On the pervasive lack of discipline and cohesion among FSA affiliates, see, for example, Vera Mironova, Loubna Mrie, and Sam Whitt, "Why Are Fighters Leaving the Free Syrian Army?," *Washington Post* (Monkey Cage), May 12, 2014; Barak Barfi, "Aleppo Dispatch: The Dark Side of the Syrian Opposition," *Atlantic*, January 14, 2013.

166. Observers have suggested that ISIS's aggressive behavior toward other rebels in Syria was specially inspired by Abu Bakr Naji's Jihadist treatise *The Management of Savagery*, emphasizing the importance of conquering territory and brutally defending it as steps toward the creation of a caliphate. By contrast, al-Nusra's more conciliatory stance might have been influenced by the writings of Abu Mus'ab al-Suri, proponent of a "softer" and more gradualist approach to Jihad, which stressed the need to win the hearts and minds of the local population for ultimate success. See, for example, McCants, *The ISIS Apocalypse*, 82–89.

167. ISIS's ideology may have steered it toward an assertive growth strategy, envisioning the squeezing of rivals out of its areas of influence, while also blinding it to the risk of provoking a violent, concerted response from the rest of the insurgent movement.

168. For the purpose of parsimonious theorizing, I make minimalistic assumptions about rebel groups' preferences, positing that they primarily care about surviving as independent actors and succeeding in the fight against the government. In the real world likely there is substantial variation in levels of aggressiveness, greed, or ambition across rebel groups, which may factor in other groups' calculus about how to deal with them.

169. See, for example, International Crisis Group, "Anything But Politics: The State of Syria's Political Opposition," *Middle East Report* 146 (2013): 11–18; Christopher Phillips, *The Battle for Syria: International Rivalry in the Middle East* (New Haven, Conn.: Yale University Press, 2016), chap. 6.

170. Similarly, Gade and her coauthors do not find evidence of a statistical association between external support for rebel groups and infighting in Syria. Gade, Hafez, and Gabbay, "Fratricide in Rebel Movements."

171. Lister, *The Syrian Jihad*, 189–90.

172. Michael R. Gordon and Anne Barnard, "U.S. Places Militant Syrian Rebel Group on List of Terrorist Organizations," *New York Times*, December 10, 2012; Bill Roggio, "Chief of Syrian Revolutionaries Front Says al Qaeda Is 'Not Our Problem,'" *Long War Journal*, April 3, 2014, http://www.longwarjournal.org/archives/2014/04/chief_of_syr ian_revolutionary.php.

173. Lister, *The Syrian Jihad*, 245–46.

174. Christia, *Alliance Formation in Civil Wars*; Krause, *Rebel Power*.

175. In late 2014 Christopher Kozak estimated that a combination of battlefield attrition, defections, and desertions had reduced the size of the Syrian Arab Army from 325,000 fighters before the war to about 150,000 (plus thousands of Iranian and Iraqi Shia militias, Syrian paramilitary forces, and Hezbollah fighters), which implies that Assad's regular forces in early 2014 were larger than 150,000. Christopher Kozak, "The Assad Regime Under Stress: Conscription and Protest among Alawite and Minority Populations in Syria," Institute for the Study of War, December 15, 2014, http://iswresearch.blogspot.com/2014/12/the-assad-regime-under-stress.html. In late 2013 the overall insurgent movement was estimated at around 100,000 fighters. See, for example, "Syria: Nearly Half Rebel Fighters are Jihadists or Hardline Islamists, Says IHS Jane's Report," *Daily Telegraph*, September 15, 2013. Fabrice Balanche estimated that in late 2013 the regime controlled 50–60 percent of the population, compared to 15–20 percent under insurgent control, with the two sides controlling roughly comparable amounts of territory. Balanche, "Insurrection, Contreinsurrection et Communautés," *Geostrategic Maritime Review* 2 (Spring/Summer 2014): 36–57; Balanche, "L'Insurrection Syrienne et la Guerre des Cartes," *OrientXXI*, October 24, 2013.

176. A possible way to reconcile the 2014 inter-rebel fighting with Krause's argument would be to posit that Ahrar al-Sham's attack on ISIS amounted to a sort of

punishment inflicted by the dominant group for attacks previously conducted by ISIS against other groups. Krause, however, does not theorize explicitly this type of dynamic.

6. Are Coethnic Rebel Groups More Likely to Fight Each Other?

1. Lotta Harbom, Erik Melander, and Peter Wallensteen, "Dyadic Dimensions of Armed Conflict, 1946–2007," *Journal of Peace Research* 45, no. 5 (2008): 697–710. Following standard practice in the study of civil war termination, I consider a rebel group as having ceased its military activity if its fight against the government does not meet the threshold of twenty-five battle deaths for two successive years; thus rebel groups whose military activity falls below that threshold for only one year are considered as active in that year in my dataset. See, for example, Kristian Skrede Gleditsch, David Cunningham, and Idean Salehyan, "It Takes Two: A Dyadic Analysis of Civil War Duration and Outcome," *Journal of Conflict Resolution* 53, no. 4 (2009): 570–97.

2. I divide rebel groups that the UCDP Actor Dataset (version 2.2-2014) identifies as "alliances" into their constituent organizations (as long as case-specific sources report them as maintaining their organizational independence while part of the alliance). For example, I break down the United Islamic Front for the Salvation of Afghanistan (UIFSA, active in Afghanistan in 1996–2001 and better known as the Northern Alliance) into its three constituent elements: Jam'iyyat-i Islami-yi, Hizb-i Wahdat, and Junbish-i Milli-yi Islami. Similarly, for cases in which the UCDP Dyadic Dataset uses collective names, such as "Kashmir insurgents" and "Syrian insurgents," I divide these into their constituent elements. I identify constituent elements by cross-examining the UCDP Actor Dataset and the entry for the corresponding actor in the UCDP Conflict Encyclopedia, available at https://www.pcr.uu.se/research/ucdp/ucdp-conflict-encyclo pedia/. For instance, I divide the Kashmir insurgents into the JKLF and the HuM. See online appendix at https://costantinopischedda.com/data-replication-materials-and -additional-materials for details.

3. Ralph Sundberg, Kristine Eck, and Joakim Kreutz, "Introducing the UCDP Non-State Conflict Dataset," *Journal of Peace Research* 49, no. 2 (2012): 351–62. The same twenty-five fatalities threshold is adopted in Hanne Fjelde and Desirée Nilsson, "Rebels Against Rebels: Explaining Violence Between Rebel Groups," *Journal of Conflict Reso-lution* 56, no. 4 (August 2012): 604–28.

4. Julian Wucherpfennig et al., "Ethnicity, the State, and the Duration of Civil War," *World Politics* 64, no. 1 (January 2012): 79–115

5. Wucherpfennig et al., "Ethnicity," 95. I code the existence of an ethnic claim if ACD2EPR reports either direct evidence of such a claim or indirect evidence (e.g., an ethnic reference in the name of the group). I code ethnic recruitment if ACD2EPR reports that either the rebel organization alone or both the rebels and the government recruited from the ethnic group. Using this broad ethnic recruitment criterion makes sense as it allows me, for example, to code as "Shia Muslim" armed groups like Amal

and the Mahdi Army, which analysts typically consider as affiliated with the Shias of Lebanon and Iraq, respectively, even if both the Lebanese and Iraqi governments recruited from the same ethnic group as well. My findings are substantively unaltered if a narrower definition of ethnic recruitment is adopted, excluding instances of overlapping ethnic recruitment pools between the government and the rebels (see tables A1 and A2 in the online appendix).

6. Data from the UCDP Actor Dataset.

7. Fotini Christia, *Alliance Formation in Civil Wars* (New York: Cambridge University Press, 2012), 221–25.

8. Christia, *Alliance Formation in Civil Wars*, 271–75. Data available up to 2011.

9. Data on government troops from National Material Capabilities Dataset, version 5.0; data on rebel troops from the Non-State Actors in Civil Wars Dataset (both available up to 2011). See David J. Singer, Stuart Bremer, and John Stuckey, "Capability Distribution, Uncertainty, and Major Power War, 1820–1965," in *Peace, War, and Numbers*, ed. Bruce Russett (Beverly Hills, Calif.: Sage, 1972); David Cunningham, Kristian S. Gleditsch, and Idean Salehyan, "Non-state Actors in Civil Wars: A New Dataset," *Conflict Management and Peace Science* 30, no. 5 (2013): 516–31.

10. Data from the Non-State Actors Dataset (available up to 2011). The original variable on leadership control takes on three values: "low," "moderate," and "high." I consider a rebel group leadership as exercising limited control if the variable equals "low."

11. Data from the UCDP External Support Dataset (available up to 2009). See Stina Högbladh, Therése Pettersson, and Lotta Themnér, "External Support in Armed Conflict 1975–2009: Presenting a New Dataset," paper presented at the International Studies Association Convention, Montreal, 2011.

12. Although these are, of course, not the only possible rebel ideologies, they are arguably the most common in the relevant time frame and certainly the most studied by civil war scholars. See, for example, Monica Duffy Toft, "Getting Religion? The Puzzling Case of Islam and Civil War," *International Security* 31, no. 4 (2007): 97–131; Stathis N. Kalyvas and Laia Balcells, "International System and Technologies of Rebellion: How the End of the Cold War Shaped Internal Conflict," *American Political Science Review* 104, no. 3 (2010): 415–29; Kai M. Thaler, "Ideology and Violence in Civil Wars: Theory and Evidence from Mozambique and Angola," *Civil Wars* 14, no. 4 (2012): 546–67; Laia Balcells and Stathis N. Kalyvas, "Does Warfare Matter? Severity, Duration, and Outcomes of Civil Wars," *Journal of Conflict Resolution* 58, no. 8 (2014): 1390–1418; Stefano Costalli and Andrea Ruggeri, "Indignation, Ideologies, and Armed Mobilization: Civil War in Italy, 1943–45," *International Security* 40, no. 2 (2015): 119–57; Monica Duffy Toft and Yuri Zhukov, "Islamists and Nationalists: Rebel Motivation and Counterinsurgency in Russia's North Caucasus," *American Political Science Review* 109, no. 2 (2015): 222–38; Barbara F. Walter, "The Extremist's Advantage in Civil Wars," *International Security* 42, no. 2 (Fall 2017): 7–39; Stahis N. Kalyvas, "Jihadi Rebels in Civil Wars," *Daedalus* 147, no. 1 (2018): 36–47.

13. Fjelde and Nilsson, "Rebels Against Rebels."

14. Data from the Non-State Actors Dataset (available up to 2011).

15. Data from the Rebel Contraband Dataset (available from 1990 to 2012). See James I. Walsh et al., "Funding Rebellion: The Rebel Contraband Dataset," *Journal of Peace Research* 55, no. 5 (2018): 699–707.

16. Fjelde and Nilsson, "Rebels Against Rebels."

17. Kristin M. Bakke, Kathleen Gallagher Cunningham, and Lee J. M. Seymour, "Shirts Today, Skins Tomorrow: Dual Contests and the Effects of Fragmentation in Self-Determination Disputes," *Journal of Conflict Resolution* 56, no. 1 (February 2012): 67–93; Kathleen Cunningham, *Inside the Politics of Self-Determination* (Oxford: Oxford University Press, 2014).

18. Gary King and Langche Zeng, "Explaining Rare Events in International Relations," *International Organization* 55, no. 3 (2001): 693–715.

19. See Gleditsch, Cunningham, and Salehyan, "It Takes Two." The variable is measured in log form.

20. See tables A3–A4 in the online appendix.

21. I obtain similar results using *preponderance2*, an alternative measure coding rebel pairs not included in Christia's dataset, with my data on the number of government and rebel troops (see table A5 in the online appendix).

22. A Wald test fails to reject the null hypothesis that the coefficients for *bipolar, tripolar,* and *multipolar* are equal. The count of coethnic rebel groups (in both linear and log form) is a significant predictor of inter-rebel war when *coethnic* is dropped, in models not reported for reasons of space. Owing to collinearity, the coethnicity dummy, the number of coethnic rebel groups, and their interaction cannot be included in the same model.

23. I cannot include as a control the dummy variable flagging proximity between rebel groups because rebel groups that are not physically proximate never fight each other. I use the UCDP Georeferenced Event Dataset (version 18.1) to code rebel groups' districts of operation. To measure the distance between rebel groups' areas of operation (towns or districts) in adjacent provinces, I use Google maps and information from the Georeferenced Event Dataset. To avoid skewing the proximity variable in favor of my argument, I do not consider rebel attacks against civilians, given that insurgent groups may be able to operate clandestinely and launch terrorist attacks in areas under tight government control (e.g., the November 2008 Lashkar-e-Taiba's operations in Mumbai), but not to engage in sustained fighting against other rebel organizations there. See Ralph Sundberg and Erik Melander, "Introducing the UCDP Georeferenced Event Dataset," *Journal of Peace Research* 50, no. 4 (2013): 523–32.

24. A comparable increase in the probability of inter-rebel war can be observed when holding *splinter* at 0.

25. Data from the World Development Indicators (Washington, D.C.: World Bank, 2017).

26. Nearly 40 percent of the rebel groups in the Non-State Actors Dataset are "much weaker" than the government, while about 47 percent are "weaker." Data available up to 2011.

Conclusions

1. Contingency probably played a crucial role in bringing about the failure of the gamble for resurrection launched by various Syrian rebel groups against ISIS in 2004. In particular, the facts that some Ahrar al-Sham fighters allowed ISIS units to escape encirclement by hostile forces and that Damascus prioritized targeting ISIS's opponents, thus providing the group with badly needed breathing space, may have saved the Islamic State from defeat.

2. The fact that the case studies yield more false positives (inter-rebel wars that should not have occurred) than false negatives (inter-rebel wars that should have occurred but did not) suggests that, though my argument identifies a set of factors that rebel groups pay close attention to when deciding about infighting, there probably are other causal paths to inter-rebel war, which future studies should theorize about. Another possibility is that my analysis may have missed some windows of opportunity or windows of vulnerability that did not lead to inter-rebel war. I cannot rule this out (though I strove to identify the presence of windows over time regardless of the occurrence of infighting) given that that even highly competent detectives sometimes struggle to notice "dogs that did not bark." Replication efforts by other scholars are therefore encouraged.

3. Arnold Wolfers, *Discord and Collaboration: Essays on International Politics* (Baltimore: Johns Hopkins University Press, 1962), chap. 1; Robert Jervis, *Perception and Misperception in International Politics* (Princeton, N.J.: Princeton University Press, 1976), 19–21.

4. On the conditions under which decapitation is more likely to have major debilitating effects on insurgent organizations, see Paul Staniland, *Networks of Rebellion: Explaining Insurgent Cohesion and Collapse* (Ithaca, N.Y.: Cornell University Press, 2014), 46–47; Austin Long, "Whack-a-Mole or Coup de Grace? Institutionalization and Leadership Targeting in Iraq and Afghanistan," *Security Studies* 23, no. 3 (2014): 471–512; Jenna Jordan, "Attacking the Leader, Missing the Mark: Why Terrorist Groups Survive Decapitation Strikes," *International Security* 38, no. 4 (Spring 2014): 7–38.

5. Stathis N. Kalyvas, *The Logic of Violence in Civil Wars* (New York: Cambridge University Press, 2006). For a claim about the limited causal effect of ethnic identities in the more specific realm of inter-rebel relations, see Fotini Christia, *Alliance Formation in Civil Wars* (New York: Cambridge University Press, 2012).

6. Jason Lyall, "Are Coethnics More Effective Counterinsurgents? Evidence from the Second Chechen War," *American Political Science Review* 104, no. 1 (February 2010): 1–20; Lars-Erik Cederman, Kristian Skrede Gleditsch, and Halvard Buhaug, *Inequality, Grievances, and Civil War* (Princeton, N.J.: Princeton University Press, 2013); Jason Lyall, Yuki Shiraito, and Kosuke Imai, "Coethnic Bias and Wartime Informing," *Journal of Politics* 77, no. 3 (July 2015): 833–48; Manuel Vogt, *Mobilization and Conflict in Multiethnic States* (New York: Oxford University Press, 2019).

7. Kristin M. Bakke, Kathleen Gallagher Cunningham, and Lee J. M. Seymour, "Shirts Today, Skins Tomorrow: Dual Contests and the Effects of Fragmentation in

Self-Determination Disputes," *Journal of Conflict Resolution* 56, no. 1 (February 2012): 67–93; Kathleen Gallagher Cunningham, *Inside the Politics of Self-Determination* (Oxford: Oxford University Press, 2014); Peter Krause, *Rebel Power: Why National Movements Compete, Fight, and Win* (Ithaca, N.Y.: Cornell University Press, 2017).

8. See, for example, the study by Jannie Lilja and Lisa Hultman arguing that ambition to establish dominance over their ethnic community drove infighting among Sri Lanka's Tamil rebel groups in the mid-1980s. Lilja and Hultman, "Intraethnic Dominance and Control: Violence Against Co-Ethnics in the Early Sri Lankan Civil War," *Security Studies*, 20, no. 2 (2011): 171–97.

9. Cf. Krause, *Rebel Power*.

10. Robert G. Gilpin, "The Richness of the Tradition of Political Realism," *International Organization* 38, no. 2 (Spring 1984): 287–304.

11. Kenneth Waltz, *Theory of International Politics* (Reading, Mass.: Addison-Wesley, 1979); John J. Mearsheimer, *The Tragedy of Great Power Politics*, rev. ed. (New York: Norton, 2014).

12. Alexander Wendt, *Social Theory of International Politics* (New York: Cambridge University Press, 1999), 95.

13. Jack L. Snyder and Keir A. Lieber, "Correspondence: Defensive Realism and the 'New' History of World War I," *International Security* 33, no. 1 (Summer 2008): 181, 183.

14. Robert Jervis, "Was the Cold War a Security Dilemma?," *Journal of Cold War Studies* 3, no. 1 (Winter 2001): 36–60.

15. Stephen G. Brooks, *Producing Security: Multinational Corporations, Globalization, and the Changing Calculus of Conflict* (Princeton, N.J.: Princeton University Press, 2005); Tanisha M. Fazal, *State Death: The Politics and Geography of Conquest, Occupation, and Annexation* (Princeton, N.J.: Princeton University Press, 2007); David M. Edelstein, *Occupational Hazards: Success and Failure in Military Occupation* (Ithaca, N.Y.: Cornell University Press, 2009).

16. David E. Cunningham, "Veto Players and Civil War Duration," *American Journal of Political Science* 50, no. 4 (October 2006): 875–92; Michael W. Doyle and Nicholas Sambanis, *Making War and Building Peace: United Nations Peace Operations* (Princeton, N.J.: Princeton University Press, 2006).

17. "Setback for U.S.-Backed Rebels in Syria," *CBS News*, November 4, 2014; "U.S.-Backed Syria Rebels Crumble Under al Qaeda Fire," *CBS News*, March 3, 2015; Eric Schmitt and Ben Hubbard, "U.S. Revamping Rebel Force Fighting ISIS in Syria," *New York Times*, September 6, 2015; Stewart Welch and Kevin Bailey, "In Pursuit of Good Ideas: The Syria Train-and-Equip Program," Washington Institute for Near East Policy, *Research Notes*, no. 36 (September 2016).

18. On this point about the Taliban, see Seth G. Jones, "Why the Taliban Isn't Winning in Afghanistan: Too Weak for Victory, Too Strong for Defeat," *Foreign Affairs*, January 3, 2018, https://www.foreignaffairs.com/articles/afghanistan/2018-01-03/why-taliban-isnt -winning-afghanistan.

19. Fabrice Balanche, *Sectarianism in Syria's Civil War* (Washington, D.C.: Washington Institute for Near East Policy, 2018), 17, 51, 64–65. Analogously, in Uganda the Lord's

Resistance Army refrained from directly expanding into Teso, owing to the region's ethnic-other population, and instead allied with the Iteso Uganda People's Army. See Adam Dolnik and Herman Butime, *Understanding the Lord's Resistance Army Insurgency* (Hackensack, N.J.: World Scientific, 2016), 54–55.

20. Amnesty International, *Syria: "We Had Nowhere to Go"—Forced Displacement and Demolitions in Northern Syria* (London: Amnesty International, 2015); "America's Strategy Against Islamic State Is Storing up Trouble: Ethnic Tension in Eastern Syria Is Increasing, to the Delight of the Jihadists," *Economist*, May 26, 2018.

Index

GPSR Authorized Representative: Easy Access System Europe, Mustamäe tee
50, 10621 Tallinn, Estonia, gpsr.requests@easproject.com

www.ingramcontent.com/pod-product-compliance
Lightning Source LLC
Chambersburg PA
CBHW021857020426
42334CB00013B/374

9 780231 198677